PRAISE FOR **THE BOLD WORLD**

"*The Bold World* reminds me of the best things we have learned from our uniquely instructive sojourn as Black people in America. To be watchful; to pay attention; to make every attempt to comprehend reality; to believe that real life flows in the direction of the real, which is to say, of the true. Not to feel daunted by almost any obstacle for which we have brains and energy to challenge. To rejoice when Life comes through us and has the courage to keep on going. It is a marvelous book."

—ALICE WALKER

"In *The Bold World*, Jodie Patterson makes a case for respecting everyone's gender identity by way of showing how she came to accept her son, Penelope. In tying that struggle to the struggle for race rights in this country during her own childhood, she paints a vivid picture of the permanent work of social justice. Written with sparkle and charm, and deeply introspective, hers is a book of refreshing frankness and great moral purpose, moving and pellucid."

—ANDREW SOLOMON, *New York Times* bestselling author of *The Noonday Demon* and *Far from the Tree*

"[An] extremely valuable book about family, gender, race, and identity. Patterson has broken the silence, and readers will thank her for it."

—*Booklist*

"A courageous and poetic testimony on family and the self, and the learning and unlearning we must do for those we love. In her stunning and moving debut, Jodie Patterson offers us all a blueprint for what it means to be a champion for our children and encourages us to be bold enough to let our babies lead the way, especially when we don't have answers. Required reading for every parent, and anyone who has ever been parented."

—JANET MOCK, *New York Times* bestselling author
of *Redefining Realness* and *Surpassing Certainty*

"This isn't a book just for mothers or mothers of trans children or folks from the trans community. This is, above all, a story about self-determination, and it is vital for anyone seeking love in its highest form. Patterson's clear-eyed recollections and poignant insights from her own transformative journey—from girl to woman, from daughter to wife, from mother to activist—inspire us all to remember and to become the people we were meant to be. This is the work we all must do in order to be free, and to love more fully."

—ELAINE WELTEROTH, journalist, former editor in chief, *Teen Vogue*

"Patterson leaves no emotional stone unturned in her powerful chronicle. . . . [This] raw tour de force illustrates the strength of a loving and determined mother."

—*Publishers Weekly*

"Jodie Patterson is the type of mom that every transgender child deserves. Her unconditional love for her son Penelope radiates throughout her book. Being a trans youth myself, I know what it feels like to live in a body that doesn't align with your heart and mind. I see myself in Penelope yearning to be understood and cheer for Jodie as she learns how to parent a transgender child in a world that often isn't welcoming. Bravo, Jodie!"

—JAZZ JENNINGS, trans youth activist,
star of the YouTube series *I Am Jazz*

"Jodie Patterson draws on the different parts of herself—the student, the activist, the family loyalist—to respond with heart, commitment, and all the fierceness required to protect her transgender child. Beautifully written, *The Bold World* is activism at its most pure level."

—CHAD GRIFFIN, president, Human Rights Campaign

"There are things each of us can't see—until we're ready. With this book Patterson encourages us to seek out our blind spots—to see who we can't see and to hear what we can't hear. Our children need us to read this book—a story of mama-bear instinct and internal awakenings."

—CHRISTY TURLINGTON BURNS, founder, Every Mother Counts

"What the book is: a woman's journey of constant transformation and fierce love for a world where her children can live their authentic selves."

—*USA Today*

"This memoir is a loving, honest and raw portrayal of the family's journey to support Penelope, even though the path ahead was neither clear nor easy."

—*NY Post*

"*The Bold World* is a wonderful read of a modern woman's approach to life, love, and family with a transgender child to raise, in this not-so-perfect world. A must-read."

—BETHANN HARDISON, fashion activist

THE

A Memoir of Family

BOLD

and Transformation

WORLD

JODIE
PATTERSON

BALLANTINE BOOKS

New York

2020 Ballantine Books Trade Paperback Edition

Published in the United States by Ballantine Books, an imprint
of Random House, a division of Penguin Random House LLC, New York.

BALLANTINE and the HOUSE colophon are registered
trademarks of Penguin Random House LLC.

Originally published in hardcover in the United States by
Ballantine Books, an imprint of Random House, a division of
Penguin Random House LLC, in 2019.

LIBRARY OF CONGRESS CATALOGING-IN-PUBLICATION DATA
Names: Patterson, Jodie, author.
Title: The bold world : a memoir of family and transformation / Jodie Patterson.
Description: New York, NY : Ballantine Books, [2019]
Identifiers: LCCN 2018039475 | ISBN 9780399179037 (trade paperback) |
ISBN 9780399179020 (ebk.)
Subjects: LCSH: Patterson, Jodie | Parents of transgender children—United
States—Biography. | African American mothers—Biography. | Transgender
children. | African American transgender people. | African American families.
Classification: LCC HQ77.8 .P38 2019 | DDC 306.874/30896073—dc23
LC record available at https://lccn.loc.gov/2018039475

Printed in the United States of America on acid-free paper

randomhousebooks.com

2 4 6 8 9 7 5 3 1

Book design by Simon M. Sullivan

To Mama, for showing me how to rise up in love.
And to Morrison, Hughes, Hurston, Wright,
and Angelou for asking me to wonder.

And look out on the world
And wonder
What we're gonna do
In the face of
What we remember

—

LANGSTON HUGHES, "Puzzled"

CONTENTS

This book is a memoir, a collection of my memories from childhood through adulthood. I chose to tell the stories that I felt shed light on my understanding of gender and race. There are things I've left out and names I've changed, simply to protect people I love. But each story is told to the best of my own recollection and with honesty. I created dialogue that I either specifically recalled or that I, today, feel is plausible and likely in order to bring the actual scenes to life and to match the best available recollections of those events and exchanges.

The South

———

I'VE ALWAYS BEEN TOLD that women are powerful, tenacious, and important. That we pull from limitless places. That we make magic wherever we go—shining light into the darkness, forming impenetrable shields with our love. That beneath moments of weakness are endless reserves of strength.

But I, woman, am feeling none of these powers.

A friend of mine once told me, "Parenthood means delivering optimism to your children." But I'm filled with only pessimism about the future. It's clear to me that dark envelops light, bad beats up on good. Women do, in fact, break. Smiling requires an effort I just don't have. And joy? It's packed up its bags and gone elsewhere.

"I need to stay with you for a while," I heard myself saying to my mother over the phone, weary from the last few years. "I just need to rest."

"I'm here," she said without pausing. "Come as soon as you can."

I bought two plane tickets to Atlanta the next day.

Although my parents brought up my sister Ramona and me in the North, my South Carolina–raised mother sprinkled our upbringing with Southern dust. We were city kids who spent summers with our grandmother in Georgia and who grew up appreciating hot bowls of grits and long family gatherings in the kitchen. These were the things that held a kind of magic for me—they were essential elements of a well-maintained soul. The South, I knew, had the power to fix anything. There was spirit in the soil. I believed that whatever my problems were, the South would always know what to do with them.

But as I grew into adulthood, that magic had gotten lost. Somehow, I needed to find my way back.

At forty-three years old, I am exhausted. Run ragged by the pressures, the expectations. Turned fragile in the face of hardship. Kept up at night by thoughts too scary to speak of during the day.

With my grown-up life in full swing, there is never time to pause. I have five children, a husband, an ex-husband, a schedule that often leads to grinding sixty-hour workweeks—and a crippling fear of the life I've created. To "cope," I simply set a goal and don't stop until I, the bullet, hit the target.

I'm in need of what the South holds, of the spirit in the earth and of Mama and her steady ways. Needing, too—maybe most of all—the women. My women. Those matriarchs of my lineage whose stories, voices, and faces I often lean on like prayers, especially during times like these. Times when I've lost myself completely.

And so I return to the South once more, hoping to breathe the Atlanta air and remember where I come from.

My mother lives in a sprawling suburb called Peachtree City. Her neighborhood is made up of neatly designed suburban dwellings and quaint dirt-covered back roads that wind around the subdivision's golf courses and muddy green ponds. She left New York for Atlanta when she and my father divorced in 1989, and after a time moved into my grandmother Gloria's house, where she remained after Gloria died. While this house isn't quite the same as the one I visited during my childhood summers, it still feels like home. And even after Grandma Gloria passed away, the place still holds affectionately to her memory: her furniture, her smell, her love.

When I'm at the house, my mother and I don't pull out all my baggage and spread it across her table, examining each piece to determine how to fix it, as my dad and I might have done. She isn't one to tackle obstacles that way, and I don't go to the South—or to her—for that. I don't go to strategize. I go because being there resets something in me.

I haven't told her everything. I haven't even had the time yet to fully put into words why I'm here. But she can see the strain on my face: My hair is thinning, I've lost weight, and I have new lines and creases she's never seen before.

I've left four of the kids at home with my husband. Georgia, my first child, has come with me. I've wanted to spend time alone with Georgia for months now, but the little ones, the business, and Penelope, my third child, demand so much of my time. Penelope, my determined toddler.

Despite the awkwardness that has grown over the years between us, I always eventually call Mama when things get bad. After I've exhausted all my own methods and relentlessly tried to push my way through the problem. After I've looked to my girlfriends for help. After I no longer even want to be saved. When I've thrown in the towel and accepted that the thing I'm fighting is just way too big to defeat, I call Mama, knowing that there's nothing more to do than yield. Mama is good at yielding.

During this visit I spend most of my afternoons alone in the sitting room. The space feels like a time capsule—there's no TV, no computer, no gadgets or telephones. Rather, it's filled with the same beautiful furniture that adorned the study in Grandma Gloria's old house—furniture that was passed down from her mother, and her mother before that. Generations of memories live inside the wooden skeletons of those pieces, and Gloria was a meticulous preservationist. There's not a tear or a scratch on any of them. After my grandmother died, my mother was reluctant to disturb anything—there was just too much of Grandma Gloria still lingering there. Instead, she opted to leave things as they were. If Grandma were to walk inside this room today, she'd know exactly where to rest her feet.

The sitting room is filled with books—my grandmother had thousands of them; her collection was enormous and never-ending. Shelves upon shelves of weathered paperbacks and sun-faded hardcovers fit snug next to pristine first editions signed by her good friend Jimmy—James Baldwin—whom she first met on a university campus in the 1960s when the South was still reeling from *The Fire Next Time*. Grandma's books were always around her, sprawled across her desk, stacked on the floor, tucked under her arm. I would often catch her in the study of her old house rereading six books at a time and scribbling notes in the pages, wondering what she was writing down.

But the true soul of the sitting room lives in the photos. There are pictures everywhere: nineteenth-century portraits of women elegantly posing in their best outfits; group shots taken at family gatherings in the old days, in which four and five generations sit closely together, not so much smiling for the camera but telling the onlooker: *We are unbothered by these times; we are steadfast and courageous.*

I want some of that. I need to know what it takes to be just that.

Digging deep into a drawer, I pull out a photo I've always loved looking at—it must have been taken in the mid-1970s. Four generations of us women traveled to a local Sears and Roebuck to sit for a portrait. My mother's at the top left corner of the frame, a young mom at the time, barely thirty. Grandma Gloria is to her right, all pointy lapels and gold dangling ear-

My great-great-great-grandmother "Ma" (bottom left) could pass for white, but she chose not to. Her daughter, Sissy (center), is seated with my great-grandmother Lurline, who would eventually become the most stoic woman I've ever known. My great-great-grandmother Ann (top right) was a sturdy woman who clearly "ran the show."

rings, a pair of glasses hanging from a chain around her neck. My sister Ramona appears on the bottom left, small and defiant, and I'm on the bottom right, age six, wearing the same polyester jumpsuit as my big sissy. Between us sits Great-Grandmother Lurline. Never mind that the dark sunglasses she's wearing obscure her eyes, her penetrating gaze is unmistakable. Lurline's signature face, perfectly captured in that photo, said—then and always—"I am *not* playing." She had a talent for communicating a lot without saying much at all. I don't remember her smiling much, either.

Lurline obtained her college degree and credits toward her master's in the early 1900s. This, during the first decades of the long reign of "separate but equal," a system that rarely translated into higher education for colored people. But she came from a long line of teachers, preachers, and entrepreneurs, who managed to work the system and carve out a place for themselves. They gained access to an accelerated track to opportunity. With that access came a deep sense of expectation. Lurline's parents made it very clear that there was no other direction to go but forward, no other measure of doing well than by being the best. No excuses for failure—certainly not the color of your skin and most definitely not your gender.

The morning of the photoshoot, Grandma Gloria had combed our hair. Ramona and I preferred our Afros in the style of my idols, the Jackson 5, an equal distribution of puff on all sides. But Grandma liked hers tapered at the bottom à la Nina Simone. And so, to our dismay, she shaped ours that way, too.

But walking into Sears, I fixed my face and strode inside with a sense of purpose. Without being told why, I knew somehow that it was a big day for all of us—more important than the hairstyle I was so desperately trying to channel. It wasn't just about me, it was about preserving the order and honoring the line: Lurline, then Gloria, then my mom, then Ramona and

*Mama and Grandmother Gloria standing; Ramona and
I seated next to our great-grandmother Lurline—
the matriarch.*

me. Arranging myself in front of the photographer, my grand-mother's hand on my shoulder, I knew I was needed to capture something important. With any one of us missing, the meaning would have been lost.

Now, years later, I can slip into any of those generations, into any of those times in my life—I can be the annoyed kid, the young mom, I can even imagine myself as the older woman. I think that's what I like about looking at the pictures. I can see myself in each of them. I've imagined my daughters stepping into the frame, and into that lineage. Penelope included. My persistent Penelope. But staring into the photo now, the image is shaky, blurred, and unclear.

I grew up feasting on the photos of these women—faded images of Lurline and my aunt Lurma, my mother, Jamelle, and their sister, Ramona, my own sister's namesake, who died in a car crash when she was just five years old. Each year I ran my hands across their portraits and learned a little bit more about the formidable women inside the frames. About their determination, their loves and losses, the sacrifices they made, and the convictions that allowed them to survive whatever they were faced with. Preserved in those images, they showed their strength in their posture—in the straight of their back, the square of their shoulders, the lift of their chin, the steadiness of their gaze.

But I am weak—shoulders slumped, back bent, eyes fixed to the ground. I haven't slept in months. I squat down on the floor, cross-legged, like a child might do—and I lean against the couch to steady myself. I continue to fixate on the photos. I know that now is the time for searching. For figuring out how I, woman, can put myself back together and be bold in this world. There is no other place I need to be than here—in the South on this floor.

My women will be the ones to answer my questions. They were alchemists, transforming the weight of expectation into drive, grief and hardship into vision. Each of them took whatever scary thoughts might have kept them up at night and turned those thoughts into power. They never imagined themselves being stomped out, and they always insisted on their freedom. They were activists, educators, leaders—women who refused to follow. And if they ever felt restraint rising up, they just got up and left—changed their circumstances and never turned back.

My grandmother divorced four times. My mother divorced twice. And Aunt Lurma, very pretty but not at all interested in being the pretty girl, opted for children without marriage, partnership without laws. She decided early on that convention wasn't for her. Lurma, like the rest of the women in my line, was guided principally by one thing: the freedom she felt in her bones.

My grandmother learned self-determination from Lurline. Gloria passed that knowledge down to Mama. Mama passed it down to me and Ramona. And I was intent on passing it down to my daughters.

Three generations later, we have Penelope. My third child, my angry toddler, who, after round one thousand of what had become a steady stream of anguished outbursts and fights, told me, "Mama, I'm not a girl. I am a boy."

Today, back in the South—with the time to move slowly, to finally reflect, I know that it's not only the demands of work and city life that have brought me here. It's Penelope. It's dealing with everything that comes after hearing my child say "I am a boy." It's grappling with my fears about what that means for the future; living with a reality that has turned me upside down. I've been running away from the chaos, barrelling forward into a future that I can't quite name. Racing through each hour, each day, each month, without a plan.

But what I do have holds value. I have these pictures of womanhood, excellence, Blackness, and freedom. And they are real and very powerful.

In the sitting room, with these stories and these photos, I see the pattern. Like his grandmothers before him, Penelope has made demands too—that his voice be heard, that the world fall in line with him. Penelope, like the rest of our clan, is more than a bundle of expectations. He is more than one thing. More than what we see. And he is most certainly not a girl. His declaration of self, his total dismissal of conformity and expectation, is elemental—etched into his DNA by his ancestors.

But with all of this comes a steady, nagging, terrifying truth. Because I know the world is unkind to people it doesn't understand—to those who don't live by its rules. I know, too, that the same America that has been divided on race and class and love for so many centuries will no doubt be divided on Penelope. A boy with a vagina.

What if the world, for the rest of his life, tells Penelope, "No"?

I think fear sometimes forces us to primal places. When we're scared, we seek comfort. We look for something, or someone, familiar. When we don't know what's next, we look to the past to give us a preview, or a road map, of what's to come. We search for answers in those memories, looking for clues within our own stories to show us how to find a way forward. And with that knowledge at our back, we hope to pick up the pieces of who we are along the way, and make ourselves whole once more.

PART I

Sleep

One day I'll grow up, I'll be a beautiful woman.
One day I'll grow up, I'll feel the power in me.
But for today, I am a child . . .

—

ANTONY AND THE JOHNSONS

ONE

Roots

AS A KID, I WAS TINY. All through my school years, I looked half my age. When girls in my class started filling out their tank tops and high-waisted jeans, getting to know the shape of newfound curves, I remained small, layering my sweaters even in the summer to hide my flat chest.

I saw weakness in my narrow hips and thin arms. They were weightless, powerless, unable to keep me from floating away. If I couldn't feel my own weight, how could I trust myself? How could I be confident that with one swift change in the wind, I wouldn't disappear into the air like a runaway balloon? In my mind I could be strong, but it was my body that couldn't measure up.

At home, in the full-length mirror in my bedroom, I'd fantasize about being an opinionated, chubby girl. Someone with wide hips and sturdy legs who demanded to be seen. A girl with presence. With my Jackson 5 album playing in the background, I'd roll my neck and wag my finger in the air, perfecting comeback lines to imaginary adversaries—"Oh, so you can dish it out, but you can't take it?"

No one was taunting me in the hallways of my mostly white Manhattan private schools. But still, it was the principle of the thing. To wield your power like a sword. To carry it effortlessly on your body and let it drip off your tongue in a well-crafted attack. I longed to be Sassy Chubby Black Girl. In my mind, big was powerful. And I wanted to be thick with power.

But I was stuck in my slight frame, and there wasn't much I

could do about it. My fate was written in my genes. And so I made up my mind early on that I would borrow weight from the people around me. To combat my small size, I kept close to anything that felt bigger than I was, to those who held a pulse louder than mine—Mama, Daddy, my sister Ramona, when she allowed. I gravitated toward them to be closer to their power, never really thinking it could be mine. Even our apartment on Eighty-First Street and Riverside Drive, a mostly white and wealthy neighborhood on the Upper West Side, felt like an anchor. I needed it, as I needed my family, in order to feel what it was like to be substantial.

In our house, Daddy was the provider and Mama was present and responsible. Together, in their distinct roles, they agreed on creating an actively Black household, where racial solidarity and pride ruled. This was the mid-1970s, when Pan-Africanism, Black solidarity, and political leaders like Kwame Nkrumah were encouraging Black people globally to fight racism by coming together and increasing our knowledge, power, and strength. I remember learning about Martin Luther King Jr. and Malcolm X as if they were each other's brother and our very own uncles. Perhaps they had opposing approaches to the struggle, but they were family nonetheless. Daddy might not have liked King's pacifism or Malcolm's religion, but he never spoke against either of them. We were raised to rally around our people as if we were all related by blood.

> Lift ev'ry voice and sing,
> Till earth and heaven ring.
> Ring with the harmonies of Liberty;
> Let our rejoicing rise,
> High as the list'ning skies,
> Let it resound loud as the rolling sea.

As children in the segregated South, my mother and her sister, my aunt Lurma, learned the Negro National Anthem along with their ABCs. Black history, for them, wasn't limited to just one month, it was woven into their every day, seamlessly, like breathing. It was used as a tool to help bring Black people together and thus make us stronger.

Similarly, Ramona and I learned our Black history at afterschool programs and cultural events that Mama and Daddy signed us up for. We learned the anthem when we were toddlers, and loved its challenging tone and vivid lyrics—lyrics that made me think about the era when Mama was a little girl. We sang it as often as we could, for our parents at the dinner table, in the backseat of the car driving to Martha's Vineyard, and for our relatives who'd gather around our makeshift stage for talent night in our living room on Saturday evenings. "Facing the ris-ing sun, of our new day be-gun!" Ramona and I would belt out, our arms flung wide in the air. "Let us march *onnn,* till victory is *wonnn!*"

Later, when Mama tucked me in for the night, she'd explain the importance of the lyrics—how the song was really about leaning toward goodness, toward love and light. Believing in the anthem, she said, was one of the many ways Black people survived. It reminded us that good always wins in the end.

The conversations we had, the music we played, the art that hung on our walls—Mama and Daddy made sure that everything we touched, heard, and witnessed contained an element of Blackness, of the inherent goodness and strength of our people. Nina Simone, James Baldwin, August Wilson, Faith Ringgold, Romare Bearden—these were our precious heirlooms, our wise teachers, and the most poignant reflection of who we saw ourselves to be. Each family, each member of every family, and every person had the support of an entire culture behind them.

My parents knew how small a little Black boy or a little Black girl could feel in this world, so they made sure we thought in numbers. In that way, one Black family could feel like a nation of comrades. One little girl could feel like a warrior tribe.

It was important to Daddy that we be confident. Confident enough to walk into any setting, anywhere in the world. He wanted us to feel at home particularly in places where Black folks dwelled—regardless of their circumstances. Beginning when Ramona and I were two and three years old, he would insist that the family go for tennis lessons every week in Harlem, where he was raised.

We'd drive up Central Park West to Frederick Douglass Boulevard, cut across on 140th Street over to Adam Clayton Powell Boulevard, and continue north until we hit 150th Street, where the Frederick Johnson tennis courts resided. There, we entered what locals termed the Jungle. The Jungle couldn't have been more different from our Upper West Side neighborhood. There, Blackness was everywhere—not just inside some homes but out on the streets, in the air, and on every corner. We could buy six-foot stalks of sugarcane for a dollar out of the back of someone's truck, listen to Grand Master Flash rapping from a boom box propped up on a park bench, and stand captivated while a Nation of Islam member preached on the corner.

Daddy had chosen those courts in particular so that every week, year after year, all four of us—Mama, Daddy, Ramona, and I—would have to travel from our fancy white neighborhood to an all-Black community in Harlem. Daddy wanted us to be around all types of people, especially all types of Black people. And he didn't want his girls afraid of anyone or uncomfortable around anything—not poverty or privilege. Daddy wanted us to know how to "flow"—from one situation into another, rich to poor, uptown to downtown. From Black to white and back to Black again.

Playing tennis together was our family time.

"Jodatha," he'd say to me as we approached the courts at the Jungle, "there's no place you don't belong. Walk like you own the joint. Because you do, baby girl. You do!"

My parents were dispelling the myth—that we were just a few strange Black people in a big white world. The reality they were teaching us was: We are many. And we are diverse. There may be differences in the way we look in Harlem, or in Cuba or Africa, or on the Upper West Side, but we are one community.

It was this kind of support structure that was meant to help me, a skinny, tiny thing, feel significant.

When we were kids, my sister Ramona literally towered over me. She's just over a year older than I am, but looking at us side by side when we were young, you would think she could easily stick me in her pocket and carry me around. Though Ramona and I have two older sisters from our father's first marriage, it was just the two of us with the same mother, raised under the same roof. But in our youth, a shared address and set of parents were about the only similarities we had.

I was ordered and methodical—a striver for perfection—and my bedroom was a shrine to those efforts. The clothes that hung in my closet and lay in my dresser drawers were carefully organized just so. I had a collection of Black baby dolls that sat on a shelf, and each one was fully dressed and accessorized from a different period. They were Victorian aristocrats and seventies B-girls, as beautiful and elegant and cool as they wanted to be. Next to them was my tribe of teddy bears outfitted in hand-me-down T-shirts, followed by my arrangement of first place trophies and ribbons from various gymnastics meets. Lined up across the center of the shelf were all my prized albums—the Jackson 5, The Sylvers, Minnie Riperton, Roberta Flack, Prince—their colorful sleeves in pristine condition, always gleaming.

Each weekend, I cleaned and dusted my room, carefully moving each doll, teddy, and record from its place. Nothing was thrown about or forgotten. Everything was important. Every time I walked into my room and saw my rainbow-patterned bedspread neatly tucked and folded, I felt an intense surge of happiness at the sight of the order I had created.

But to get to my room I had to pass through Ramona's, wading through the chaos she seemed to revel in. Ramona would lie in bed all day, stretched on top of rumpled sheets while she picked up books from the many piles strewn across her floor, devouring chapter after chapter. She was lost to us in the pages of *Catch a Fire: The Life of Bob Marley,* or the latest Judy Blume novel, inhabiting whatever worlds existed there. Ramona had taught herself to read at age five on the floor of Bank Street, in our school's bookstore, and never stopped. She was constantly feeding her mind with information.

When she wasn't reading, Ramona was a tornado that spun through the apartment's long corridors, taking out whatever and whomever she touched as she passed. When she'd wake—which was usually late—she'd whirl into my room, where we shared a closet. Each morning Ramona stomped over to her clothes and tried on nearly every item she owned, discarding the rejects on my floor. She'd finally settle on an outfit unlike anything I'd ever seen before—shredded jeans, an oversized men's shirt, a cropped bolero jacket, cowboy boots—somehow making it all work. Each ensemble was a work of art. She was bravado personified, and I regarded her mostly from a distance. Get too close and she would run, but if I made myself quiet and still, I could drink her in. Ramona was brazen and stubborn and full of attitude, and I desperately wanted all of what she had.

"Let the child be free!" Daddy pushed whenever Mama tried to get Ramona to behave nicely. Mama was a stickler for manners and hated whenever Ramona would do things like eat with her fingers at the dining room table.

My father wanted us to celebrate who we were, as we were. He showed a lot of pride in his brown-skinned girls, and we

I liked precision. *Ramona preferred flair.*

were encouraged, even rewarded, for expressing ourselves unapologetically. If one day we felt like wearing jeans under our
dresses, he'd support it. "The girls are happy, Jamelle, who cares
what they look like?" Or if Ramona refused to brush her hair
before going to visit family on a Sunday, he would challenge us to
an Afro contest—seeing who could grow the biggest one by Easter. For him it wasn't about us acting right or speaking well. He
cared only that we rebel against the status quo. Defiance had always been in Daddy's blood, and he nurtured it wherever it grew.

Coming up Black and poor, my father faced years being told
about all the things that he could not achieve, and he ended up
achieving them anyway. He was a self-made millionaire—
"smart, Black, and rich," as he often liked to remind me. He
emerged from his tough childhood in Harlem as a person who
wore his success like a middle finger to white America.

With his impeccably made suits and his spirited laugh, Daddy
charmed and elbowed and clawed his way into the bureaucratic
(white) boys' club. He'd come a long way from the tenement
walk-up he called home all those years ago, and by the end of
his life he'd amassed a small fortune and left behind a long list of
successes. Each milestone opened a new door for him, and he
was often the only Black man walking through to claim the
prize.

In 1955, when he was just twenty-seven years old, he co-
founded the first Black-owned brokerage firm on Wall Street,
Patterson & Co., providing wealth management services exclusively to Black families. Six years later he published the *Citizen
Call,* a Harlem community newspaper that spotlighted the social, political, and personal lives of Black folks in the neighborhood. In the early 1970s, when Blacks and Latinos in New York
were dangerously divided, he became the founder and president
of a nonprofit that revitalized much of the South Bronx's poor-
est Latino neighborhoods, putting jobs back into brown com-

To us, Daddy was bigger than anything we could imagine.

munities. And less than five years after that, he and my mother founded the Patterson School, a private school in Harlem aimed at nurturing excellence and confidence in Black children. We knew, with no one ever having to tell us, that our Daddy was king.

In every one of his achievements, in every lesson he taught us, was a taunt to the other side: *You thought this world was yours? Well, I just took it.*

Nothing in my father's home would be suppressed—not his

thoughts, his ambition, or his children. "Don't let white people confuse you, Jodie!" he'd whisper roughly in my ear whenever the neighbors and doormen mistook our family for the help. "Stay focused." He saw those people as both enemy and gate-keeper to the life he wanted—and the life he wanted for us. People to win over, then to snatch the keys from their hands without a second thought.

John Patterson realized fast that you couldn't rely on anyone telling you how to get what you want. When I was eleven or twelve I remember once asking for his permission to do something—what, I can't remember now. We were in the TV room of the house, and I stood leaning against his chair, wig-gling nervously. He peered at me over his glasses and said, "It's your life, Jodie. I'm going to die one day anyway—you need to figure it out on your own." That was Daddy's approach to par-enting: throwing us into the deep end and commanding, "Swim, damn it!"

Ramona took to Daddy's limited restrictions and just-do-it attitude—she could go and do and be whatever she pleased. But I struggled; freedom to me felt like abandonment. It accentu-ated the point that I just wasn't capable yet of standing on my own. I preferred tight walls and even tighter rules—the more structure I had, the safer and more nurtured I felt. But Daddy wasn't focused on our comfort, he was grooming us to be strong—and to live for no one but ourselves.

That is, unless what we wanted infringed upon his control. "Be free," he'd tell us in the house, on the tennis courts, and in confrontations with my mother. There wasn't much he wouldn't allow us to do. But if we needed his time, money, or patience, he had only a limited amount of each to give—and he used them only as he saw fit. Challenging Daddy was unacceptable, and asking for more was asking too much. At home, the final word was his alone.

I spent much of our childhood trying to avoid the trip wires of my father's anger, but Ramona walked through his minefield without ever slowing down. Daddy valued Ramona's stubbornness because his children were another symbol of his defiance. But when that bravado was aimed at him, they went head to head: "In this house, I'm king!" he'd tell her. "Get it together, young lady."

Ramona was just as loud as he was when things didn't go her way, refusing to get dressed for tennis lessons on a Saturday and vowing to stay home alone under her covers all day if that's what she wanted to do. The point she was making was very similar to Daddy's. To him, to Mama, and to anyone who got in her way, her message was the same: "You can't make me."

We had a clear view of Riverside Park from the windows of our apartment. It was giant and overgrown, spanning more than eighty city blocks and dense with tall oak trees and winding, dimly lit paths—nothing like the manicured Central Park on the other side of town. Not far from our building, at the edge of the park, was a huge hill with jagged boulders jutting out on one side. In the summers when Ramona and I were young, around six and seven years old, we would climb those boulders—clawing and stretching like wild animals on the hunt for food. In the wintertime after the snow fell heavy, Mama would take us back to the other side of the hill where the surface was smooth, and we'd whiz down on our red sleds. When we were little, the park was good to us.

But for Ramona at thirteen, the park wasn't as giving.

"Just stay where I can see you from our windows." Mama gave us permission in the afternoons to sit on the stone wall that bordered the park. "And then come home in an hour."

We were just to sit there with our friends, safely within Mama's sight, so she could check on us every so often. But after five minutes, like clockwork, Ramona would get bored and swing her legs over to the other side of the wall, facing a steep drop-off below, turning her back to our apartment windows. It was a small first act of defiance, but when she did it, I knew more would come.

"Who wants a smoke?" Ramona asked one day as she pulled out a pack of Parliaments from her jeans pocket, gesturing to her two best friends, Gabby and Stacie.

"Where'd you get cigarettes from?" I asked, stunned and a bit impressed.

"Uhh . . . at the smoke shop on Broadway, where they sell *ci-ga-rettes*?"

Gabby laughed at my naïveté and Ramona's sarcasm.

"You know Mama can see you?" I ventured nervously.

"So what?" Ramona shot back. She was fearless.

Ramona lit the Parliament and took a few puffs, and then, without warning, she jumped—eight feet down onto the craggy earth. Gabby and Stacie looked at each other, stuck their cigarettes in their back pockets, and did the same. Ramona and her friends took off into the park and disappeared behind that same hill we'd used for so many years as our jungle gym. I assumed they were just smoking, but I didn't dare jump off the wall to witness it with my own eyes.

Eventually, I made my way back to the apartment and waited for her to return. Hour after hour I watched for Ramona from my bedroom window. Night came, and the young moms and their babies in strollers, the joggers doing their after-work runs, and the school-age kids had all gone home, but there was still no sign of my sister.

This became Ramona's regular routine—jumping the wall, disappearing behind the hill and out into the night for hours, leaving me behind. Mama would pace the house, looking out her bedroom window every few minutes to see if Ramona had reappeared. Eventually she'd search the edges of the park and smoke shops nearby, trying to sniff out her daughter on the streets she may have passed along, asking if anyone had seen her child.

After that, Mama would return home to start calling Ramona's friends. "Gabby, have you seen Ramona? No, she hasn't come home yet." Short, tense pause—their answers were never quite satisfying. "Well, if you speak to her, please have her call. I'm worried." Mama would go down the list of Ramona's friends, one at a time, calling their houses and asking for any information they had. "When's the last time you saw her?" "When you went home, where did she go?" Just as Mama reached her peak panic, Ramona would appear at the front door, eyes red, giggling in the way someone might do when they couldn't care less what you think.

Exasperated, Mama demanded answers. "Damn it, Ramona! You can't just leave for hours unaccounted for—Where were you?"

"With. My. Friends!" she'd bark back, then stomp to her room, slamming the door behind her.

Where my sister wanted to disrupt, I wanted to please. This was especially true when it came to Mama. She understood my need to be anchored and never asked me to separate from the things that secured me. With her, my size was my biggest advantage. It allowed me to follow her around the house wherever she went, a happy little barnacle swept up in her current. For years, I would crawl into my mother's bed at night and lie on her back. Burying my face in the back of her neck, I'd breathe in her scent, feeling myself get bigger with each inhale. Aligning my body with the shape of her curves, my heartbeat found the rhythm of hers, and the *thump-thump* of our bodies working to-gether rocked me to sleep many nights. In those moments, I felt whole. In her calm, Mama set my tone.

Unlike Daddy, she never barked, or spanked, or got mad and walked away. She was always and infinitely available. Whatever I wanted, she helped me get. What I lacked, she gave to me without question.

I loved to watch her. Stretched out on top of the kitchen counter doing homework, I kept one eye trained on her as she seasoned chicken in a brown paper bag. Or, sitting cross-legged on the toilet in her bathroom, I'd study the way she leaned toward the mirror as she applied makeup at her vanity. Four slow, deft strokes and she was done—that was all she needed. There was always a dramatic red lip, an arched and defined brow, loosely blow-dried hair. My own mother was Sophia Loren in the flesh, working her magic in slow motion, and she was all mine.

In the kitchen of our prewar apartment, she often liked to cook in just her bra and stockings. Stirring something in a bowl, she'd look at me and smile. During the summers, she'd walk over to the window at the end of the kitchen, stand on her tippy-toes, and reach one arm up high to turn on the air condi-tioner, her lean body stretched out like a ballerina. That little act—her moving to flick on the A/C—contained all the beauty I thought existed in the world.

Observing Mama moving through our apartment, I was watching womanhood in action. She taught Ramona and me how to feel our beauty on our limbs, and discover how it sounded in our mouths. Too many times to count, my sister and I were instructed to stand in front of a full-length mirror in our underwear and study what we saw. I would trace the form and outline of my body—inch by inch, curve by nonexistent curve.

I memorized my gymnastics-made muscular thighs, my

Mama at nineteen, a beautiful senior in college.

Peter Pan ears, my upside-down-banana lips. On cue, Mama would then make us wrap our arms around ourselves and repeat: "I love myself. I love myself. *I love myself!*" until we dissolved into giggles. Though I wrestled with my less-than-ideal frame—my lips too broad, my arms too long—playing this game always felt like a reprieve.

Caring for our hair was also approached like some sacred ritual—every part and plait was suffused with my mother's love. The more perfectly she parted my cornrows, the more I knew she cared. The more she redid my braids, the more active her love was. The more precisely she remembered my favorite styles, the more she understood me. It was that direct. In some families, hair was trouble, or pain, or ugliness. In my family, hair was love.

Bathrooms and bedrooms have always been the places where

School pictures meant I could spend extra time with Mama the night before, while she braided my hair.

our women have done the best talking—our best loving and sharing. Closing the doors to the men and to the rest of the world, we found our voices between hair strokes, stories, and thoughts while making each other feel beautiful.

And with Mama, it was all about feeling. She massaged our limbs at night to relax us into sleep. Sang us songs in the morning to make those first moments of being awake a little less disorienting. And she acted as Daddy's benevolent interpreter—wrapping his often-harsh words in love and allowing them to sound, for a moment, as he himself had perhaps intended. "Baby, Daddy just wants you to be strong." Mama would climb into the backseat of the car with Ramona and me during road trips to tell us stories about princesses with kinky hair and the dark-skinned princes who loved them, to make us understand there was no universe in which we didn't belong.

Though their methods were different, my parents both had the same aim: putting us at the center. But over time, their influence and good intentions seemed to work less and less on

Ramona. My mother—who had grown up being deferential to her own mother, who had listened carefully and stayed in line—struggled to understand this wild child that had begun to emerge. This brooding daughter who greeted us each morning at the kitchen table by slumping into her chair with her arms folded tightly across her body, refusing to eat much of anything. And my father, who encouraged our freedom but demanded his control, started to feel that Ramona could not be contained.

At the kitchen table, in her room, at the front door, I watched Ramona war with our parents, and watched our parents at a loss about what to do with her.

Throughout middle school, Ramona's spirit was fighting with everyone in the house so explosively that my parents decided it best that she go live with my grandma Gloria for a while. That's when I first started to think that the South must have the power to fix things.

During the year Ramona was gone, I started sleeping on my bedroom floor at night, wrapped tightly in my blankets. That was the year the monster invaded my dreams. I would find myself in my nightmare being chased by something so powerful that I had to conjure superhuman strength to stave off being consumed. Although it was faceless and voiceless, it was very real.

The backdrop of my dreams was the urban maze of New York City, transformed into an obstacle course. With my extraordinary powers, I'd hurl, climb, and fling myself out of harm's way, swimming across the choppy Hudson, climbing up and over the giant black cherry trees that lined Riverside Park, catapulting myself from the Empire State Building to the Twin Towers. I sprinted across the entire length of Manhattan, soaring from skyscraper to skyscraper. But no matter how far and fast I ran, I always felt the monster's breath on my neck. I'd wake up exhausted, drenched in sweat—and sometimes urine—my body clenched like a fist.

Each night, knowing the nightmare would surely return, I'd try my best to close myself around myself—hands between my knees and chin tucked to my chest—breathing in my own scent as a lullaby. Cocooning myself from the disorder all around.

Ramona, I hoped, would return home happier. Perhaps we'd even grow closer. But on the day she came back from Grandma Gloria's, my sister carried the same anger she'd had with her when she'd left months earlier. She walked down the hallway to her room, quietly closing the door behind her, and crawled into her bed.

A dry silence rose between us, and tension settled over our entire house like a thick fog.

After Ramona came back from the South, I felt the rub between her and each of us intensify. Give Ramona a curfew and she would break it. Ground her and she would simply jump out our first-floor window. She did it dozens of times—on a school night if need be—because she had places she wanted to go and boys she needed to see, neither of which were sanctioned by Mama and Daddy.

Daddy became more and more forceful, quicker each day to snap at us over anything—the wrong meal served by my mother at dinnertime, a spilled glass of juice in the TV room, or anything, really, that required a little patience and understanding. From my tiny corner, I witnessed the push and pull: Mama pulling for Ramona's love. Ramona pushing back. Daddy taking turns in both directions, trying to gain control of his household, pushing back on all of us when our presence threatened to reverberate louder than his. And I existed somewhere in the middle, holding myself together while the family started to fray.

"Mona, did you borrow my red sweater?" I tapped lightly on the outline of my sister's shoulder one morning. She was buried from head to toe, deep under the covers—her mattress pushed, randomly, into a corner of the room. "Mona?" I tried again. She was a heavy sleeper, everyone in the family knew this; almost nothing could wake her, and you never wanted to be the one attempting the impossible. But it was already seven o'clock, and Mama was in the kitchen making breakfast. And I wanted my sweater back. "Seriously, Ramona. I gotta get dressed now."

"Get the *hell* out of here! I'm sleeping!" she yelled, snatching the covers back over her head. It was her typical response to anyone trying to wake her.

On any other day, I would have left her alone and not made any more fuss. But for whatever reason, on this day, I was prepared to get back what was mine, by any means necessary. I sat on the edge of her bed, ready to wait it out. A few seconds passed, and then Ramona sprang out of bed like lightning, landing a hard, blunt punch to my shoulder—knocking me to the ground.

"Get *out*!" she roared as she pulled back her fist, winding up for a second attack.

"Ma-maaaa!" I screamed, running to my parents' room for backup. I found Daddy standing by his dresser, putting on his cuff links in the mirror.

"What are you running from, Jodie?" His question was rhetorical.

"She won't give me back my sweater. And then she hit me. And I need my—"

Daddy put his cuff links down on his dresser and grabbed my shoulders, squaring them with his. "Go back in that room and *deal* with it." He lowered his face to mine and looked directly into my tear-filled eyes.

"Don't let her bully you, Jodie. Put your hands up; defend yourself. You have to hit her harder, faster. Like *this*—" He jabbed with his right arm just past my ear. I tried to protest; I didn't want to fight. But Daddy was always priming us for a battle—against the world, against each other, whatever the war might be.

"Ma-maaaa!" I yelled for her again. She needed to step in and make this all right.

Mama came running into the room then. She took one look at the two of us facing each other—Daddy in his boxer stance and me with tears in my eyes—and she exploded: "We can't teach the girls to fight each other, John. This is just too much!"

My mother had had enough—enough of Ramona sleeping through the days, acting out, talking back; enough of her over-bearing husband, forcing his drill sergeant ways upon us; enough of me, I think, looking scared. She turned from us and made a beeline toward my sister's room, Daddy and I trailing behind her.

"Ramona, you need to wake up! *Getuprightnow!*" She said it as one word—fast and charged. Mama yanked back the covers, reaching down to force Ramona out of the bed. But the sudden move jump-started my sister into action—she sprang to her feet, daring Mama with her eyes to make a move like that again.

Ramona's room was small and shaped in a perfect square. We each took a position: Ramona and Mama facing each other, Daddy and I on either side of them.

"You may not sleep through this day, or any day—not one more minute, Ramona. And you may *not* hit your sister." Her words came shooting out like bullets, penetrating the entire room. I'd rarely heard Mama sound this way.

"Yes, Jamelle. I will." Mama, who was all patience to Daddy's fire, all love to Ramona's resistance, had reached her limit. It was Ramona's disrespect—clear, calm, and intentional—that did it. Mama pulled back her hand and opened it wide, prepared to smack her own daughter across her mouth, for the first time in her life.

But Ramona was faster. My sister smacked our mother across the face with such force that Mama's tortoiseshell glasses flew off and sailed clear across the room, hitting the wall and dropping to the floor.

After that, not one yell or curse or cry came—out of anyone. Only silence, and an acknowledgment of the shift. In that single smack, Ramona flipped the power in our home. The only movement thereafter was of Mama clutching her face, and of me scampering to the corner, frantically looking for her glasses on the floor.

In the moments that followed, I don't remember seeing Daddy, although he was there in that room. The world in front of my eyes dwindled down to just the three women: my mother, who had been defeated, Ramona, who had come out victorious, and me—invisible and scared. It was unclear from where I stood which of us held the better position: to be the ruler, or to be ruled.

In phases of discord, people separate. Couples decide to go on breaks. Friends don't speak for years. In families who live together, that separation can be more challenging—but even they can find their ways.

In the time after Ramona and Mama's showdown, we all retreated to our corners. Daddy went to play tennis. Ramona wandered around with her Dominican friends on the seedier streets along Amsterdam Avenue. And Mama escaped to a little duplex apartment in the West Village each week, where she and a hodgepodge group of hippie housewives sat in a circle and chanted in the dark for hours, practicing transcendental meditation.

I rarely saw Mama and Daddy kiss anymore. Most of their time spent together consisted of just a few seconds in the morning passing each other in the kitchen, one quick pursed-lip kiss goodbye. No eye contact or warmth. They'd go about their separate days, and then at night sit silently at either end of the dinner table. Their tension became ours.

For my part, I threw myself into routine. Three hours a day, six days a week, I trained across the state in gymnastics. I came home from practice after dark, took a bath, ate dinner, finished whatever homework I hadn't completed in the car, then fell asleep—usually too exhausted to dream.

Unlike the rest of my family, though, my salve was proximity. I needed to be close to them, as complex and as dangerous as they were, even if just physically. Staying close meant staying connected to my power source. So I did my best to try to avoid conflict, taking refuge in Mama, staying close to her. I remained small and good, safe and amenable—creating not one ripple or problem that might cause the family to finally, irrevocably, fall apart.

Just thinking about being without them gave me anxiety. I started developing a series of bizarre tics. While doing homework, I'd start quickly cracking every joint in my body—snapping, cracking, popping, rolling, from neck to toes in a way that made me look like I was convulsing. Standing in line at the grocery store with Mama, I'd rub my thumbs over my other four fingers, tapping them once, then twice, in a pattern. These were little rituals I'd learned in gymnastics that many of my teammates and I would use before executing complicated tricks. On the mat, they were for good luck. But I applied them to my everyday life to keep me calm and safe, and feeling balanced.

When I wasn't near my family, I carried them in my head. They took up more space in me than I owned for myself. Flooding my brain, filling the silence between my ears with sounds. Mama's comfort, her perfection and her fragility. Daddy's imposing presence—forcing his weight on me even when he wasn't in the room. Ramona's untamed spirit, her bravado—who she was that I wasn't, what I wanted to be but couldn't.

I'd hear their voices turning over and over in my mind. I was always absorbing them, taking in everything they said to me, even things they didn't know I was hearing—an argument, something my parents revealed in confidence to another adult, a plan Ramona was making to sneak out late at night after Mama and Daddy had fallen asleep. I was always recording, notating, rewinding, and playing them over again. On the outside, I was pulled together, but on the inside I was a ball of tightly clenched nerves—all rattling and shaking to get out.

By the time I turned sixteen, I felt crowded. The power and presence I once craved from my family to make me feel complete started to suffocate me. I felt owned by my parents, by this idea of being good, owned by structure and order. Owned by the routine of home to school to gymnastics.

I had spent the first fifteen years of my life not breaking a single rule. Being nice, staying small, simply absorbing. But by the time I was in my junior year of high school, I craved to be someone other than who I was—someone less in control.

While my parents kept their eyes fixed on Ramona, their "problem child," I started quietly rebelling, stepping away from good behavior for an afternoon, or an evening, in search of whatever lay beyond. They didn't know that I smoked pot for the first time with my three best girlfriends by the Hudson River boathouse, or that I sat in the back corner banquette at Mikell's jazz club on Columbus Avenue and Ninety-Seventh Street, getting drunk on white wine while I listened to Whitney Houston belt out "Saving All My Love for You" on the small stage. I didn't tell them that I lost my virginity after school one day to Claude, one of only three Black boys I knew, on a neat pile of blankets on Ramona's bedroom floor, minutes before my mother came home.

Outwardly, nothing changed. I remained the steady hum to Ramona's big, loud bass. But those secret experiments—setting aside who they thought I was to try out whatever else was inside me—loosened something. I wanted more than stolen moments at the boathouse or in my sister's room. I wanted a whole world to get lost in, an environment where no one knew me and I could try things out on my own.

At eighteen, Ramona was spending most of her evenings and weekends traveling downtown to the Village with her friends to shop and socialize and sometimes dance the night away. Hearing her come in after a night out, I fantasized about the adventures she was getting into.

By 1987, downtown New York had become an amazing mecca of music, style, dance, and decadence. The neighborhood was only a quick subway ride from where we lived on the Upper West Side, but to me it felt as far away from my reality with my family as I could get without purchasing a plane ticket. Downtown could be the playground that I'd been looking for.

Ramona had started going to Nell's, a new nightclub on the edge of Greenwich Village that everyone was clamoring to get into—and only a handpicked few were allowed in. In the year since it opened, Nell's had become more than a club, it was a culture. It represented what New York aspired to be: a beautiful, egalitarian oasis where Black and white, straight and gay, young and old, rich and poor all gathered. I desperately wanted to go. My sister, being an eccentric extrovert, had friends who were artists and actors and dancers, and the first in line to pass through Nell's doors. For me it wasn't that easy. Although our parents allowed me to go out on the weekends without a curfew, I knew that getting *inside* Nell's would be difficult. Without Ramona, I'd have no chance of making it in on my own.

One Friday night, without any advance warning, Ramona invited me to tag along.

"Stay close and follow me," she directed as we walked toward a posh crowd corralled by red velvet rope.

On any given night, there were no less than fifty well-dressed people gathered around the entrance, hoping to get picked. Skintight Azzedine Alaïa dresses were the style—body-hugging minis with stitching that accentuated every curve. Sleek, sexy, and expensive was what everyone was going for, in the mode of Robert Palmer's "Addicted to Love" music video featuring the girls playing instruments, stone-faced and swaying from side to side like pretty zombies.

Because I was a high school kid who didn't have an account at Bergdorf's or Barneys (although many of my peers did), Alaïa wasn't an option for me. Instead, I paired my favorite black tube skirt with a little black tank top I'd found in the back of my closet, and put on some sheer black stockings. The only designer things on me were the red Chanel lipstick I'd stolen from Mama's vanity and my shiny lace-up Doc Martens. Not exactly sleek and sexy, but they had attitude—and that's what mattered most.

"Let Ramona in . . . and that pretty one," the doorman announced to the bouncers. In order to make it past the front door, one had to either be someone or know someone. Celebrities rolled through the club all the time—Mike Tyson, Lisa Bonet, Prince—but Nell, the club's owner and namesake, didn't cater to celebrities. She preferred the painter and the architect, the restaurateur and the fashion stylist, the start-up music label executive and the up-and-coming comedian. And—luckily for me—if you were "cute, female, and underage," you, too, were considered somebody.

Walking through the unlit vestibule two steps behind Ramona, I was immediately enveloped by the sounds of Soul II Soul reverberating throughout the club's interior: "How-ever do you want me? How-ever do you need me?" echoed throughout the hall. My shoulders started bobbing before I could stop myself—it was electric.

Taking in the scene before me, I kept my head low and mimicked whatever Ramona did. When she moved, I moved. When she smiled, I smiled. And when she smoked a cigarette, I asked for one, too. She led me through the velvet curtains and into the performance room. There was a small stage and a grand piano, and banquettes lining the walls. We made our way down the narrow staircase at the back of the room and into the main lounge.

The setup downstairs was dimly lit and cozy, like an old library, with people draped over worn leather couches and area rugs—talking, listening, leaning into one another. Then there was the dance floor. It wasn't a fancy space, more like someone had cleared out all the furniture and turned off the lights in their living room late at night, dancing with their friends until the sun came up. In this room, it was only the music and the movement that mattered. Time was irrelevant, names were unnecessary, and there were no barriers between people. That first night at Nell's, I took it all in, absorbing every last detail.

Going out on a Friday night, coming home Saturday morning and sleeping all day became routine. I danced and downed cranberry and vodkas and experimented with drugs in club bathrooms. I held secrets from Mama, things I would never want her to know. Things no one asked me about because I'd never given anyone cause to worry.

If my parents had looked closely, they would have seen that I wasn't just the put-together one, the in-control one—the daughter Ramona was not. But I was never punished, or even spoken to, about my behavior. My parents were consumed with Ramona's consistently loud rebellion, and with the demise of their own relationship—which later ended in divorce.

My late nights out and early morning returns went unnoticed, and the assumption remained that it was only Ramona who needed minding.

During my senior year and the summer that followed, I spent much of my babysitting money on finding freedom—in boys and clubs, and after-after-hours parties in dingy dens in the East Village, where I laughed with Boy George and Madonna look-alikes. Towering drag queens, scruffy artists, cocky B-boys—for that exhilarating summer, those people became my people.

To own my identity, I was starting to feel I had to touch it, feel it on my own. And so, night after night, I reached my arms out into the smoky, strobe-lit dark, hoping to catch a glimpse of myself in the shadows.

TWO

The Women

IN LESS THAN A YEAR, I'd be off to college—finally on my own. Freedom to me looked a lot like an East Coast women's institution like Smith—or maybe even Wesleyan, where my mother studied French in graduate school. Some place where uninhibited women walked around untethered, with fierce intellect and wild spirits. I wanted to be among unpossessed and unaffected people who refused to alter themselves for anyone. It was *that* kind of freedom that I aspired to. I was looking for my tribe.

"The world is yours, baby girl," Daddy said one morning, winking at me in the rearview mirror of his car, a smile in his voice. I cracked my own smile thinking about how freeing that sounded. Soon I'd be in college, without the weight of my family pushing down on me.

"But here's the thing, Jodie," he continued, looking straight ahead as we made our way toward my high school. "I'm only paying for a Black college."

Like all things, it appeared that we'd be doing my college experience John Patterson's way, or no way at all.

I looked out the window, barely listening as he continued his speech, watching the trees recede into a blur as we crossed Central Park into another world.

Moving from the West Side of Manhattan to the East Side was like being transported. My parents chose to raise us on the Upper West Side primarily because, while it was predominantly white, it was also home to people of all walks of life—Blacks, Jews, Dominicans, Asians, musicians, actors, professionals, educators, both the rich and the poor—all living together between Ninety-Sixth and Seventy-Second streets. Yes, people still acted on their prejudices. Black boys might be followed in a neighborhood store, Black girls mistaken for babysitters instead of residents in their own buildings—but those same people were forced to confront the truth: that this neighborhood belonged to us all. Eventually, we had to think beyond race, class, and religious lines and allow for diversity. The East Side, by contrast, had none of that rub between cultures. It was glaringly white, wealthy, and Christian, with the largest percentage of brown people being nannies, doormen, and chauffeurs.

Reluctantly, Dad had allowed me to be among the "tony East-Siders" at the all-girls private school Convent of the Sacred Heart mostly because of my determination—I'd applied and gotten a scholarship without his help or his approval. Although he wasn't pleased with my choice of schools, he appreciated my willpower and effort and allowed me to attend. But he was constantly, every day, every moment of his life, battling that Upper East Side white world, and what he thought it might do to me if left to its own devices.

On our way to school, driving through the park toward Fifth Avenue, we'd talk about the impressive prewar buildings that hovered above the treetops. He'd point out all the places over the years where he wasn't welcomed, the co-ops that denied him access, and the people who had surpassed him in their careers, all white men. The East Side reminded him of things he didn't have, and of limitations that were forced upon him.

To me, those same buildings looked beautiful—they reminded me of the places I planned to live in one day with my own family, places where a lot of my friends from school lived. But Dad never had any friends who lived in those buildings while he was growing up on 145th Street. He'd never visited anyone there as a kid, never had lunch overlooking the Metropolitan Museum, never sunbathed on terraces with his class-mates.

He hadn't even entered any of those buildings on Fifth Ave-nue until he was well into his forties, while visiting an old friend from his early career days who'd gone on to make a fortune. He took the elevator all the way to the top floor, and when he walked out after the visit, he knew he wanted that for himself, and for us one day. The space, the high ceilings and long hall-ways, the sunlight that came into every room, the doormen who took your bags and watched out for your kids walking home from school—he wanted all of that.

Daddy did try to buy all of that once, in the form of a pent-house on Ninety-Sixth Street and Fifth Avenue. But the mostly male co-op board, none of whom shared our skin tone, said no—*No, you may not purchase this penthouse. You may not have this view, this plot of land, this level of power. No, you are not one of us.* Not because of what he did or didn't have, but because of who he was. So he took his money across the park and bought a home on the Upper West Side instead.

"The world is yours, baby girl" was his brilliant opening line to me that morning as we drove to school. But Daddy knew that for Black people, grabbing what you want in this world is not easy. And more often than not, the effort it takes will break your spirit in two.

Going to a Black college, to Dad, meant fortifying ourselves for that journey. It meant going where you are wanted first, to gain strength, before battling a world that doesn't want or choose you.

And so it was that I ended up in Atlanta, at Spelman College. Trading in my image of northeastern feminism for something else entirely. A foreign land where, rather than being one of the few, or the only, I would be face-to-face, shade-to-shade, with hundreds of my kind—a skinny Black girl among the many.

• • •

Walking onto Spelman's campus for the first time, in 1988, I began to truly understand how little I knew. Going to a mostly white high school, I understood a certain standard of beauty and wealth. Is your hair straight enough? Is your frame petite enough? Do you have a doorman, a nanny, a housekeeper? Do you vacation? Where do you vacation? The rules of the Upper East Side were quite familiar to me.

But at Spelman, in this new arena where everyone was a shade of brown, I knew that each part of me would be scrutinized from a million different angles, in ways I'd never conceived of before.

Plus, I was a northerner, and I'd already had an idea of how poorly that translated while visiting my grandmother in Georgia over the years. No one down south wanted to be like, dress like, or act like Woody Allen and Diane Keaton, two of my icons. I liked their imperfections and quirkiness, but down south those things didn't go over well. I learned that lesson while visiting my aunt Vicky's hair salon in east Atlanta one summer. Her place was in an all-Black neighborhood, situated at the center of an outdoor mall way past its prime. I walked into that shop sporting rolled-up jeans and a collared shirt buttoned all the way to the neck, thinking I looked *cool*—but I was immediately met with raised eyebrows.

"Girl, *what* are you wearing?" Vicky always had a streak of eccentricity in her, and I could tell she at least got a kick out of my taste—but her customers, it was clear, thought differently. I could see them scrunching down in their chairs from underneath hair dryers so they could get a better look, then shaking their heads in disapproval after properly taking me in.

In those initial weeks on campus, I did all the wrong things, beginning with inviting a friend from home to help me settle in.

Monique was half Black, with hazel eyes and wavy dark blond hair down to the middle of her back. Together, we walked through the long corridors of HH—or, more formally, Howard-Harreld Hall—the school's biggest dorm and my new home, where we were greeted with cold stares from everyone who passed us. As we approached, gaggles of girls grew quiet, tightened their faces, and rolled their eyes in our direction. I later discovered that people thought Monique was white, and that I was crazy—crazy for bringing a white girl with me for support during a time when the sisters were supposed to be bonding over our greatest achievement thus far: entering the holy ground that was Spelman.

Mistake number one of one thousand.

Every girl at Spelman seemed to be at the top of the mountain. They were smart *and* well put together. Pretty *and* outspoken. Eighteen-year-olds who spoke about themselves in bullet points, each new sentence punctuated with a "Top of" this, "Best of" that. Their résumés made their way into each conversation, and it was all you needed to understand that they had been preparing for this moment all their lives. While I was still poking skeptically at my self-understanding, it seemed that everyone else was well acquainted with their best assets, and not only that, they knew how to package those assets to the world.

The classroom was a place teeming with a kind of confidence I'd never seen before. In a very basic way, these women, my classmates, were *impressive*. They communicated more self-possession in a raised hand than I had been able to muster in all my years combined.

Theirs was a necessary confidence—a confidence that I had yet to tap into. One that was built on something our parents and grandparents tried their best to teach us—that there are no safety nets, no institutional elevators that take us to the top. That we have only ourselves. We are the only ones who can determine our worth. These women understood that self-worth was to be our greatest tool.

I'd been raised on these ideas, too. I heard my parents' lessons in confidence and self-love, and I understood those lessons, in theory. But at Spelman I saw, up close, what those teachings looked like in practice. My classmates had ingested the wisdom and knew our power: that we are equally smart, beautiful, and capable of anything.

On campus, your confidence was displayed in your appearance as much as it was in class. The expectation was to come correct in every detail. It meant always stepping out with a made-up face and a good shoe—a pretty heel or a pump, never anything that looked worn or raggedy. It meant "night styling." Girls spent the hours right before bed wrapping their hair with bobby pins or twisting it into curlers, pinning each roller into place before moving on to the next. After dark, the dorm hallways smelled faintly like a beauty salon, of setting lotion and hot curling irons.

You were never to be spotted in public smoking a cigarette, or uttering a swearword. And your greatest accessories were the baubles on your key chain—a sorority emblem, a simple silver cross, a small framed picture of your grandmother—plus keys to the car you obviously had. Key chains were the Grown Black College Woman's crown jewels. Dangling yours from a bag or the crook of your finger announced that you, the Grown Black College Woman, had arrived.

Then there was me. Without a car, still in my downtown club kid phase. Clunky Doc Martens, layered strands of fake pearls around my neck and wrists, and a plaid miniskirt gone askew was the cool New York teen's standard uniform. But here, down south, it was awkward. A month or so into my time on campus I remember sitting on the quad steps with my lips pursed around a cigarette, thinking I was finally grown and free, when I was approached by one of my older schoolmates. "We don't do that here," she said, waving the smoke away from her face. Then she turned around and disappeared into the crowd.

I was starting to understand the signs—that the protocol was real, and the nuances of this campus culture ran deep: The language. The hair. The clothes. The academic excellence. It was the cadence and vibe of a people all operating under a set of rules I didn't know.

As much as I wanted in, as much as I wanted to be part of this magic, this community of confident women, I was ill-equipped. Everyone seemed to be chanting the same mantra—"We're here for a reason! For a purpose!"—while I was still without words, without direction, and without the faith to understand what I was capable of.

To celebrate my acceptance, my grandmother Gloria and my mother, in town from New York to help me move in, took me and my friend Monique out for dinner to Piccadilly's, an all-you-can-eat buffet-style family restaurant—one of Atlanta's many. We all sat down at a large square table, Mama and Grandma Gloria chattering happily about the wonderful Spelman experience I was about to embark on.

"You'll need a white dress and gloves for the Freshman-First march through campus, Jodie," my grandmother said.

"Oooo, yes!" Mama chimed in. "We can get something nice at the mall—and then we can also find your bedding."

They both looked at me, beaming, while I stared blankly back, my eyes full of tears.

For Mama, my attendance at Spelman brought out a pride that went far deeper than me. Her sister, my aunt Lurma, had gone to a Black college, Grandmother Gloria and Great-Grandmother Lurline both went to Black colleges—and Grandma Gloria even returned to a Black college to become a tenured professor. I was stepping into a strong tradition in our family, and they could think of nothing other than how happy they were for me to be part of a history of triumph, determination, and excellence. But all I could feel was that I didn't belong.

"Jodie, you know Lurma was Freshman Queen at Clark. Maybe you'll run—I bet you'll win, as dynamic as you are!"

I started to tune out Mama's cheerful ruminations as my throat tightened and the tears started to fall. I wasn't going to run for Queen—I wasn't even going to make it through the first semester.

I was terrified of the girls who stared at me in the hallways, and of all the things I didn't know. Terrified, most of all, that this sisterhood I wanted to belong to so badly, these rituals and traditions that my matriarchs embraced so easily, wouldn't want me.

I sat there quietly at the table while my mother continued to talk with Grandma Gloria—talking through me, around me, detecting none of the fear on my face. I excused myself and found the nearest pay phone to dial my father.

"Daddy . . . I . . . want . . . to . . . come . . . home." Each word was separated by a deep, exaggerated sob—I was losing it. "I hate it here. They hate me. I want to come back."

"No, Jodie," he said. "This is exactly where you need to be. It may not be what you want to do, baby girl, but it is what you need to do. Toughen up and handle it. You'll be fine." *Click*.

Daddy knew something I didn't. He understood that Spelman would eventually change me, move me forward, as his experience at Lincoln University, another Black institution, had for him. "Handle it. Put your hands on it. Work through it. Toughen up!" This was the closest thing to providing comfort that I would get from him.

Lucky for me, our school's president, Dr. Johnnetta B. Cole, was a staunch believer in commune. We were asked—demanded, even—to think and learn collectively. As freshmen, we had a ten o'clock curfew every single weeknight and on the weekends we had to be in by midnight, no exceptions. This meant that instead of exploring the streets or Atlanta's other college campuses like Morehouse or Emory, we were made to explore ourselves, and to befriend one another. We were encouraged to really get to know each woman, and each story that came with her.

We ate, slept, and imagined together every night, learning about one another between teeth brushing, hair washing, and study sessions. Communing together day after day allowed the walls to come down. Surrounded by these girls, slowly, I began to straighten my back when I talked, and I learned to state opinions without a floating question mark in the air—a bad habit I picked up from my private school friends back home. I dabbled in roller sets, started carrying lipstick, and purchased a long white cashmere coat to wear with my combat boots—a touch of elegance to the edge. I nodded to strangers while walking through campus, and called out "Hey, girl!" to people I knew. And I started stepping into every room prepared to be my own hype man. Never downplaying, always dialing up. I even got myself a car, a beige hatchback hooptie that my grandmother sold to me for a dollar.

Dr. Cole insisted we nurture our spirits together, each week, in Sisters Chapel. Filing into our campus's chapel on Saturdays to attend convocation became something I looked forward to—and a time to learn things beyond what was on the classroom syllabus. Dr. Cole called upon her own band of women, her "*she*roes" as she liked to call them—luminaries like Toni Morrison and Sonia Sanchez, Octavia Butler and Susan Taylor—to put something useful in us. They read us stories and told us about the world— what it would expect from us, take from us, and give to us if we put in the effort. They also told us about hope, and about creating a world not yet imagined. We sat in solidarity each week—row upon row upon row of young women eager to hear words meant for both the mind and the spirit—words specifically for Black women and for future leaders.

Of course, we knew most of Dr. Cole's sheroes before they even stepped onstage. They were famous, and we admired them from afar, as did the rest of the world—reading their books and the articles that chronicled their careers. But seeing them in person, walking about on our small campus, and standing onstage in our hot, sticky chapel without air conditioning, meant something more intimate. It meant that these women, these luminaries, belonged to *us*. Live and direct from our humble corner, Dr. Cole's band of famous women sent a message to a world that watched their every move: These girls are our girls. And if you honor us, you honor them.

These women were giving us what Daddy had wanted from the Jungle, and what Mama had wanted from our bathroom time. It was a feeling of belonging to more than just oneself, of belonging to a warrior tribe.

Behind those large wooden chapel doors, closed to the outside world, it was like being right back in Mama's bathroom getting my hair brushed one hundred times, where the words flowed easily and the love was obvious. We, Black women, were allowed to be all in our feelings, whatever they were—grateful, angry, inquisitive, bold, righteous—and whenever they surfaced. There, we learned how to simply be.

There is a moment in each of our lives when all we want to do is jump off a cliff, Thelma and Louise style. Or over a wall. Or out a window. Abandoning what is and surging forward—up and out—into the winds of possibility.

It is a typical freshman night on campus. And although I'm

supposed to be in bed, I'm more focused on figuring out how to see Aaron. I'm willing to do whatever it takes, even turn my back on Southern protocol, in exchange for his hands—all over me.

My room sits on the second floor of HH, the biggest dorm on campus, spanning half a New York City block. We comprise the most concentrated amount of freshman women—all seventy-five of us could easily get out of control if the opportunity allowed. Academic challenge, political protest, sexual exploration—you name it, we are 'bout it.

Tonight, I'm perched on the back window of my dorm while my unsuspecting RA thinks I'm tucked in bed for the night. HH is built like a fortress—it has more bricks than windows or doors—and it's where I must remain when the clock strikes midnight, according to Spelman rules. All freshman women have a curfew.

I dangle my legs out the window, just as Ramona dangled hers over the park wall when we were young, and I smile to myself. *It's now or never,* I think.

The back windows of our dorm overlook a quiet courtyard. There are no streetlamps, just the moon providing its glow. I like the courtyard because these back windows conveniently allow for a different type of Spelman behavior—like, say, anonymously catcalling the cute Morehouse boys as they pass by during the day: "James, Jaaaames! We see you, cutie!" Even better, these windows are perfect for escaping into the night.

The Georgia night air is still and warm on my arms. The oversized T-shirt I'm wearing drapes off my left shoulder, exposing just enough skin to assure my guy, when I see him, *I am not a virgin*. And that bare shoulder alone gives me a strange confidence. WAKE ME UP is written on the front of my tee in bold black letters, and BEFORE YOU GO GO on the back—the lyrics to one of my favorite songs.

I hold on tightly to my window frame and look out across the courtyard, then down at the steep drop below. I don't dwell on the distance between me and the hard ground, or on the fact that my car has only a drop of gas, and I have even less cash in my pocket. I close my eyes, remembering how bravely Ramona used to jump off the wall around our park.

What's making my heart race and the sweat drip down my spine is this boy, who is not a Morehouse student—or a student at any college, for that matter. He's a drifter who lives downtown in a small, dark apartment with a handful of other people. He doesn't work, he hangs out each night and sleeps all day. And when he calls my dorm hall phone, his voice is muffled and raspy, barely audible over the chatter of women near me. Often I can't understand a word he says. But I can always pick up on what he's conveying, which is: *I want you*.

Aaron's told me he's a rock star, but I've yet to see him perform. Nor do I care to. What I care about are his eyes and their smudged eyeliner, and the way his pants hang off his bare butt (Aaron doesn't do underwear). And the way his hair is undone and slightly smelly, and the fact that he is always a bit dirty, especially his hands. And that he is wild.

What's pulling me out of this dorm window isn't the sex, although I'm sure we'll have some tonight. What tugs is the promise of something I haven't yet had enough of. Something Spelman and Dr. Cole and Sisters Chapel surely can't teach. It is that thing that made Ramona jump over the park wall: reckless abandon.

There was something about the way Aaron inserted himself into the middle of our girls' circle at an off-campus party one night that caught my attention. Without formalities or even a "Hello, my name is," he interrupted our conversation and began talking, practically *at* us, clearly amused by his own arrogance. All the while he looked me dead in the eye, head cocked to the side, smirk visible on his face, as if to say *Just watch. You'll be mine.*

And although from the moment I saw him at that party, it was obvious we'd never be a couple, I wanted him. And so I decided I would sleep with him, frankly, just to see what it was like. Not to fall in love but to experience his kind of sex, in his apartment, on his floor, with his strange friends in the room next door.

Aaron is the furthest thing from my parents I've ever met.

So I jump out the window into the night. Leaving behind all the good girls tucked nicely in their pretty little beds.

This was the end of the 1980s, when feminists took the form of lyricists. It was the era of Queen Latifah's "Ladies First," Salt-N-Pepa, and Monie Love. Black women were stepping onto the front lines and declaring themselves. Queen Latifah moved me, a Black teenager, in the same political way Gloria Steinem ignited a whole generation of white women to grab what was rightfully theirs. Female rappers during that time were powerful. Strong. Sexual. Complex. They spoke mantras that we could not only blast in our rooms and at parties on Saturday nights, but that we could use to empower ourselves.

It was also a time when media began reflecting life as I was experiencing it. For the first time we were seeing our complex selves on television—reaffirming what we were feeling inside. *A Different World,* a network television show that followed the lives of students at a fictional historically Black college modeled after Howard University, showed an ethnic mélange of kids who defied easy characterization. They tackled taboo topics like HIV/AIDS, and they were unapologetic about their individuality. Spike Lee had also just released *School Daze,* putting a spotlight on Black colleges like Spelman and Morehouse.

And amid all this, our Dr. Cole—Spelman's first Black female president, breaking a hundred years of the institution's exclusively male leadership, both white and Black, was in her second year. As Spelman's new leader, she was shaking up the school in the best way possible. We didn't see her as an agitating disrupter; she was loved by all. And it was her forward-thinking vision wrapped in the affection she had for us that allowed our school to evolve with the times.

Dr. Cole understood what we were craving: more diverse narratives, a louder political voice, and broader definitions of ourselves. Our sister-president understood exactly which aspects of the school's tradition needed to remain and which needed to be updated. She deemphasized sororities and pushed for higher GPAs. She asked us to be thoughtful and respectful, but not too polite—and never quiet. She pushed us to support our own community, and to simultaneously think globally. Dr. Cole was replacing the white-gloved ceremonies that dictated campus culture before her with a culture infused with activism.

We could feel it, how important she was—the first president in our school's history ever to physically reflect our predominantly Black and female student body.

Spelman was founded in 1881 with high ambitions. Eleven illiterate students and a meager $100 grew to six hundred students within a year. In less than five years the college was debt-free and backed by two of the wealthiest and most powerful abolitionist families, the Rockefellers and the Spelmans. And roughly a hundred years later, Spelman had become the highest-ranked institution among all historically Black colleges—and among the top ten women's colleges overall.

Dr. Cole was the newest and most radical leader of this legacy. With her encouragement, we joined the antiapartheid movement, boycotting Coca-Cola products in support of South Africa's divestment. We protested the Rodney King beating and took STOP THE HATE signs to the KKK rally that marched through downtown Atlanta every year. We were emboldened to take a stand for something, to have a voice. Dr. Cole removed some of the filters through which we saw ourselves, destroying outdated stereotypes of the "well-behaved" woman and connecting the shifts taking place in our culture with what we were experiencing firsthand, every day, at school.

She ushered in a new guard of students who were energized by change—who had aspirations that did not just stop at a topnotch education, proper etiquette, and the prospect of marrying a Morehouse Man. There would be a new type of Spelman Woman during Dr. Cole's tenure: women who respected and understood the culture as it was, while bringing something new to the table. Not just the desire for education and marriage—but for education, marriage, *and* activism. We were asked to challenge the world, and be vocal in our opinions—but to do so with grace and decorum, as our mothers had wished for us.

Dr. Cole saw women as being defined by their actions. She saw tradition as something to disrupt if disruption was called for. She could identify the better in something that had been one way for too long—and she reigned not from up high, but from down in the trenches. With us and among us.

Wrapped in Kente cloth, wearing her hair in a short natural, she'd walk the halls and touch each of our faces with the palm of her hand as she passed. Imbuing each of us with the strength she possessed just from walking through life as she did, as only truly great leaders can do. Because, as I was starting to learn, sometimes the king is a woman.

"How did your mom end up running the Panthers?" I asked as I stretched across my friend Ericka's bed one afternoon during our sophomore year, staring up at the ceiling while De La Soul played from her CD player.

"Because she's a badass. It was after Huey went to jail, got strung out, and the Party needed a leader. But those fools couldn't handle her." Ericka shot straight. "Men," she smirked.

I sat quietly with that answer: "Because she's a badass." I sat with it for hours in Ericka's room that day, mulling it over in my head, turning it around on my lips, practicing in words what I wanted for myself in truth: "badass."

I used to spend hours tucked away in Ericka's dorm room, comparing notes on our lives before Spelman. Sitting on her bed, we talked a lot about traversing worlds. The effort Ericka described when negotiating different spaces was a feeling I knew well. How it felt to conform or switch whenever we entered our mostly white schools—and then at the end of each day, crossing back through the cultural divide to reenter the familiarity of home. Home, where Jacob Lawrence images and African sculptures adorned the walls and the Negro National Anthem was sung before bed. Where Donny Hathaway and Gil Scott-Heron—or Kathleen and Eldridge Cleaver—weren't just figures we read about, but people in our everyday lives.

My father taught my sister and me about the importance of self-determination as a form of revolt, and for the same purpose, Ericka's mother taught her how to literally be a revolutionary. Ericka's mom was Elaine Brown, an involved member of the Black Panther Party, who often conferred with Huey Newton, Stokely Carmichael, and Eldridge Cleaver during late-night strategy sessions. In true revolutionary form, Elaine eventually moved up in ranks and became the Party's first and only female leader. Radicalism was the backbone of both Ericka's and my experiences.

Some people assumed my dad was the American Dream,

starting from nothing and making his way up in life so that he could offer his kids more. But of course, he was just as radical as Elaine. My father saw, thought, and acted through the lens of race—always. His mantras (Don't let white people confuse you; Let the children be free), his decisions (I'm only paying for a Black college, Jodie; Figure it out for yourself); even his career path—were all centered on his desire to disrupt. His approach to life was radical; in everything he did he was going straight at the problem, tugging at its root and eventually destroying it.

Ericka's mother felt the same, believing that the only way forward was to destroy an unjust system and rebuild with an eye toward consciousness. Neither was concerned with accommodating or fitting in. Progress, for both of them, meant making people feel uncomfortable in whatever space discomfort was required. Ericka and I, each in our version, were daughters of the revolution.

The more I learned about Ericka, the more I learned about Elaine. Elaine Brown was the first complicated, unexplainable, "bougie-ghetto" (in her words) badass Black woman I'd ever encountered. She was all things: a radical thinker, a kept woman, a strip club waitress, a mother, a lover, undeniably Black, ambiguously exotic, marginalized, politically active, and more than anything else, someone who just didn't give a fuck. Ericka didn't open up much to people about her mother, but she told me these stories in the deep, raspy voice she inherited from Elaine, and I ate them up like candy. The dessert at the end of my hearty meal of Shirley Chisholms and Rosa Parkses. Elaine was the decadent complement—sumptuous and satisfying, and so, so necessary. A heroine not included in most history books.

What I had begun to experience was the sensation of personal freedom, like the tremor before orgasm. The Black Panther Party

had awakened a thirst in me. And it had given me the power to
satisfy it. For a black woman in America, to know that power is
to experience being raised from the dead.

—ELAINE BROWN, *A Taste of Power*

I read Elaine's autobiography and learned how she went from "a rather unconscious, silly girl to someone who knew things." *I*, Jodie, felt like an unconscious, silly girl with no big thoughts of my own, and I desperately wanted to be someone who knew things. Who cared about things. I learned how she made room for herself at the head of the table in the Black Panther Party and demanded recognition and respect. Like my dad, what she wanted, really, was more than just a taste of power—she wanted it all.

Elaine had recently left the Party because she'd had enough, exhausted from fighting the Man, beat down by the blatant sexism of her Panther men, and simply tired of being broke and tired. She was well known all over the world and was often in the company of the most well-to-do people, but in many ways Elaine was still a marginalized Black woman who could barely pay her rent and Ericka's tuition. So, after meeting a wealthy Frenchman named Pierre at a high-society party in L.A., she threw in the towel, accepted his invitation to move to France, and became his lover. Unconcerned with how it might look, or how her legacy might be rewritten, she headed for the hills to try on another life. One filled with maids and a chef and a driver. It was a life in which she got up each day only when she felt like opening her eyes.

"It was a superficial and frivolous time," she told me much later. "But I loved living life as a princess." Here was someone who rebuilt herself, and rebuilt herself, and rebuilt herself again. She held her oppositions all together in one body, and she proudly showed them off. Elaine refused to be defined by one narrative, or to let one thread of her existence discount another. I wanted exactly that for myself.

My feelings for Elaine, the complex revolutionary, the sexy badass, the woman who gave zero fucks, bordered on obsession. And when I'd return home to New York on holidays, I took it as an opportunity to play out some of her stories, becoming what I thought a 1990 Elaine Brown would be like.

I was twenty-one years old when I became a true lover—capital *L*—for the first time in my life. I started dating Serge during the summer after my junior year at Spelman, though we'd first met years before in the thick of New York's nightlife scene, when I was sixteen and he was twenty-five. I'd see Serge out with a slew of women draped around him, saying hello as I made my way to the dance floor to stand in a circle with my high school girlfriends, bopping and swaying self-consciously to the beat. His eyes were always on me, quietly watching. But I was still interested in high school things, and boys my age—the ones with George Michael haircuts or gold teeth like Bobby Brown. I was certainly not interested in gentle, soft-spoken Serge—a man much older than I was.

But we kept in touch through the years and built a friendship. He'd call every so often to say hi, and we'd talk about things—about theater and architecture and design. Stuff I knew nothing about, but desperately wanted to learn because Serge made it all sound so exciting. When I'd come home to New York during breaks at Spelman, he'd take me to art openings or movies in the East Village. With Serge, I remember seeing a play about the Black Panther leader Huey P. Newton—it was the first time I'd gone to the theater without my parents.

He was patient, willing to put in years before we ever dated. He never demanded anything of me. In the beginning, he only gave—a phone call, a conversation. A dozen white roses with a note reading "I miss you. Please call." He checked in on me every month for years, and over time I began to see him differently. By that summer after my junior year, I had grown tired of the possessive, cocky men I was typically drawn to—the Aarons, and the young men at the college across the street, those who resembled my dad in a lot of ways. And so I opened myself to him.

Serge was a free-thinking European—mom a Swiss German, dad Vietnamese—and he possessed a quietly chaotic spirit that took him from probing conversations to long stretches of deep thought. When I was back home from college during breaks, I lived with Serge. We'd walk through the streets of Tribeca and I'd watch his mind at work. The graffiti on a wall reminded him of Basquiat, whom he knew in the early eighties when all of downtown New York looked like that block we had just passed; the architecture of that building on the corner made him think of a book he was reading, which made him think of love, which made him think of me. He'd grab my hand and smile, overcome with emotion. The entire moment conjured for him a Nina Simone song, the two of us singing "My baby just cares for me" as we floated down Church Street.

I was fascinated by the things he knew and the way he gave all of his information to me. As though life was to be shared, not divided up and conquered. I had never heard my parents debating ideas together for the pleasure of it. But with Serge, we'd talk as if everything were entirely made for our exploration. We were theologians in search of learning more—about religion or sex or art, or each other.

We'd go back and forth on topics that had no answers, just to see where the conversation would take us. With Serge, I was learning not to be bound by tradition and how things are, but instead to explore for the sake of finding new ways and new stories.

It was Serge who encouraged me to cut off my hair the summer we started dating. He wasn't concerned with length or texture or night styles—as so many of my schoolmates were. He thought my nose was one of my best features, and that a short pixie cut would highlight it. So I did, I cut it all off to try on a new, more daring form of beauty. And in doing so I took a radical stand in the "good hair" versus "bad hair" debate on campus, where long, straight hair was the optimal standard of beauty, and watched everyone stare while I walked the halls completely shorn.

Whenever we were together, Serge would take dozens of Polaroids of me, stretched out across his black leather couch, or in bed, or of just my profile while I sat at the kitchen table. And then we'd look at them together. "I love your back, Jodie. It's so defined. And your hips, too—they're strong."

I loved how he placed the word "strong" next to my hips. I hadn't ever thought of them as strong before. Serge made me look at, touch, and acknowledge my own self. I began to think about my body and, for the first time, to feel rightfully attached to it. Before then I had regarded it mostly with disdain. But from then forward, my body—my everything—started to come into focus. And I was roused awake. Aroused by adventure and challenge, by Blackness, by my own sexuality—and by a brand-new love.

Who am I in this world? I began to think. *What does it mean to be a woman? Is it my body, my mind, or my spirit? Or maybe it is defined by the power I wield.*

By the time I entered my senior year, I was fully exploring—crisscrossing barriers and mixing references, pulling from all the women I had read about—Toni Morrison, Zora Neale Hurston, Maya Angelou, Lorraine Hansberry, Audre Lorde—and those I was getting to know at school. I joined an African women's group and took African studies classes, amassed a collection of ankhs and started writing protest poetry (because, why not?).

I recited my uncle Gil's lyrics while wrapping my head each morning in African cloth. *You will not plug in, turn on and cop out . . . Because the revolution will not be televised.*

It was all a little clumsy, as to be expected from a college-age revolutionary. But I was catapulting myself from a silly girl with no big thoughts to someone empowered—whose possibilities were suddenly limitless. This idea of power and purpose was something my dad tried to teach me growing up, but his version lacked what I needed most: the crucial element of feminism—where I, a young woman, could be the king.

It was the women in the stories I read, and the women sitting next to me in class, and the women writers, and that woman I called Grandmother, who imprinted on me. All strong-voiced and strong-willed. All defiantly optimistic. All lovers of the word. All believers in transformation. Those women spoke to my heart and made me feel not only seen, but exalted.

During my four years at Spelman, my classmates and I had become sisters, unfolding and waking up in the world. We had been nurtured and groomed by sheroes and kings, and now, sitting in formation in the Atlanta Civic Center, just minutes away from receiving our diplomas, we were Black Girl Magic in the flesh.

Maya Angelou, one of Dr. Cole's most trusted sister-friends, took to the stage as our commencement speaker. "I belong to you," she began. "I have given birth to you. You are absolutely mine. Because . . . I have loved you."

Maya Angelou's voice was raspy. She didn't sound professorial or academic. She spoke to us as if we were in her kitchen, sitting around her table, while she cooked us a meal.

"You are already paid for. You do not have to pay for yourselves."

I had no clue what she was talking about—it was way over my head. But I was intrigued, so I shifted to the right a little so I could get a better look at her between my classmates sitting in front of me.

What did she mean by "paid for"? Dr. Angelou had sung a slave auction song as we filed into the auditorium before the ceremony began: "Bid 'em in, get 'em in; Bid 'em in, get 'em in." Maybe she was talking in metaphors, about self-ownership—taking ourselves back from slave owners and now owning ourselves. But I wasn't sure.

She continued—singing, speaking, laughing, reciting poetry she had written years ago. Even dancing a little.

"When you walk into an office you don't go alone," she was saying. "Bring your people with you. Bring everybody that has loved you with you: 'Come on, Grandma, let's go. Come on, Auntie.' When you walk in, people don't know what it is about you. They can't take their eyes off of you. They say, 'She has charisma'—No, what you have is all those people around you."

I started to understand what Dr. Angelou was telling us. She was talking about family and memory, and the power of both combined. About holding on to collective energy and to a love that surrounds us—and to the blood, sweat, and tears that our mothers and mothers' mothers spilled for us so that we could attend Spelman.

She was talking about the same thing Daddy had been instilling in me with his trips to the Jungle: connection—to all the women and men, relatives and loved ones who have cared for me and worked for me and lived for me, and already paid for me, many times over. Maya Angelou was telling us, 250 Black women—we belong.

During the course of her speech, my eyes never left hers. I

heard every word she spoke and every thing she asked. Of us she
asked that we stop and wonder about our great-grandmothers.
She asked us to work now, very hard, so that we can pay for our
granddaughters. She asked us to always know that we are loved
and to always bring our beloveds into every space with us so
that we know we are not alone. Each poem she referenced, each
spiritual she sang, every validation of my existence, would be
with me forever.

"However I am perceived or deceived," Dr. Angelou said, in
closing, "lay aside your fears that I will be undone, for I shall
not be moved."

*Dad giving me a pep talk on life, moments after
I walked the stage at graduation.*

And then it took hold of me, snatching me faster than the boys and the wild abandon—and even more forcefully than the tug of freedom I felt in high school: the idea that I could own myself, could be my own anchor. In that moment, in a stadium that dwarfed me in size, surrounded by hundreds of people, I felt every bit of my strength. It surged up through my legs, humming in my belly. I could feel how fortified I was—how fortified I'd always been. "You had it before you earned it," Dr. Angelou had told us. "Because it is your inheritance."

I no longer worried that my skinny legs might not make it across the stage. I was not at all scared of strutting past the rows and rows of distinguished guests and faculty, past our ferocious Dr. Cole and our mystical Maya Angelou—past our parents, holding their breath. And past grandmothers and aunties, sisters and friends, all beaming as if our diplomas were their own.

When my name was finally called out over the loudspeaker— "Jodie Miishee Patterson"—I took a deep breath and strode, with new confidence, across that long stage. Because at the other end was not just my hard-earned diploma—it was the whole world awaiting.

THREE

Serious Daring

Clap-clap-clap. "What's your next move, Jodatha?" Daddy stood in front of me like a drill sergeant, trying to jolt me into action. I lay sprawled across the couch in the den of his apartment one afternoon—basking in my most recent achievement, feeling confident that life was on my side.

I shrugged, unconcerned. "Not sure." It felt as if I had all the time in the world. I had a college diploma from Spelman, and *the* Dr. Maya Angelou in my corner—how could things not fall into place? To say the least, I was hella optimistic about my future, but unlike many of my multitasking classmates, I hadn't lined up a job, or even an interview, during the last months of my senior year, and I hadn't a clue as to what my career might be.

"Well, make a list of all the things you love. And then *do* one of those things. You need to get a move on it, baby girl." I could tell from Daddy's tone that if I wanted any of his respect, and perhaps a bit of his help, I'd need to land a job and stay in the game. Daddy didn't tolerate inertia.

Over the next several days, I began making what turned out to be a very short list:

1) Reading
2) ?
3) ??

Yep, reading was about it.

Serge had a subscription to *The New Yorker,* which Serge and

I plowed through religiously. We had stacks and stacks of *The New York Times*. And I had hundreds of books: used and worn ones from Grandma Gloria's collection, and brand-new ones that I'd scooped up from various bookstores across the city. Aside from my library, I had very little else to my name when I moved back to New York after graduation and into the loft I shared with Serge. Just a few pieces of clothing, three pairs of shoes, and no valuables to speak of. I wanted for nothing more, really, except to read—and then to think about, talk about, or write about what I had just read. How those passions would translate into a job that didn't involve teaching or freelancing for magazines—neither of which particularly interested me—I wasn't at all sure.

With no concrete post-Spelman plans on the horizon, I decided to spend the summer traveling through Europe with a best friend from college. We bought Eurail Passes and round-trip tickets to Vienna, where my sister Ramona was living, intent on seeing new things, thinking new thoughts, and returning with a solid plan for the rest of our lives.

That summer of 1992, we visited cities I'd never seen: Prague, Budapest, Madrid, Paris, Venice, Corfu. While my friend saw the sights, I'd sit in the same café from morning till early evening, poring over *The Unbearable Lightness of Being,* absorbing each word, sentence, and punctuation mark. Then I'd write in my journal about what I'd read. I liked the pace of the book, how it read slowly and methodically, almost putting me in a trance. I connected with the idea of needing more weight to one's being. And I understood how miserable it is to feel without substance.

Those long days spent alone, with words swimming around in my head and endless cups of coffee in my bloodstream, were some of the most romantic hours of my life. I had fallen even more deeply in love with books, and by the end of our trip I knew I wanted nothing more for myself than to be a book editor—a master of words.

After six weeks of youth hostels, cafés, and backpacks, I returned to New York that fall and began the job search. I sent out dozens of persuasive cover letters and samples of my own writing, looking for any entry-level position in publishing that would take me. Nothing was too small, I thought—I just needed my first break. In less than two months, I landed a job at Scholastic, the well-known children's publishing company. I was to be the administrative assistant to the director of communications, and although I was unclear on what the communications department actually did, Scholastic—certainly from where I sat—was at the epicenter of publishing. I felt I had hit the bull's-eye.

The job, I soon found out, consisted mostly of faxing, copying, scheduling, and cleaning up both my and my boss's mistakes before anyone could catch on. Every day I went into the office with a tiny kernel of promise, hoping my days of administrative grunt work would finally be rewarded with something substantial—at the very least, writing for the company's news bulletin. But, to my disappointment, I never wrote or read anything beyond a memo.

To keep my brain from completely shriveling, I enrolled in evening writing and modern literature classes at the New School, and then at City College, where I read Eudora Welty for the first time. I fell in love with Welty's writing style and found myself rereading passages just for the pleasure of revisiting her words. Lines like "It took me a long time to manage the independence, for I loved those who protected me" and "The memory is a living thing—it too is in transit" resonated so intimately that I thought she'd written them just for me. Those lines validated many of the thoughts I'd been turning over since I was a teenager. I took Welty everywhere—to bed, to the park bench for lunch, on the subway home. I even sneaked her into my desk at work, pulling her out between tasks to ingest just one more page.

In the bathroom one day at Scholastic, my eyes lingered over Welty's last sentence in her book *One Writer's Beginnings:* "Serious daring starts from within." That night, bent over a stack of loose-leaf paper, I handwrote my final essay for class. "I can't help but admire Welty's demand for freedom and self-definition," I scribbled down in closing. Eudora, like many of the authors who'd come into my life over the last few years, had spoken to me, and set me in motion.

A few days later I returned to my father's apartment with an idea.

"Daddy, remember last year when you asked me what I love?" I sat in the side chair of his long oak dining room table and cleared my throat, prepared to finally give him an answer.

"Well, I figured it out—I love literature! I've looked into the best schools and programs, and I've narrowed down the ones I think would be perfect for me. Dad, I want to become a *master* of the *written word*!" I lingered on the word "master" for effect, hoping my enthusiasm would be contagious. I knew I'd have to sell this pursuit of a master's degree in writing to him in a big way.

If there was one thing I knew about John Patterson, it was that he hated spending his money—and even more, he hated other people spending his money. Graduate school, no doubt, would be expensive. But Daddy himself had received an advanced degree, a J.D. from Brooklyn Law School. He'd spent years studying the law not for the purposes of practicing it—he went for information, for mental dexterity, and for the connections a law degree provided. I assumed he, of all people, would understand the importance of learning to learn, mastering as a way of becoming stronger, better, and wiser. This would be my crucial piece of leverage. But instead of the enthusiasm I hoped for, Daddy sat next to me in silence, a deadpan look on his face.

"Grad school is for gay, fat, or ugly women. There's no place for you there, Jodie."

It was as though a sword had sliced through my knees, dropping me to the floor. He hadn't said much, but those two little sentences spoke volumes. His intentions were clear: Not a dime of his money would be spent on my ideas, or on my dreams. Whatever he had planned for me was not up for debate. His words felt final.

I started rambling, trying my best to hold myself together while I appealed to his rational, educated self. "Daddy, you went to law school and look at how much it's helped your career and your life. I just think it's hypocrit—"

"Listen, do what you want, Jodie. But don't think for a second that I'm going to pay for any of it. Zero."

He turned in his chair to face me, looking directly into my eyes. "Stay focused. With *your* skin color, you can marry well."

He left those words right there on the oak table for me to parse on my own. Then he flashed a smile that under any other circumstances might have smoothed everything over. But this time, it disintegrated me into a million tiny pieces. My own father had distilled me down to just skin—something I had no control over. And then he squeezed me down even smaller, to a color. And then he smiled at me as if it were all okay.

We weren't equals, not in his mind. And we might never be. Men pursued degrees, as he had, so they could change the world. But women need only be smart enough to marry well, raise outstanding children, and run an efficient household. To Daddy, my endgame was solely family. I absolutely wanted family. But I also wanted to do things—big things—that would take me beyond the walls of my household, just as he had.

Gay. Fat. Ugly. He threw those words at me to stop me from doing what he didn't think I should do. And he threw them so confidently because in his mind they could do only one thing: shame me out of my own confidence and make me change my mind.

I placed both hands on the table to stabilize myself. If I hadn't, the clarity of the moment would have knocked me down. And then I cried, silently, facing him with tears streaming down my face—because I knew this was a battle over who would have final control over me.

My mind flashed back to everything Daddy had told me about the world being mine, and about fortifying myself against all the bad that was working against us. And I knew, then, that Daddy was part of it—he was a small piece of the bad that I was preparing myself for.

What if I *were* gay or fat or ugly? Did Daddy have the power to tell me "No, you can't be those things"? Did he even have the right to define those three words?

The mountain of a problem that arose that night was not the lack of funding for my dreams, or that we disagreed. It wasn't even confronting the idea that he would always take more for himself, leaving less for everyone else. The worst offense was finding out that my own father was part of the other side. The side where men and their residual sexism dwell—the kind of sexism that is passed down through generations. And I was squarely on the opposite side, where women fight for just about everything we want and any damn thing we need.

Staring at him at the head of his big oak table, the king upon his throne, looking down at his child asking permission for a bit of power—I couldn't find any words. I couldn't tell him how horrible he sounded, or how much I wanted him to be open to another way. Sadness came instead. Sadness for him, a man stuck in his ways. And for me, a young woman being arranged.

So I ran—out of the dining room, out of my father's house, across Eighty-First Street and clumsily down the subway steps. I ran from the strongest provider I knew, and from a house that once made me whole. I ran because I couldn't trust them anymore. I ran so hard and fast that the details of that frantic sprint have totally disappeared from my mind. I don't remember the sounds of the street, or the faces of the subway passengers, or how I made it from the train to my loft. I don't know what I told Serge when I burst through our door with tears in my eyes. All I remember is that I traveled as far away from Daddy and his ways as I could. I vowed to stay away until he understood— knowing that that time might never come.

That day, at twenty-two years old, I learned a valuable lesson: Once you give someone the power to judge just one tiny part of you, you invite that person to define all of you. I had allowed my father to make decisions about my life, on my behalf. And in doing so, I opened the floodgates of his judgment. The truth of it smacked me in the face: If I didn't insist on defining myself, someone else most certainly would.

I would have to distance myself from my father—and anyone who needed me to be different from who I was or who I wanted to be. That, I believed, was the price to pay for owning myself. What I stood for that day, what I aspired to become, and all the moves I'd make in between would depend on it. For self-determination, there would be loss. Daddy was that collateral damage.

I stopped seeing, speaking to, and thinking about my father as best I could. Months went by when I didn't answer any of his calls. A letter arrived in the mail one afternoon:

It may seem as though we are forever at odds. I love you too
much, forever, to accept that. Please allow me to keep trying in
order to make our relationship better. See my love.

Forever, Dad

I read it, folded it in half, and tucked it deep into my desk
drawer.

Being at odds with him left an immediate and massive void.
When a problem came up that I'd normally ask my dad to help
me solve, about life or friends or a bothersome and competitive
coworker, I didn't have anyone to turn to. No one seemed sharp
enough or qualified enough to advise me. But still I wouldn't
reach out.

And then, a few months later, as if the season had changed, I
let go of him completely. He'd become too painful, and I had
someone else now to put all my energy, belief, and love into. I
had Serge, and he became my everything. I drew him entirely in
with just as much conviction as I extricated my father from my
life. Where Daddy felt like a wall around me, Serge was flowing
water. He seemed to love me for me, and for everything I
wanted to be. I was ecstatic when I was with him.

Watching me with Serge, there were flashes of hesitation in
my mother's eyes. She, more than anyone else, knew the effects
of a broken heart. My parents had been divorced for several
years at that point, and Mama knew firsthand how the soul
wanders after a break, trying to find stability. She saw me bending toward Serge, noticing how I smiled at him when he spoke,
how I lapped up his words and his laughter, giddy with the
thought that this exciting, free-spirited man was all mine.

"Are you sure about this, Jodie?" Mama would ask, forebod-
ing in her voice, knowing how it might all play out—how it did
for her, at least, after she and my father had separated.

But it was too late. Life with Serge was exhilarating. We were perpetually guided by the chase—of new ideas, new experiences, and new opportunities. If my dad was stuck in his old ways and habits, I absolutely would not be. Serge and I together had a chance to rewrite the story. He was a designer in the nightlife business, so his entire career revolved around capturing the zeitgeist, then embodying it in brick and mortar—hoping people would come, revel, and pass on the good word. That meant we were constantly surrounded by creatives—artists and writers, musicians and chefs, who thought only in the realm of possibility, driven exclusively by the challenge of manifesting their wildest dreams.

I was putting in eight soul-sucking hours a day at my communications job at Scholastic, then rushing home to come alive again with Serge and his friends. We'd eat out every night and talk for hours over several bottles of wine. Their new ideas would soon become restaurants or plays or paintings; their musings would turn into projects that had the entire city at attention. It was intoxicating. Serge's life held a mirror up to my own boring existence of faxing and copying and reading copy from my desk.

I thought a job in publishing would feed my love of stories and pull me closer to the smart, engaged people I wanted to surround myself with. I entered the workforce with a romantic picture of what it would be like—I envisioned something similar to my English Literature classroom back at Spelman, where we enthusiastically read and dissected great works for hours. But in reality, the career I thought would tap into my creativity, bringing me closer to myself, actually stifled me—chaining me to my desk, to the manuscripts and their deadlines, and to a mostly older, white conservative world of which I wanted no part. Every time I walked into those publishing offices, I felt as though I was stepping into their grid and out of my own. It was the rigidity of the work that bothered me—it felt, once again, like walls closing me in.

In less than a year, I left my job and bounced around to other niche publishing houses, trying to find that exact energy I was craving. I was sure Scholastic wasn't indicative of the entire industry, and with a little hard work I believed I could find the right company to match my desire to create. The collision—between work and personal life, reality and aspiration—happens so often as we feel our way through life. And it was happening to me again, and again and again. But with each time my ideal didn't quite match up with my day-to-day life, I could also feel myself inching a little closer to what I needed.

Almost everyone Serge introduced me to was creating a career that mirrored their passions and personalities. Up-and-coming clothing designers, fashion stylists, DJs—they were all originators and explorers who flowed without restrictions. With them, there was no separation between their "work" selves and their "real" selves. I'd look at them and then wonder about myself—*What is my special thing, my mojo? What story am I going to tell one day?*

"Serge, you've been so quiet recently—what's going on?" I asked him one morning at our kitchen table.

I knew his work took him to far-off places in his mind: Area, MK, Bowery Bar, Time Café, Fez, Sticky Mike's. Creating those places meant he would disappear inside his thoughts for months at a time. Serge wasn't just opening up restaurants or lounges, he was creating iconic moments that would shape our city and culture. They were other worlds and different times, and they had the special ability to synchronize people. I knew what he was spending his time on was important, but whenever he zoned into his work, it made me feel left out. I wanted to be a part of whatever he was brewing, to understand the behind-the-curtain secrets to his magic, to know exactly how he created. I'd been observing Serge's process since we moved in together, but I needed him to spell it out for me.

"I don't know what's going on with me," he said casually, sipping his coffee. "I'm just in my head, I guess. I have this idea, of a venue that changes every night—like, completely transforms." Serge had pages and pages of torn strips of tracing paper thrown about the house with images he'd drafted. Banquettes that would become intimate corners in his next restaurant, lighting fixtures that would set the mood in his newest lounge, bodies and silhouettes and faces—many of which looked like me in various formations.

"I'm working on something big, Jodie. It's still rough—I need more time to make it all happen." I had no idea what he was talking about, or how it would all turn out, but I knew, by the way he spoke and from what he'd done before, that it would be amazing. It made me realize just how desperately I wanted to make things happen, to actualize a dream.

"You know, babe, I've never lived on my own. I've either been with my parents, or my roommates, or now, with you. I've never brought anything to life, not by myself. Not an empty apartment, or an idea—nothing." Serge looked at me across the table as if he knew the inevitable was coming.

Later that night, under the covers, I blurted out what I'd been mulling over all afternoon:

"I think . . . I need to move out. I need my own bed to spread out in, and my own walls to hang art on. I need something all mine."

Serge shifted his pillow and turned to me, putting his hands on my face. "I get it, you should have your own space." He responded in true Serge fashion—softly and without conflict.

"It'll probably be good for you." He paused for a beat to remember. "It was for me when I was in my twenties." His eyes told me that he would miss us snuggled together, the way we were that night, and that he wasn't naïve about what could happen with new space between us. But his arms around my body told me he would, in the end, be supportive of my decision.

Within weeks I moved to the East Village, into a tiny, shabby but gloriously all-mine studio. I bought a vintage fire-red leather couch from our favorite outdoor flea market, constructed a loft bed that extended from wall to wall, and bought cheap daisies from the bodega around the corner to adorn the only table I had. It was a baby step to independence, but a powerful one—having my very own set of keys that no one else had copies to, locking the door behind me each night knowing that no one else was expected. For that year, every penny I scraped together for my rent felt well spent.

Eventually, when I got tired of the dirt and grime of the East Village—and the teenagers sleeping in my doorway, high on whatever drug they'd taken—I decided to move to Fort Greene, Brooklyn, where the Black bohemian scene was starting to emerge. It was an electric community where everyone wanted to be amazing and beautiful. The positive energy on the streets of Fulton and South Elliott, my block, was palpable—I swear I could feel it on my skin. Digable Planets, the underground hip-hop group known for their breakout hit "Rebirth of Slick (Cool Like Dat)" were my neighbors, the indie film director Spike Lee lived just around the corner, and the music journalist Touré, who had an apartment across from Fort Greene Park, became like a brother to me. We were all a tribe, looking out for one another. Salif, the owner of the Senegalese restaurant downstairs from my apartment, would offer me dinner on the house, knowing my funds got tight toward the end of the month. And the Brooklyn Moon Café, where a young Erykah Badu was known to test out new material, had the support of the entire neighborhood filling the space each night. We sustained our local businesses, watched out for one another, and kept the vibe just right.

Living in Fort Greene was like living in the mecca of magic. Rents were still low and life felt easy. On any given Saturday, all I needed to do was step out my front door, make a right onto Fulton, and wait for something amazing to come my way—and it was bound to. Amazingness could be the perfect conversation between friends, or a belly laugh over a moment that had just passed, or an instant of connectivity between you and whoever happened to be on your right or left. Spontaneity was the theme of each day. Sometimes I'd sit outside the laundromat between South Elliott and South Oxford for hours while my clothes spun 'round and 'round, chatting up my friends on music and fashion and food as they passed by. Then I'd make my way over to the barbershop to get my hair cut with the fellas and laugh for a solid hour while five guys I knew from the neighborhood cracked jokes and talked smack. We would eventually roll over to one of their apartments, smoke a joint, and listen to Al Green late into the night, dreaming of what could be.

Working in an office, at a desk, typing letters into a computer all day, felt futile in comparison to what was happening in Brooklyn. I was beginning to realize that office structure and protocol, plus the slow pace of editing, just wasn't for me. All I wanted to do was marinate in the surprise of each Brooklyn day, in my electric community of Fort Greene.

One day, I decided to quit my publishing job. I just couldn't go back there. It was a crazy idea, considering that I had very little money saved, but living frugally among my friends, without much structure, felt lavish to me. I slept in most mornings and went out most nights. When I came home, I'd stretch out in my bed, using all the pillows, and stare at the ceiling until I fell asleep. And when I woke up, I would weigh my options and decide, casually, selfishly, how I'd spend the next several hours of the day. This sudden free fall into autonomy felt entirely new, and I appreciated the ability to float around my neighborhood on my own terms.

I searched out new friends with interesting stories. Sometimes I'd imagine life without rules and boundaries, a life where money flowed in—somehow—and work's only obligation was to feed the soul. I made my way less and less frequently into Manhattan, and inadvertently saw Serge and his friends less as well. I grew a mild distaste for the "big city"—instead reveling in *my* community and *my* tribe and the daily rhythm I'd created on my own.

"You're not the person I thought you were," Serge said to me late one afternoon in his loft. Weeks and weeks had passed after leaving my job, and I still hadn't made any plans to find a new one. Although I didn't let on, what Serge had said was a gut punch, all the more wrenching because there was no malice there, just sadness—as though he was mourning the loss of a great potential he saw in me. He was so sure that I could do anything, like eventually becoming a famous editor of great books, or maybe even a writer myself. But none of that seemed to be happening for me. What Serge had said was true. I was not the person I used to be, nor the person I wanted to be precisely. I was roaming somewhere in the middle, my identity still out of focus. And although I couldn't bring myself to admit it, I needed to be fully on my own, with no backup plan or backup person to figure out which way I was headed.

Serge and I struggled under the weight of this knowledge for a while until he painfully, reluctantly broke up with me. I believe that, to him, it seemed like the only thing he could do to help.

• • •

Months passed, and I floated through my life without a compass.

At a dinner party one night in the city, I met a woman who was an exotic dancer. Jacinda lived in a small one bedroom apartment in Brooklyn near the Atlantic Avenue subway station and gave piano lessons to rich kids during the day. She was a plain girl, not the type you would necessarily pick out of a crowd, but she was smart and she was tough—and her fearlessness, particularly with her body, impressed me. She seemed to have what many of the people I admired had, a belief in herself and in her own kind of magic: one that commanded the body.

I walked away from that dinner with Jacinda and spent the next few weeks imagining how it would feel to be so publicly uninhibited. In my eyes, Jacinda was *living,* really living—and I was pitifully wasting time.

I worked up the nerve to call her one afternoon out of the blue, and proceeded to unleash a series of questions that I'd been storing up in my mind: How did you start dancing? Where do you get your outfits? How did you learn the moves? One by one, she answered every question I asked. Over the next hour or so, Jacinda became my professor, walking me through the business of stripping.

Before we got off the phone, I asked if I could come with her one night to the club where she danced. It was a spontaneous idea that just popped into my mind, and the question came out before I could reconsider. I needed the money, sure. But even more than that, I needed an experience that might make me feel accomplished. Dancing half naked in front of strangers in some far-off part of town seemed exactly what I needed. Jacinda laughed, taken aback by the proposition. But she agreed to let me tag along. The next day I purchased a black pageboy wig at a hair boutique in downtown Brooklyn, two glittery thong and bra sets, and a pair of over-the-top black patent leather heels.

A week later, on a Saturday night, Jacinda and I set out for the South Bronx to make my debut.

We took the 6 train to Hunts Point, an area in the Bronx I'd never heard of before. While we walked the half mile in the dark toward the club, we transformed. As we adjusted our wigs and applied our lipstick, Jacinda coached me on how to shift my mind to adapt to a very different set of rules from what I was used to. "You'll be fine," she told me, as long as I kept three rules in mind:

Rule #1: Folks are crazy; always keep your eyes open.
Rule #2: When you're dancing, pick a person in the crowd who shows interest in you, and focus only on him. It'll give you confidence.
Rule #3: Figure out your special move, and do that move confidently.

I thought about Sade and how she always did the smallest of motions when she performed—a flick of the wrist and the audience went crazy. *Tonight,* I thought, *I'll channel Sade.*

The club was an unfancy oasis at the edge of a desolate neighborhood. Block after block was dark and quiet, but as we approached the strip joint, the music from inside spilled out onto the street, where easily thirty men, all Black and Latino, formed a line to get in. When we arrived at the door, we were met by two large and very unfriendly looking bouncers. They rifled through our bags, checking for drugs, presumably, before ushering us through a metal detector, checking for any weapons we might have on us, I assumed. Jacinda had warned me that the club was wary of women coming in to prostitute, distracting the patrons and "stealing" potential money from the club owner. She predicted that the bouncers would ask me why I was there. I shouldn't take it personally, she explained. "Just say, 'I came to dance.'"

Moments before, when we were walking from the train station, I was confident I could handle what I was getting into. But now, in the moment, it smacked of a realness I wasn't prepared for. I was out of my element and terrified—and somehow, at the same time, intrigued. I wanted to know everything about this danger. I saw it as an obstacle to navigate—to get over or work through—and that possibility pulled me in.

As I walked onto the main floor, my eyes adjusted to the dimness. The low lights cast weird shadows on everyone, and I struggled to see people's faces, making out only their silhouettes. Everyone seemed so much bigger than my friends back in Manhattan and Brooklyn; the men more buff, the women more fleshy and curvy. They all seemed to tower over me. The room was crowded; every corner, walkway, and chair was occupied by bodies—some dressed, others not.

"All right, y'all, get ya bills out—Next up: Baaaaby Gucci!" The DJ put on an up-tempo Latin song I didn't recognize while all the eyes in the club followed a very thick, very short woman with wavy hair that hung down to the middle of her back as she sauntered up the staircase to the narrow stage. A few men clapped loudly when she began. Baby Gucci snaked to the middle of the stage, her long hair swishing behind her, and then dramatically she dropped to the floor into a full split. She bobbed up and down in that split several times while the crowd shouted out their appreciation. I was impressed by her flexibility, and remembered from my days in gymnastics how much training that move actually demanded.

There were maybe seventy-five men in the club, outnumbering the women by far. But it was the women onstage, like Baby

Gucci, who stole my attention. They were the ultimate per-formers, confident with their curvaceous bodies, aware of and pleased with themselves. They glided with intention across the club's floor, entrancing whomever they passed, stopping only for those who dared to speak. And when they were called on-stage, they *danced*—the way a lot of us do only in the privacy of our own homes, in front of our own bedroom mirrors. Unin-hibited, the girls climbed to the top of the pole, releasing their hands and arching backward—dangling upside down on the strength of their thighs alone. Then, slowly, they slid their way down, inch by sweaty inch. I wondered how they got to be so strong, how their feet held up for hours in those six-inch heels, and how their bodies obeyed all the moves. The entire scenario seemed impossible.

"Stop staring, Jodie. Let's get changed," Jacinda directed, bringing me back to reality. I was here to perform, not gawk. I followed her down the hallway at the far end of the club into the makeshift locker room, and immediately the theater of the last few minutes disappeared.

Behind the scenes, the dancers were all business. There was no sexiness, no sisterhood or solidarity, no laughing or girl power. These women were competitors—for the men, for the best outfits, for the choicest spots in the club, and of course, for the money. Their objective, the only objective, was to be the biggest, shiniest object there.

In the dressing room, the neon track lighting was bright, and once again I had to adjust my eyes. The space looked like a laun-dromat without the washing machines—there were a few long tables, some folding chairs, royal blue walls, concrete floors, and that unforgiving lighting, which showed every square inch of cellulite along with dirty floor and chipped paint.

I spotted an empty chair and put my bag down to start get-ting dressed. It was at that point that they started to notice us. A dozen or so pairs of suspicious eyes watched me as I quietly folded my street clothing into my bag, pushed it deep under the chair, and bolted for the door as quickly as I could. *One more competitor in the ring,* I'm sure they thought, seeing me.

Back out on the main floor, feeling very exposed and inadequate, barely filling out my silver bikini top and thong, I managed to push my shoulders back and walk—scoping out the men as I passed. As I wove through the crowd, several of them tapped, tugged, and pulled at me to get my attention, but I didn't stop. I needed time to look around and assess everything I was seeing before making any moves.

I spotted three guys at the bar who looked friendly enough and took a seat in the swivel stool next to them. The sticky leather on the seat rubbed strangely on my bare butt and legs, and I wondered how many others had sat bare-cheeked on this same stool.

"Hey," one of the guys said to me. They looked about my age, like they'd recently graduated from college. Their worn T-shirts and khakis reminded me of the boys from Morehouse.

"Hey," I replied, assuming that was all the intro needed in a place like this.

We sat together drinking many drinks, dulling my senses and laughing about what I was preparing to do. I shared with them that this would be my first time onstage and they asked me, "Why now?" I didn't have any answers, but I did tell them that after a few more vodka tonics we'd all know if it was worth it or not. An hour or so later and several additional cocktails in, I walked over to the DJ booth and motioned with a nod that I was ready.

All prospective dancers had to "try out" in front of the crowd in order to be allowed back to perform. I was seconds away from being judged on my first dance, and depending on the crowd's response, I would know where I stood. My heart raced with the realization that I had only minutes to show people what they wanted to see.

Walking toward the stage steps in my too-high black heels, I ran through my game plan one more time. I had determined that I would stay clear of the pole and remain with feet, knees, or hands firmly on the floor. No ambitious jumps or elaborate pole tricks. No fast twirls, shimmies, or shakes. I would keep it as basic as possible. My goal, I thought, was simply to flow. To glide my way through the next three minutes.

I adjusted my sequined thong and closed my eyes. The only way I could make it up those stairs and onto that stage was to tune out the hip-hop music blasting overhead. Inside my head, I switched the record to Sade's "Sweetest Taboo," and immediately my shoulders started to relax. I swayed all the way across the stage and back again on the thought of the song's opening drums. Looking out into the sea of faces, some of them eager, the rest mildly bored, I locked eyes with the recent college grads and saw that they were smiling, cheering me on. I sang to myself: *There's a quiet storm, and it never felt like this before*. I imagined myself as that storm, and I smiled and gazed and moved slowly to Sade—over the loud music and the macho men and the thick women sucking their teeth at me from their spots in the room. I tuned it all out, and thought only about the words in the song, *Will you keep on lovin' me? Will you keep on bringing out the best in me?* I watched bills land on the floor and I kept smiling. I watched eyes on me and I kept singing to myself, dancing with the stage.

Ten minutes later I had a new job and a hundred dollars in my hands. I performed several more times that night, and each time I did, I locked eyes with someone who seemed to be in awe of me—of my skinny frame, my Sade subtlety, and all the courage I'd mustered to make my way into this moment. The feeling of being admired, and more important, *seen,* was priceless. The men knew nothing of my family, of the school and the classes I'd attended, they didn't have a clue about me other than what I had pulled from inside—that quiet storm I brought to the stage.

In publishing, I could work or not work, try or not try, and still get the same paycheck. But there, on that stage, I was determining the outcome. If I did another dance I could make more money, if I worked really hard in that hour I could make hundreds. As sexist as stripping for money sounds, I was dictating my worth. By the end of the night I was sweaty and exhausted, feet torn up—but I had made my rent for the month. All in crumpled singles, but I had succeeded. It was the first time I felt I had really *earned* my money. Sweat and tears earned. Adrenaline earned. Burning with fear earned.

I made so much money on that first weekend that I gave myself a goal: In a month, I'd go on a cross-country road trip with my grandmother Gloria. We'd drive her yellow Cadillac from Texas to the West Coast and back, weaving in and out of all the national parks and monuments. And so I returned to that same club over the next three weekends and danced.

Every time I got onstage I thought I was going to fail, or fall, or be so scared that I'd have to walk away with my head dropped in shame. Every single time. But then I'd remember Jacinda's rules—"Eyes open. Find your customer. Do your move." I'd always play my own music in my head and create my own vibe. I'd find the one or two admirers who seemed to understand me, and I'd dance for them, pulling them in. In every performance, I'd move from fear to exhilaration, from failure to being in control.

I told no one about my trips to the South Bronx. Not my roommates, not my best friends. Only my mother and one guy friend, just in case something happened to me. They were concerned, of course, and voiced their disapproval. "Jodie, this isn't you. This is beneath you," Mama warned. But I didn't ask for permission. I only said I was doing it, and that it was research, "for personal growth." And that wasn't a lie, it *was* a research experiment—a way for me to understand and work with my body, to process fear and to earn myself back. Being onstage half-naked forced me to confront questions I'd been asking myself. *What does it mean to be a woman? Is it sexual or mental? Or is it in the power I have over others to mesmerize?* Stripping makes you think about all of that. And in the end, for me at least, it made me feel valiant.

There was something more happening on those Friday and Saturday nights than just taking off my clothes. It was something that everyone around me, for years to come, would be forced to witness: the constant motion of someone refusing to sit still long enough for others to grab hold of and define based on their own narrow and ridiculous terms. I would stay in steady motion, feeling every bit of life, because seeking shelter in other people's lives had become too painful. The truth, I knew now, was out there to find.

Those weeks of dancing in the South Bronx taught me that the body is powerful—not to be underestimated; that the mind can do anything it determines; and that fear is impermanent, it's just one of many emotions, and it will always shift. Most important, it taught me that one's path is never obvious.

At the end of the month, I threw my glittery outfit, high heels, and pink lipstick into the garbage and set out on a cross-country adventure with my grandmother, feeling powerful and in control.

FOUR

She

———

FIRST TRIMESTER: COSMIC ENERGY

"Hey, baby!" I shout as I open our front door. Home is only slightly bigger than a shoe box—even the smallest noises can be heard from any corner of our 250-square-foot apartment. I shout because I'm happy, and I need Serge to feel this excitement, too.

We live in a five-story walk-up on Sixth Avenue in SoHo. It's a bustling street dotted with small antique and art shops, but our building is set back a bit, making our block feel quieter than it really is. A former factory space, the building is outfitted with heavy wooden double doors at the front entrance and a steep, narrow staircase that zigzags from floor to floor. I have to use all of my energy to make my way to the top, where Serge and I live. On every landing, I lean against the wall and catch my breath like an old lady. I look down at my stomach, smiling, and keep climbing. My legs feel like fifty-pound weights, and I enjoy every bit of the exhaustion I'm experiencing.

"Hi, Jo." He smiles, craning his neck to look at me. I love coming home to find Serge sitting on the vintage red leather couch that used to be just mine. For the past year now, it's become ours.

"Babe, I ate pancakes and hash browns again at my desk this morning! It. Was. *Great.* And then—and *then!* I went into the studio with the guys. Electric Lady is like, *whoa.*"

I drop my bags at the door and kick off my shoes, walking

barefoot across the wooden floor. His lips are pretty much all I need in this moment, so I bend down to kiss his mouth, his hands reaching up to find the curviest parts of me.

Serge has never shied away from my body, and with the extra flesh I'm now carrying, three months into our pregnancy, things haven't changed.

"You're so juicy," he says, squeezing my thighs. "It's like your friend said the other night: Pregnant Jodie is the tricked-out version of Jodie!" We laugh, his hands gliding up my leg, resting on my butt. I stay put so he can look at me, my growing belly, my big smile—and let him take it all in.

Serge and I have finally made our way back together.

Post–South Bronx, post road trip across America with Grandma Gloria, I got a new verve. Over the three weeks we spent together, joyfully living out of her car, we experienced so many firsts, in places I'd never much thought about as a city girl, like New Mexico, Arizona, Nevada, Utah, and Colorado. We'd driven into their sunsets, climbed their mountains, strolled through canyons, deserts, and ruins alike. And in just about every state we visited, we slept roadside once or twice, when our yellow Cadi just couldn't go another inch. We'd wrap ourselves in blankets and watch the stars from our car window until daylight emerged and we could safely walk to the nearest gas station for help. With so many stunning moments under my belt, I returned to New York and jumped back into my life with a vengeance. It was time, I thought, to get to work.

Soon after my trip I made sure to run into Serge. One night I went to his restaurant, hoping he'd be there but not knowing what to expect. We hadn't spoken to each other in months, but after our eyes met across the crowded dining room, we sat and talked for hours, shoulder to shoulder, catching up. I told him about Jacinda and the college boys who had cheered me on, and all about my adventures in Grandma Gloria's yellow Cadillac. I told him everything I had gained—the confidence, the strength—along with what I felt I still didn't have but wanted. Him, mostly. Serge listened without judgment, focusing on the stories and the bravado and the lessons learned—all the while holding my hand, letting me unfold.

"I really miss you, Serge."

"Me, too, Jo . . . I miss you a lot."

I went home with Serge that night, and we spooned in bed as though we hadn't missed one evening together. His soft skin felt the same, his sheets smelled just as they had months ago. Half-read newspapers were still thrown about his bedroom floor, and the paintings of naked women he so loved were still propped up beautifully against one wall, creating a collage of images in his room, Serge's feminine shrine.

It was as though time had stood still for us, as if the other men and the other women, and all the experiences that had manifested in between our "goodbye" and "hello again," were food for thought, forcing us to think about life and ourselves in new, better, more insightful ways. The next morning, Serge asked me to move back in, and I agreed.

Life moved forward. Just before my twenty-seventh birthday, we got married at the courthouse in lower Manhattan on a Thursday with my best friend, Amani, as the sole witness. I wore black leather pants, Serge wore jeans. We bought rings in Chinatown on our way to the courthouse, and when we said our vows, we felt every moment of happiness in the kiss that sealed a new "us."

Soon after we married, I landed a job working for a friend of mine who had started his own music label, Cheeba Sound, and needed an assistant. It felt like an opportunity of a lifetime—to work on something from the inside out, to finally, *finally* create.

I was quickly thrown into the center of the action. I did everything from answering phone calls to writing press releases

Our weddings couldn't have been any more different. Serge and me, low-key at the courthouse. Mama and Daddy dressed to the nines at church, in Virginia.

for our one and only artist, D'Angelo. Even the mundane elements of my job thrilled me. We were helping someone we believed to be one of the most righteous artists out there do what he did best: make beautiful, iconic music. We knew D'Angelo was special, that he represented something we didn't see often enough in the public landscape: a Black man who—as my friend once said—"debunked the stereotype that Black men dwelled in only two emotions, lust and anger." Sonically, lyrically, aesthetically, D'Angelo combined both masculine and feminine, pretty and ugly, tough and tender. It was our obligation to share D with the world—and I was excited, finally, to set out to work each day to meet the challenges of that task.

Just months before D's album was completed, I found out I was pregnant. Serge and I hadn't planned it—and I was terrified. "I can't have a baby, Serge—we live in a walk-up!" I protested, sitting on our bed, cross-legged and sobbing. "And I have a job!" Another good reason, I thought, not to upend our lives. The list went on. But in our tiny room on Sixth Avenue,

Serge struck down all my points with reason: *Jobs are a good thing when people have children—and if you don't want to work, that's fine, too; A move might be smart anyway; We can do this.* Serge held my hand in his hands. *This is a great thing.* He nudged at my fears with promise, picking them apart with hope.

"This baby's going to be special," I told my dad over the phone, breaking the coldness that had existed between us for far too long. We hadn't been in the same room without noticeable tension since he'd squashed my graduate school plans a few years before. Most of our interactions were buffered—we communicated through notes delivered by mail and over sit-down dinners in busy restaurants with plenty of ambiance to distract us. When Serge and I eloped, I sent Daddy and the rest of the family a very simple note relaying the news. Whenever a new life event happened to me, I'd shoot him an update and he'd tell me he was proud, or happy, or surprised: "You're something special, Jodatha." There was love between us, always, but there was also strain.

But this baby, I thought, meant something bigger than either of us. And I wanted him to be part of this life I was creating.

Late into my first trimester, the golden-haired child entered my dreams. Over and over in my sleep, visions of the baby would come to me—a boy with hair the color of gold, enveloped in a warm light beam. In those vivid dreams my baby felt strong and determined and independent, as though he was going to take on anything. We would name him Malcolm or Isaac or Toussaint—something befitting the gifts he would no doubt bestow upon us all.

I've wanted to be a mom from as far back as I can remember. When people asked me what I wanted to be when I grew up, I would say: a mom, a teacher, and a businesswoman in a suit. I *loved* the way my mother mothered us, and I often daydreamed about what I would be like with my kids when I had them someday.

I always envisioned myself having daughters. My family was surrounded by female trilogies—me, Ramona, and my mom. My grandmother Gloria and her daughters. My older sisters from my father's first marriage and their mother. Girls were what I knew.

Matriarchy defines our family—all the women, from my great-grandmother all the way down, were leaders. Church congregations listened to them speak on Sundays, students were inspired by them in the schools where they taught, husbands and children leaned on them at home. We were Blackwells, Rackleys, Pattersons. When I look back at what our family had amassed in life, much of it was built by the hands of women.

And yet, when I felt my baby's strong spirit in those visions, when I thought "unique," "blessed," "purposeful," the image that manifested was "boy." A woman's strength, I thought, is seldom gifted to them, it must always be nurtured. But a man's is written into his DNA before he's even born.

In retrospect, when I was conjuring this boy child, I think I was actually dreaming of someone uninhibited and free. And that was certainly who Georgia, my baby girl with blond, bushy ringlets—the golden-haired child of my dreams—would eventually show herself to be.

SECOND TRIMESTER: CREATING

"Go around me, people. Move along!" I murmur under my breath as I move through town, making my way to work each morning in no particular hurry. I'm not changing my pace for anyone. Joined with this baby, I walk with a slow, steady purpose. Girth has freed me from my anxiety—the old fear that I'll float away or be overpowered. It's as if those worries never existed.

I enjoy witnessing my body morph into something else,

something I've decided is more beautiful. I take long showers and watch the soap drip over this new shape—my thickening thighs and legs, this ever-expanding middle—and I feel euphoric. Sometimes I break into a stupid grin when I get undressed. Finally, I am the Chubby Black Girl I've always wanted to be! At almost two hundred pounds, I *am* the weight and substance I've always envied. I carry them for the first time, not just as a feeling, but physically, on my body. I've never felt so aligned.

By the fourth month, I've gotten to know the baby's rhythm—when she sleeps, when she wakes. I eat two gummy bears and feel her start to wiggle, a sugar rush dance she likes to do. She and I, we have lots of conversations: what she might do with her life, who I will be for her. This being growing inside me, gaining strength with my own blood and bones, is the best thing in the entire world. I hold on to the feeling like a delicious secret. I feel lucky—lucky to be pregnant, to be growing. Lucky to be creating. Together, we start plotting our future.

At work, as in my body, I feel integral. I leave the office each night feeling that I've put my hands on every big idea, every decision and challenge that lands on our desks. Our team is a close-knit, motley crew, full of the frenetic, excited energy that often comes when you're young and every experience feels brand-new. We do things our way, not bothering to follow the rules of the industry, not thinking one minute about protocol or repercussions. Protecting D'Angelo and his creativity becomes a kind of mission. A preview for me of what it means to safeguard something that others don't quite understand.

At home, Serge and I are a force. His somewhat vague idea of a "venue that transforms" has finally come to fruition. He names it Joe's Pub, an intimate, beautiful live performance venue housed inside lower Manhattan's legendary Public Theater, established by Joseph Papp, where musicians, actors, comedians, and spoken word artists of all stripes will have a home. Joe's Pub is our enterprise—our second baby in addition to the one getting heavier by the week inside my belly. With Serge at work building the space, I set about the task of filling it up. Musicians like Questlove, from the Roots, and Bilal, whom I'd met through D'Angelo, become among the first artists I book for Joe's inaugural set of shows.

For the first time Serge and I work together professionally, and it makes me feel womanly, responsible, and capable. And when Joe's Pub finally launches, the response is overwhelming. Hundreds of people line up, swarming to get in. It feels as if my life is on fire and my nerves are exploding each day.

THIRD TRIMESTER: LIFE

On July 31, 1999, after thirteen hours of intense back labor, our spines scraping against each other on her way out, she finally comes. And simultaneously, I commit my first godlike act: birthing. Childbirth is beyond what all the yoga classes prepared me for, eclipsing the coaching and the massaging, immune to the Reiki my mother attempted to perform on me in the birthing room, and the Sade I insisted on playing in the background. The birth plan that Serge and I had so meticulously crafted, detailing the perfect conditions for our baby to enter the world, was cast aside after hour eight.

There's no borrowing of perseverance or will or motivation to get you through the act of birthing, I realize. There's no easy way around it, no ducking the pain or the fear. You feel it all, because you have to. And in the process, you understand what it really means to move between giving it your all and giving in to nature. That ability—to go from one extreme to another—feels almost supernatural. After creating Georgia, I'm convinced that I am invincible.

Toward the end of the pregnancy, I made the decision to press Pause on the record label job and Joe's Pub until after Georgia was born. My feet had ballooned to almost double their size and I couldn't keep up with the physical pace my work required. But now, confronted with the prospect of picking up where I left off, I'm not sure I want to.

In the many, many quiet hours spent alone with my new daughter, I begin to think—about what we might do with our day, with our lives. About what I want for her, and what I want for myself. Laying eyes on this baby and thinking about what I did to get her here casts everything around me in a powerful new light. If I can birth, I can dream—and more than dream, I can *do:* I can navigate around obstacles. I can make plans. I can take the lead. I can oversee. With Georgia, I've had my first taste of real power—life-creating, life-sustaining power—and I want more.

It's time, I think, to dream forward.

Dreaming forward, as it turned out, landed me in the world of public relations, an arena that worked well with my love of stories, and with the relationships I'd created with writers and editors while working with Cheeba Sound and Joe's Pub. I named my company Jodie Becker Media, and it was my first opportunity to put ownership firmly in my hands.

My plan was to keep my business small, intimate, and based at home, because the flip side—scaling and expanding—would mean getting office space and leaving Georgia at home to go to work each day. I wanted just enough clients, three to five, to keep me engaged but not overwhelmed. The goal was to have one fluid life like many of the people Serge and I encountered every day—a full life that smoothly flowed between family and work.

My manifesto became "I choose clients that I naturally gravitate toward." I went into business with big corporations and young fashion designers, eccentric musicians, brilliant writers, film festivals, fashion events, and avant-garde magazines, all—somehow—while keeping Georgia close by my side.

I learned to multitask during these years, working at my desk for eight, nine, sometimes twelve hours a day—sometimes juggling nursing, cooking, and holding a meeting simultaneously. I'd throw a little blanket over Georgia's head to offer a bit of privacy but otherwise keep it moving.

Just a handful of hours of sleep each night became the norm. By the end of the workday I was spent, I had used up all my nice emotions keeping Georgia occupied and happy, and my ability to think rationally and calmly was depleted by my clients. At night, if any little thing went askew, like, say, Serge coming

*Georgia was content, as long as she was nursing or
snuggled in my arms.*

home an hour after he promised, I would flip. I'd scream and throw things across the room, a book or a framed picture—anything that was in arm's reach.

Serge standing there quietly in the midst of my tantrums made my chest feel as if it were about to burst open. So calm in the midst of my storms, so nonchalant about everything, coming and going as he pleased—it all made me furious. And his intended compliments—"But it's so sweet seeing you and Georgie always together," or "The apartment looks great, babe!"—felt like daggers flying straight at me. His sweetness landed on me like a threat.

While Serge could put on and take off one hat at a time—wearing "father" sometimes, then "boss" or "lost-in-the-clouds-creative" at other times—I was learning that that kind of versatility wasn't open to me.

One night, I came face-to-face with my rage. "You said you'd be home five hours ago! I've been holding Georgia in my arms all day, Serge!" The clang of the metal as the scissors hit the bookshelf and fell to the floor startled us both. I stood still while Serge looked at me to see what I'd do next. His eyes shifted slightly down to Georgia and softened. Without saying a word, he walked slowly, coldly, over to me, taking the baby out of my tensed arms. Then he turned and left the apartment, leaving me to sit in my shame.

You would think we'd change our routine after that incident, that my anger would have told us to do things differently. But going forward, Serge's schedule didn't budge, and mine didn't, either. Meanwhile, the anger kept piling up.

I'd snidely joke with Serge that I needed a wife, someone to assist me and keep all my balls in the air. He'd look confused and walk away, his mind on something else.

As much as I loved my work and my family, I was starting to

understand that "wife" was often synonymous with "administrative assistant"—someone who pulled it all together but never, ever called the shots.

The tension between Serge and me grew. We argued over his freedom to come and go as he pleased versus my always-on-call reality. It was partially my doing; I felt Georgia needed my touch and my protection. She came from me, grew out of me, had shared my blood for months. Even after she left my body, I couldn't fully separate. Even the mere idea of a nanny or even Serge taking her where I couldn't see her, smell her, touch her, sent me into a panic. Serge, on the other hand, could easily disconnect from us and go about his day at the office, not worrying or checking in until the evening.

I was seeing that my life as a woman was very different from Serge's as a man. That the obligations, the expectations—both spoken and unspoken, even our internal compasses—were fundamentally different. And at times, I felt trapped. This "womanhood," I was learning, came with an extra layer of responsibility.

All my life, my environment had been created by the people around me. I'd asked everyone important—Mama, Daddy, Ramona, Grandma Gloria, Serge—to have purpose in and over my life. Up until this point, the point of motherhood, they had led my way.

But with Georgia, I would do things differently.

I loved her fiercely, and I felt for her with the passion of a possessive lover. I knew that if Serge and I didn't allow her the space to be big and free, as girls so often don't get to be, people would try to tell her who she was and what she needed to do. They might try to explain her power with caveats, as it had so often been done with me. Be smart but not grad-school-smart. Be opinionated but not inappropriate. Be self-sufficient but not an old maid. So I vowed to give Georgia what I had only sometimes—room to wander, to experiment, and to learn to be imposing. For her, I would create an environment for her freedom to grow.

And luckily, Georgia proved never to be a dainty girl—she was born heavy and dominant, and I was determined to push those traits to the forefront. As she got older, she was athletic—always swinging on the scaffolding around New York City, doing flips and cartwheels from corner to corner. I never put her in Mary Janes or ballet flats—I wanted her to stomp around and feel the weight of her feet. I tried my best to move things out of her way so she could take up as much space as she desired and take it with her wherever she went.

I brought her with me everywhere: to big brunches with my best girlfriends, her "aunties," to intimate dinners at her father's restaurants. In any setting, she could tap into the subtext of our conversations. Nothing slipped past her. During gatherings with my female friends, I'd watch Georgia watching us. Even without knowing what we were saying, she was vibing off how we were saying it. At not even half my size, this little girl held all the possibility in the world. I saw in her a mighty force that would not, should not be stopped.

On her first day of preschool, I dressed her in her favorite pink tutu and scuffed high-top sneakers, and we strolled down Broadway heading toward school, just a few blocks away.

"Do you think we should go back home and get under the covers, Mama?"

I looked over at Georgia as we walked, seeing a flash of apprehension across her golden face.

"Ladybug, here's what we'll do. We'll march with our head

up to the sky, like this." I demonstrated, stretching my neck. "And with our chest poked out, like this!" I thrust my torso forward, like Mighty Mouse.

"Why, Mama?"

"Because *this* is the walk of self-determination," I said, smiling reassuringly.

"What's self-demer-min-ation?"

"Determination is when you know what needs to be done, and you *do* it."

Georgia looked up at me—a new look of resolve on her face, as though she understood, deeply, what I was trying to tell her. Without missing a beat, she picked up the pace, strutting up Broadway from Spring Street all the way to Bleecker, singing, "This is the walk of self-de-*ter*-mi-na-tion!" Chin to the sky, arms swinging wildly, and heart leading the way.

I called Georgia my Wise Soul—my free-spirited soul, my fierce soul. Watching her gave me faith in my own strength—not the borrowed kind, but the good stuff, the kind that comes from within.

She was something special—a totally uninhibited me. Me, unrestrained, unrestricted. A better version of me. She.

FIVE

Santa Claus Is a Black Man

A YEAR OR SO AFTER GEORGIA'S BIRTH, I found myself at my father's bedside in a small town in Germany, attempting to massage the life back into his dying body. Prostate cancer had taken over his bones and his blood, invaded his organs, and snatched his breath and speech when the pain was at its worst. That part—the speech—came easy only after the morphine settled in to do its work.

Our days were spent developing a new and visceral language, navigated by touch and sight and things better left unsaid. Each day, I tried to decipher where it hurt and adjusted his body into more comfortable positions, working to avoid erupting his bedsores. We moved silently together, me rubbing his hands and feet, rolling him onto one side or the other, while he guided me with soft grunts, or a sharp intake of breath—maybe a few coded words. I understood eventually that "three o'clock" meant the pain was on the *left* side, midpart of his body. That when his breathing sounded like air being slowly let out of a balloon, he was being suffocated by the fluid that constantly filled his lungs. I communicated his discomforts to the doctors and watched Daddy look in my direction, wearily winking his approval.

Over the past few years I'd received handwritten notes, about every six months or so, from the "spa" where my father was getting a "tune-up": "Miss you, Sunshine!" he'd write. "See you when I'm back in the States." I assumed he was living out his retirement years extravagantly, traveling to remote places for a little R&R. But this "spa" was actually a progressive cancer treatment center in Bad Aibling, Germany. He'd been quietly receiving care there on and off for years. Apparently, Daddy intended to fight the sickness his way, in the most radical form he could find. He'd told no one—not me or Ramona, or our two older sisters from his first marriage. No one except his girlfriend, Dorrett, who traveled with him everywhere. I was sure he had kept the cancer to himself for all this time so he could manage it as he pleased: without pity or tears. With only his grit and determination to get him through.

When I first arrived at the center, Daddy made clear that his cancer was yet another thing he would wrestle into submission; Dorrett and I were there to help execute his plan. "You didn't come here to sightsee!" he growled at me from beneath bright white blankets when I made the mistake of taking a couple hours away from the clinic to grab dinner the night I flew in. "Come on now—we need to get organized!" He demanded that we make up visitation and medication schedules, create spreadsheets to monitor the room's temperature, and catalog his sleep patterns, his pains, and his improvements.

Death had already begun to assert itself, staking its claim on what was left of my father. He couldn't walk, he could barely breathe, and his organs were failing—one by one by one. And so it became my mission to revive him. Daddy appointed me to uphold order and manage his recovery, for there would of course be one. Every moment of the day we would find ways to grab at his life—begging it to come back to us.

Daddy's room was on the second floor of the clinic, looking out onto the gardens. His bed took up most of the narrow space, and it faced the room's only window. When we were not adjusting his position, trying to give him some relief, I sat in an uncomfortable wooden chair by the bed while he stared outside at a single tree, moving only his eyes. From our height, it looked as if we were floating inside a canopy of clover-shaped leaves. When the wind blew, they danced and danced, making shimmery sounds. The leaves were varying shades of lime and emerald green—brilliant, vibrant, explosive colors that looked unreal. Lack of sleep, I think, will do that to you. Without sleep, the lighting changes; the dark gets darker and the light becomes blinding. Your adrenaline fog—the only thing keeping you standing—distorts reality and tweaks all your senses. A soft shuffle sounds like a stampede, a whisper grates like nails on a chalkboard.

Georgia had come with me to Germany. At a little over one year old, she was the one well of happiness that we frequently drew from; her joy swept over us all. Often too tired to rove the room with his eyes, Daddy searched for her with his ears whenever she fussed around the room. "Where is she?" he'd say weakly from his bed. Hearing his voice, Georgia would move toward him proudly, confidently, as kids that age often do—climbing on chairs and then on me to get a better look at her grandfather. She'd grin when she'd catch his eyes finally watching her, and he'd smile in return, despite the pain. "Jodie, take a picture," he'd direct me, raising his chin a bit as Georgia moved closer to him. Together, they posed for what would be the very last set of pictures I would take of Daddy with his golden girl.

Georgia affected my dad as though she owned his happiness. I watched him being lifted out of his misery every time he watched her, every time she toddled into the room, babbling, smiling, and laughing at the birds outside. This little girl just being happy, young, and agile brought my father life—maybe only minutes more life, but it was more. So I brought Georgia to him throughout our days, and even some nights, bundling

*Georgia was the sun for me, Daddy, and
everyone she met.*

her in blankets on a narrow cot next to his bed so that when he
woke up, he could see Georgia sleeping nearby.

But the pain always, eventually, took over, and it was then
that Daddy started to moan, and the doctors began filing in.
Whenever I heard those sounds, I took Georgia out of the room
as quickly as possible—away from Daddy, away from the clinic
and all the sickness, to a small patch of garden outside where the
children of other dying patients liked to play in the grass.

Each minute, each hour of any given day was filled with the
kinds of unhappy surprises that racked my insides like a seizure.
Daddy teetered closer and closer to the edge, and his team of
lifesavers—the doctors, me, and Dorrett—tried different methods to reel him back in.

Our second week in Bad Aibling, I called my sisters. "The
doctors don't know when," I told them, "but they do know

that eventually he'll drown in his own fluids." When I relayed this, I imagined a bobbing waterline slowly creeping up his neck, his chin, his nose and eyes, ultimately taking him under.

I was the most awake at two or three in the morning. After I put Georgia to bed and Daddy settled into quiet, semilucid moans, I sat on the floor outside his room with my knees against my chest, watching the empty hallway. The clinic was not a machine-driven place; the typical beeps and buzzes of heart monitors and intercom systems were replaced with hush, with muffled conversations, or the creak of a bed as someone shifted around in their slumber—sounds often heard through closed doors but rarely experienced in full view. There, each room was a private universe, everyone fighting in their own way against death.

It was during those early-morning hours that the nurses removed the bodies of the people who passed that day. I saw it once—two nurses walked past me down the hallway to a door I hadn't seen anyone come in or out of in quite a while. They walked inside the room, then moments later wheeled out a body on a gurney, covered with a sheet. I watched them roll the gurney down to the end of the hall, then disappear around the corner; the whole thing couldn't have lasted more than four or five minutes. They were there, then they were gone. The next day at lunchtime in the cafeteria, people passed around the news that so-and-so had died.

I imagined that it was done this way so as not to disturb people—the trick with these kinds of places was to forget the death part, or at least be reminded of it as little as possible. People were sick, yes, but there, we all desperately needed to believe the sick do get better—that the remedies do work. And the sick needed to feel hopeful, that maybe it wasn't as bad as it appeared.

Every day I watched pieces of Daddy drift into some other dimension, come back, and then drift out again, a little further than before. His hazel eyes started to change color, turning a light, frosty blue; his pupils became less and less focused. And the whites of his eyes started to film. The commands he'd been delivering to doctors, nurses—anyone around him who would listen—started losing their oomph. Usually the words shook with authority—"Keep it together!" "Make a plan!" They were up and forward in their feeling. But as he drifted further inside his morphine haze, deeper inside the pain, his words began to sag, saturated with fatigue.

From my post in the wooden chair next to his bed, I listened as a steady stream of aphorisms I'd heard all my life tumbled out of his mouth in an endless loop: "You got this, J.P."; "Eye on the ball"; "Toughen up"; "Lean in"; "Don't let people confuse you." Day and night he repeated them. But in that new context, the phrases sounded strange.

I'd grown up hearing those mantras all the time on the tennis court—Daddy was my first and most persistent coach. He loved to throw me into uncomfortable moments and force me to deal. Once when I was about ten, he surprised me as we walked onto the tennis courts at our country club in Queens with the news that he and I would be competing in a doubles match against two of his fiftysomething friends. "I thought you said we were just having fun today, Daddy!" I said, looking around anxiously at the two adults walking toward us on the court. "Why didn't you tell me it was a *match*—with your *friends*?"

"One game, baby girl. Just one game of doubles." He nudged me into position next to him. "Then you and I'll hit balls back and forth, promise. We got this, Jodatha!"

We were already on the court. The adults were all staring at me. There was nothing to do other than to get my head in the game. Backing out was not an option—and losing wasn't an option, either. I looked at Daddy, nodded in acceptance, and started twirling my racket in my right hand. He smiled—that was all he needed to know that I was ready.

"That's right, Jodie. Okay, eye on the ball—stay low, knees bent, and follow through. Your backhand is your winning shot. I'll get them with my cross-court—then you attack with that volley. Lean in!"

With my father, tennis wasn't just a sport, it was the blueprint for life. Life, like tennis, was made up of serves and volleys, unexpected moves, and opponents to conquer. Stay flexible, focused and open, and you can master anything. Don't, and you will buckle under the pressure of the game.

As Daddy spoke to me that day on the court, I could see the match playing out. Every shot he described, I could feel myself executing—my muscles pushing through each stroke, anticipating every move. We hadn't even served the first ball, but the whole match was unfolding in my mind in real time.

It wasn't an easy game—my serve was the weakest of the bunch, and my confidence was not quite turned up all the way—but we won. Daddy talked me through every move, pushing me to run ahead and volley, or shuffle faster across the court to slam the ball as best I could down our opponents' throats. Every time I'd make a mistake and they'd score, Daddy would laugh so loud that they'd get distracted and think this was all for fun, laughing right along with him. And then we'd sneak up on them and score the next point, and then the next. By the end, I was exhausted from the pressure of keeping up, but we came out on top, and Daddy was proud of us.

Growing up, I was always receiving little jolts of John Patterson wisdom, often disguised in sports analogies, that I didn't fully understand until years later. Shortly after Daddy moved to Boca Raton, Florida, following the divorce from Mama, I went to visit him for the weekend. He took me to lunch at the posh country club he belonged to, a place as white as the tablecloths in the club's dining room. The only other people of color there were the waiters quietly passing by with their eyes trained on the floor. In the midst of all this, I remember feeling very Black, and uncomfortably small. I leaned over to him and started cracking jokes about this one's lopsided toupee, and that one's caked-on makeup, hoping for a bit of outsider camaraderie. Being a cocky guy from Harlem, I assumed Daddy would want to take a couple of jabs, too.

Instead, without looking at me or altering his expression, he continued to face the crowd. "You're so busy, Jodie, looking at what those people have on that you're missing the point. Look around," he said, scanning. "These are some of the wealthiest men you'll ever meet. Their companies run the world, and I'm going to learn everything they know. Don't let small differences confuse you. Focus on the big picture."

He then stood up from our table and walked directly into the crowd, weaving between people, working the entire room. He shook men's hands, kissed their wives on the cheek, and disarmed everyone with his laughter. I watched people's faces as they listened to him, rapt by whatever story he was telling. And I watched his face, too—he was engaged, attentive; just enough of that brilliant smile, that body language. He was absolutely confident.

Looking back, I don't think my father particularly enjoyed that country club—it was an obnoxious bastion of white privilege. But it wasn't about that, it was about boldly telling this world how he wanted to be seen from the very moment he stepped into a room. It was about dialing in on the thing you wanted and not getting distracted by the noise.

In his prime, Daddy was electric. He was six feet tall, but his lanky arms and legs easily made him look two inches taller. Just as much as I watched my mom in her gorgeous womanhood,

Daddy could light up any room.

absorbing everything she so easily shared with me, I watched my father, too. A big song in our household when I was a kid was "Santa Claus Is a Black Man." We played it all the time, virtually every day, regardless of the season. More a Black pride song than a Christmas carol, in it the Black man is the Dream. He's handsome, he's the provider, he's strong, capable, and loving—he's what we all want. He was Daddy. The writer of the song was a close friend of my parents' and he had written it for families just like ours, who needed to believe in their men. The song became our family's anthem, and Ramona and I loved singing along.

But we saw our dad through a kind of double consciousness: as he wanted to be seen, and also in a way he couldn't see himself. We knew he was amazing. But he put barriers around his greatness. Where my mom's beauty was for all of us to enjoy, and even to become, my father's power was only for him. We could be strong, but we were never meant to be stronger than he was. I envied his toughness but feared his power, and I stood back in wonder every time he asserted himself.

But at seventy-two years old, the indomitable man of my childhood, my adolescence, and my adulthood was now bedridden in Germany, too weak to hold up his own head. Stripped of his vitality, of his health, of his control, the only pieces left in his arsenal were the steady stream of mantras he summoned to battle through another day.

It got harder and harder to look at him toward the end. Looking meant truly coming to terms with what was obvious: that our efforts were failing. His body continued to swell and break and corrode. He woke from a nap once and found me sobbing in my wooden chair, hands clasped over my mouth. "What? Is there something I'm missing?" he asked, impatient with my display of emotion. I told him, point-blank, "It's bad." Did he not see that? He chuckled and looked past me and out the window, as if he knew something I didn't. *It's not over until I say it is,* his expression told me. In his truth, the cancer didn't exist. He was certain that he could change the facts with his words, and with his thoughts.

A few days before, I had walked into his room and found that his whole body had ballooned and he needed to be drained immediately. The clinic had an all-hands-on-deck ethos, and family members were encouraged to participate in their loved one's care. We sat on his bed facing each other and I let him lean against my chest while the doctors drew fluids from his lungs, his head slumped over my shoulder like a baby's. Every time the needle went into his back, I'd tilt my head close to his ear and tell him a story, taking him back to the tennis courts.

"We're standing cross-court from our opponent. We have the serve. We're going to dribble the ball twice, then toss it up. Now arch your racket back—and swing! Run in for a sharp cross-court volley. He can't get it back. Dribble, dribble, serve. Keep your eye on the opponent, Daddy."

Each jolt of pain was a whack of the ball, a sprint down the court.

"We're tossing up the ball again. And we've slammed it into his backhand. We're gonna stay at the baseline and nail him with a forehand—*swoosh*. Now follow through. Get your knees low. Two side steps to the left, get back into center court. He lobs it up. We're going in for an overhead smash. The point is yours!" I let out a soft *raaahh* into his ear, imitating the cheer of the crowd.

The doctor's work finally done, we laid Daddy on his back and I wiped his forehead with a towel. "That's my girl," he sighed without opening his eyes.

We fought death together until I couldn't take the fight anymore. Worn out and depleted, after three weeks at the clinic I came up with excuses to leave. "Just give me four days," I told him. "Georgia needs her dad, and I need to tie up work that's been lingering for weeks."

What I didn't tell him was that I needed to fall apart for a day, needed someone to take Georgia from me so I could break into a million pieces. I wanted to get as far away from that place as possible—where practically everyone was sick, or dying, or dead. Where everyone had a sad story and a sad family member holding on—where I was one of those sad people, too.

I also didn't say that I was angry—furious that with all we'd done, all the hours spent on charts and conversations with doctors, all the love around him, he was still dying. The ultimate boss man, the leader, our Black Santa Claus, cut down in the most human of ways, by disease. When I most needed him to be superhuman and pull through, he was going to leave me to deal with my grief alone. He was, at the end of it all, human and finite and vulnerable. And that pissed me off the most. Because it meant the same for me.

Standing by his bedside, I was quick to assure Daddy that I'd return next week. "I promise, I'll be back before you know it." But that slow, unfocused look he gave me before turning away to stare at the clover-leaf tree outside his window told me that he knew, finally, what was coming.

Less than a week later, my aunt called to tell me that Daddy passed away, shortly after getting his morning massage. One of my sisters and I returned to Germany to cremate him, and we brought his ashes back to the States, to spread across the sea near Long Island.

The king, our own Black Santa Claus, was dead.

SIX

Resurrection

───────

I WAS THIRTY-TWO WHEN MY FATHER PASSED. His death forced all my little anxieties from childhood to the surface. Independence started to take on an unbearable weight. Smallness dominated my thoughts once again. Any disorder in my life—an uncontrolled emotion swirling around in my head, or even a shoe out of place in the hallway—felt unbearable, like fire to my skin.

And then there were all the questions that kept circling in my head—about love, faith, even God. It wasn't that I didn't believe in them anymore. I did. In fact, I fell more in love with my father after he died. The fraught and fractured relationship we had had my whole life fixed itself during those grueling weeks in Bad Aibling. Every bit of anger for him disappeared. The confusion around his chronic heavy-handedness no longer pulled at me. Instead, all I could feel for him was love. A giant-sized, persistent, lonely love. What I did question was the *point* of it all. Why welcome love when in the end it will be pulled from you and leave you crippled in its absence? If I could have asked for one thing in life at the time, it would have been for the return of my dad. But he was gone.

And so, as a mere second best, I asked for only a few of Daddy's things to keep with me: his wooden pipe, still fresh with the scent of tobacco; his worn and faded wallet, full of his IDs; his files—some work, some personal; and a few pieces of art.

There was one picture I couldn't stop looking at. I kept it against the wall by the front door of our loft. It was the only piece of valuable art Serge and I owned, yet it sat, unhung, on the floor.

The serigraph is called *Slave Ship,* and the artist is Romare Bearden. Taking up much of the serigraph's canvas is a woman's face and torso, etched with simple lines. She's looking off to the side—possibly to the past, maybe toward the future. Next to the woman is an outline of the continent of Africa, just slightly smaller than the woman herself. Also visible are a thin cross, a handful of black and brown male bodies in protest—knives and bats raised high above their heads—and one white man with blood on his chest.

I remember the evening Mama and Daddy bought *Slave Ship;* Ramona and I must have been eight and nine at most. It was stunning to me as a young girl, this woman at the center, bigger than an entire continent, bigger than the revolt of men— bigger than anything in her orbit. For years, all through my school days, when I looked up at her hanging on our living room wall, I asked myself, *Who is this woman?*

Years later, I discovered that the woman in the painting isn't a woman after all; he's Joseph Cinque, a free man who was stolen from Africa and illegally enslaved in 1839, three decades after the transatlantic slave trade was legally abolished. Two years after his enslavement, he was released and allowed to return home to Sierra Leone. It was Cinque's legal persistence that caused the U.S. Supreme Court to rule that all men held in illegal bondage should be treated as free men.

"We're not making a shrine for your dad out of this house, Jodie!" Serge yelled after I'd asked him one day to help me properly hang Dad's art. I'd never heard him speak to me with such venom. "He was a great man, but we're not hanging it— not a framed picture of the continent of *Africa.*" That's all Serge saw in the art: a continent.

For me, everything I'd lost when my father died—a patriarch, a Santa Claus, a rebel, a king—seemed to be resting in this frame. The perseverance, the greatness, the active Blackness—were all just sitting there, barely propped up on the floor. If we couldn't hang *this* in our home, if we couldn't pay homage to this Black man and every Black man—my dad included—who fought the battles for our freedom, then nothing would hang on any of my walls. Not the "high art" pictures of women Serge had collected over the years, not the Polaroids he snapped of me and tacked up with pins, not even Georgia's beautiful princess art. I, we, needed John Patterson's energy—that Harlem, that Race Man, that hot-tempered, you-can't-stop-me attitude protecting us. Until all of that was cherished, enshrined, resurrected—nothing had more urgency. Hanging *Slave Ship* became a declaration.

If Daddy were alive, he would have told Serge to hang the damn thing and stop getting in the way of our Black pride. Serge, I realized, would never be that kind of king—the kind that protects his family when under siege.

In those initial months after his death, Dad's specter hovered over everything around me. He appeared in my sleep, popping up on top of my nightstand, then the dresser, then on the wall behind me like the Cheshire cat with his enigmatic smile. As the executor of Dad's will, I resurrected him every time I pulled a piece of paper from one of his files—a newspaper clipping, a business contract, a to-do list scrawled on the back of a receipt. I held on to his things and strategically placed them around me—the credit cards, the cuff links, the handkerchiefs, the wallet, the tobacco-scented pipe—wanting to be near little reminders of him, touching the things that he had touched each day.

In the presence of those reminders, resentment trickled in. I became furious over the loss. Angry about the investment I'd made in our relationship—livid that all the love I felt for him now had no place to go. I stopped the activity of love, and I started pulling away from everyone, closing door after door on family and friends, retreating inward.

My mom would call for weeks at a time trying to reach me, and I'd never pick up or return her calls. I'd watch the phone ring and it would send a wave of panic through my body. I imagined her watching me watching the ringing phone, and I'd feel exposed. I'd try moving the phone out of sight, but the ringing just continued—first her, then an auntie, then a sister, then Mom again. The phone became my enemy, the thing that allowed others to get close to me. I just wanted to be invisible, to curl up and sleep. Needing it all to stop, I sent my mother an email one day that very simply said "I don't like talking on the phone. Just email me if you have anything important to say, and I'll get back to you."

At work, I could barely concentrate. The marble desk I once worked from for hours, brainstorming, writing press releases, reaching out to editors, planning photoshoots, now felt like a cold, blank space. My enthusiasm dwindled and so did my clients—my steady flow of jobs had trickled down to two.

"Let me get back to you next week," I'd answer when they'd request my standard weekly update. "I'm a little under the weather today."

Clients seemed silly and self-indulgent, friends seemed self-ish and unaware. Only Georgie, my Ladybug, brought the faintest reminder of possibility to my days. She was my only reason to get up in the morning. Georgia needed to be taken to music class, or spun around at the park, or read to or fed or hugged or tucked in. Aside from those moments, I felt zero at-tachment to anything.

"Jodie, I have a doctor who can help you," my mom wrote to me three or so months after Daddy passed, catching me off guard. "I'm fine," I responded, then moved her message out of sight to the Mom folder on my computer.

Another message, an hour later. "Well at least call her, she's cured a lot of people. Dr. Queen can cure any ailment, whatever it is. All you need to do is send a photo of yourself and she processes it through her computerized system and it cleanses your energy . . ."

It felt as though my mother was always selling me something. One year it was the mattress that had done wonders for her back, "only three thousand dollars." Another year it was herbs that helped when she was sick. And now, to cure my grief, it was this "soul work" that her doctor could do with a photograph. I didn't need a mattress or a Photoshopped picture to save me. What I needed was control over my life. My mind kept returning to my father—if nothing else, he knew about control.

I found myself, in those months, looking only for grounding. For something to tie me, hold me down—like a weight on top of paper in a windstorm. Being an entrepreneur wasn't helping; it offered too much looseness. While before I thought that running my own show was what I needed for my happiness, in my current state of grief, it gave me too much slack: I could choose to work or sleep in, to take on another client or no clients at all. I had no boss, no structure, no deadlines other than the ones I agreed to—and to date I wasn't agreeing to much of anything.

Serge, I decided, couldn't solve the problem, either.

"Could we actually not go to dinner tonight?" We were sitting in the back of a taxi, heading downtown after seeing a show at Lincoln Center. I was turned away from him, ignoring his hand on my leg. Serge didn't attempt to answer. "A friend is in town," I continued, still looking out the window. "We're gonna grab a drink and catch up." Serge mumbled his disappointment and we drove down Broadway in silence.

We scheduled couples therapy, but Serge regularly called ten minutes into the session, saying he couldn't get away from work, leaving me on the couch to fill up the next fifty minutes by myself. I arrived hours late or not at all to his restaurant/store/bar openings. Time and time again, we were both halfway showing up in each other's lives.

In more obvious ways I avoided intimacy. Come home late, climb into bed, find the farthest corner from him on our king-sized mattress, turn my back, fake sleep. Every night we fell asleep on opposite ends of the bed, without saying a word, not even good night.

The end was coming—had already come. By the summer of 2001, Serge reluctantly moved out. This time the breakup was for good.

After our separation, Georgia and I existed lockstep, as a single unit: eating together, sleeping together, reading books on the floor together. We ordered takeout from our favorite spot, eating rotisserie chicken dipped in salt and pepper while sitting cross-legged on a pink picnic blanket spread across my bed. We laughed and sang and snuggled, all while I quietly panicked inside.

Many nights I'd lie awake, mind racing with thoughts of Dad, and then my uncle, his brother Raymond, who'd passed in the month that followed Germany. Sometimes I'd tell myself that I had to step up, now that the men were gone, and be that strong figure our family needed so badly. I'd imagine what that would require of me, then break down in tears, knowing I was in no shape to lead anyone. I scribbled down meandering thoughts on loose paper during those nights, then tucked the pages away under the mattress or in an old purse, secret places where no one would find them, not even myself. I prayed for something to change, for someone to come into my life and fix things.

• • •

Just as my last few Jodie Becker Media jobs were winding down, I got a call from a friend of mine who was the publisher of *VIBE* magazine, the bible of urban culture. He was reaching out to me about a sales job he thought I'd be perfect for. He was impressed by my work with D'Angelo, my PR company, and all that I'd contributed to Joe's Pub.

"I've been watching you for the past three years, Jo. What you're doing . . . it's hot. And important—people listen to what you have to say."

My friend went on and on for an hour, refusing to get off the phone until I at least agreed to consider his offer. The truth was, I felt stuck, weighted, and direly in need of a reset. This job could be the switch I needed—more than I would allow myself to realize.

Three weeks later, I took the job at the magazine as the director of fashion sales, even though it would mean having to get a part-time nanny for Georgia. Georgia was older now, and I felt she (and I) could handle the separation. The upside—and it was big—was that the job offered a steady and substantial paycheck, a great title, the stamp of an established team, and fabulous work trips to Milan. To top it all off, I had an office. I felt that the dream I'd had as a kid was being realized—of being an executive in a Donna Karan suit, sitting in her own office, ready for anything that might be thrown her way.

I took the job despite knowing the obstacles I'd face tackling new and unfamiliar territory. In fact, I took it specifically *because* it was all new and unknown. The people, the requirements, the deadlines, the pressure—I knew none of it was going to be easy, but I welcomed the challenge. And still feeling fragile and untethered from loss—of my father and his brother, and of my marriage—I liked what *VIBE* offered: stability, community, and commitment.

The exterior of it all was very beautiful—I was invited into luxe conference rooms overlooking Madison Avenue, where chilled water was presented to me in Baccarat crystal, and I dressed up daily in high heels, statement bags, cashmere, cashmere, and more cashmere. But the hard truth was that the job was hard—*grueling*—with demands and requirements that I hadn't yet mastered as an entrepreneur. We were required to go on sales calls each week, and no matter the state of my nerves, I was forced to present the magazine, all by myself, to the most critical people—the fashion-folk.

"As you can see from the pie chart"—I pointed to papers spread out on the table in front of us—"*VIBE*'s audience is made up of urban trendsetters. Our median income is Blah. Our racial demographic is Blah-Blah, and despite turns in the economy, this group never shies away from purchasing luxury items." I sounded like a tape recording. My success at the job depended on my being vivacious and clever, bringing to life the nuances of our readers, a relatively misunderstood group of dynamic young urbanites. It was up to me to help established fashion brands like Chanel and Ralph Lauren see our readers as viable customers, and then to persuade them to advertise in our magazine, for the big bucks.

It was difficult explaining how this particular person, the *VIBE* reader—who had a modest income of maybe forty thousand dollars—would, without hesitation, spend their money on luxury items time and time again. It was also difficult explaining the urban mindset to suburbanites. And it was even more difficult for me to muster enough confidence and conviction to convince anyone of anything at that time. Although I dressed the part of a smart and together businesswoman, I was still stuck in my grief, falling apart inside. I stumbled and fumbled and flatlined each week, then licked my wounds and started all over again Monday morning.

"Jodie, do you want to walk Deborah through the presentation we made for her? I think she'll like what we pulled together." Three months into the job, Carolyn, my boss, had decided to sit in on all my presentations for the day, there only to "assist and help if need be." I hated when she did that.

"Jodie . . . ?" She prompted me again. My throat clenched, holding hostage the words I'd memorized the night before in my bathroom. The woman sitting across from us, staring at me, had it easy. All she had to do was listen, ask a few questions, listen some more, then say either yes or no. She held all the power, and she knew it—looking at me, arms folded across her chest, swiveling in her swivel chair. My boss did nothing to help, either.

"Jodie?" Still, no words would come, not a partial sentence or a phrase. Only a grunt, and then another grunt.

Quickly and dismissively, Carolyn began filling in the silence with all the numbers and humor and insight I should have had. I disappeared into the chair, as if I weren't even there and as if I hadn't just royally screwed up, until they finished talking and shook hands goodbye.

Outside our office building, on the street, I gave my best apology to my boss.

"Carolyn, I just want to say I promise to work harder, to be more focused. I'll memorize everything and pull it together. This will never happen again."

She looked down at her watch. "It's got to be better than just memorized. You have to *know* it, Jodie." She was right. I excused myself and went back inside, directly to the handicapped, single-stall bathroom, where I could be alone. I locked the door behind me, bent over the toilet, and sobbed like a child over the predicament I was in.

There wasn't a month at *VIBE* that I didn't fall short of my sales goals, or a day when I didn't scramble trying to catch up. I can't remember one time at the magazine when I felt at ease. *At some point they're going to fire you, Jodie, and you will have nothing to fall back on.* I prepared myself for the worst but I stuck with it, failing and trying, then failing and trying again. I'd coach myself: *Watch long enough and you will see something. Study long enough and you will become.* I knew I wasn't ready to master anything, but I also knew I had to keep trying my ambitions on, even if they didn't fit quite yet.

I came to work every day because on some level, I knew that from my efforts, something good would come, it always does. We have to keep facing the sun, as Mama taught us. I also came to work every day because it was one of the few things in my life that brought an ounce of weight to me. I felt so tiny, so fragile, so alone, that borrowing a bit of substance from *VIBE* was a blessing. I was, if nothing else, two important things: Georgia's mom and the fashion director at a major magazine.

I went out a lot during those months to escape, taking advantage of the free time I had when Georgia was with Serge. I'd work in the office until late, then find something to do that usually involved eating, dancing, and drinking lots of red wine— just so I wouldn't have to go home. I stayed busy and social and slept very little, deciding that motion, even when frantic, was always better than being curled up under the covers, broken for the rest of my life.

It was in that place, where I had just about convinced myself that running was a sustainable state of being, that I met Joe.

It was summertime, just before Georgia's third birthday, and I'd left my summer rental in the Hamptons to venture out on the town with a girlfriend. It was not long after Serge and I had separated—just twelve months prior—and I had vowed to take every opportunity to go out and meet people, refusing to sit at home and cry another day. I walked around the crowded room, scanning for someone interesting to talk to.

And then I felt someone tug at my elbow.

After spending so many years in Atlanta, I was very familiar with the elbow grab—it was *the* signature Black male move to get a woman's attention without causing a scene. More intentional than a tap on the shoulder, which could be easily misinterpreted as a signal to let someone pass—but far less brazen than a pull at the waist, way too risky. A move like that could earn you a slap across the face. The elbow grab at a party is at once very intimate and holds its own form of formality. It's an odd place to be touched by a stranger, but not an altogether unwelcome one. Slightly intrusive, but not; slightly sexual, but not. And if nothing else, it at least commands you to turn around and make eye contact with the pursuer. Regardless of whatever variation of "Ma, can I talk to you for a second?" follows, I had always found that initial move endearing—private, sweet, a little bold. Ripe with the kind of physical language Black folks happen to be fluent in. It was an old familiarity I'd come to miss.

So, lucky for Joe, the moment I turned around to look at him, I already had an enormous smile on my face. *I'm so very glad you found me,* it seemed to say. And I was. In Joe, I saw the promise of something familiar, I saw our whole story foretold.

That night, we stayed up late talking for hours. He described growing up in a family that put African solidarity first. He grew up with Kwame Nkrumah, too, the African nationalist who believed all Black people around the world, throughout the diaspora, should unite.

"My mom was this petite white woman from Canada who'd never been to Africa," Joe said to me, leaning forward in his chair, laughing a little as he said the words. "But when my dad asked her to move all four of us to Ghana, alone, to raise us there while he stayed in Boston developing his eye practice, she did it."

Joe was proud of his mom's commitment to his dad, and to the family. She said yes because she knew how important culture was to family life. She also said yes, perhaps even mostly so, because she was devoted to her husband and believed in the traditional structure of families—where a man leads and a woman follows. Joe and his siblings learned to speak Twi, ate traditional foods from roadside stands, grew up going to local schools with their cousins, and then eventually made their way into the Ivies—all the while understanding fully and completely that Black family is everything.

It was as though he was seducing me with his enthusiasm for Black nationalism and that A-team mentality that I was raised on. Where other people might not have paid much attention to these stories, or might have written them off as having sexist undertones, I was drawn to them and thought they were sexy. I could already see Joe leading our future family. It was in the way he spoke of men, women, and commitment all in the same breath, in how he conjured family memories with an emphasis on what parents *did* for their children. It was his body language and his eyes, and mostly it was his strength—both physical and mental—that got me. He looked like the type of guy who would move the world out of my way if ever I needed a little help.

It took two years for us to officially start dating, given that I was coming out of a marriage and he was coming out of an on-again/off-again relationship. But the seed was planted that night in the Hamptons.

I had used my months at *VIBE* to gain some time—allowing me to move away from my old life and toward something new.

After an intense year there, just when the long days were starting to get the best of me, a friend recommended me for a position at a fashion company—the director of PR for the fashion designer Zac Posen. It was a dream job in many ways, tapping back into my work experience in PR and publishing and into the relationships I'd developed over the years with writers and editors. I believed I could actually bring value to Zac and his team, a feeling I'd been missing at *VIBE*. And so I took the job without hesitation.

I was impressed with how Zac and his family ran the business. His mom was the CEO and my day-to-day point person. His big sister and head of the design team worked with me on the wording and branding around each season. And even Zac's dad, a well-known local artist, strolled through the offices, giving his input. It was a family affair, which had begun several years back in the living room of their downtown loft. Now, many seasons and runway shows and accolades later, Zac Posen was a globally recognized name.

The upward climb, the success, the determination, even the attitude (of which Zac had a ton) were alluring to me. He was King Entrepreneur. I paid attention to how he kept close to every aspect of his business, from inspiration to design to manufacturing to PR to sales to runway. Everything went through Zac's hands. He was only in his twenties, ten years my junior, barely out of school, and yet he'd accomplished way more than I had, leading a multi-million-dollar operation.

What impressed me most was how connected Zac was. One of his most surprising partnerships was with Sean "Diddy" Combs, a lead investor in the company. The two were like brothers in some ways, and polar opposites in others. Both were extroverts who could switch on their inner light and charm so brightly that entire stadiums of people would be under their spell. But Puff was forward and brazen, while Zac was sophisticated and highbrow. Diddy was all Harlem, Zac all SoHo. Both had a temper that could ignite in a second if things didn't go their way.

I often found myself caught between two kings.

"I'm sorry, Mr. Combs, but Zac's schedule won't allow him to present at the MTV Awards this year in Miami. He's so very honored that you've extended this opportunity. However, Mr. Combs, we need to respectfully decline." I sounded like someone's B-level secretary, but Zac's instructions were clear and we would *not* be going to Miami under any circumstances. We had the new collection to focus on.

There was a long pause over the phone.

"Baby girl. Baby girl." The tone was familiar. "You 'bout to slip on the banana, baby girl. Don't slip on that banana."

Weirdly, I understood what Diddy was saying. You have to see what's in front of you, both the obstacles and the opportunities. If you can't see it—the banana or the blessing—you will fall, fast and hard.

I leaned into the job, keeping my eyes open and my time busy from the moment I woke up, to the second I fell asleep. I reminded myself to stay on my toes and keep a "Yes I can" outlook. But I was always feeling overwhelmed—by the constant zigzag between work and Georgia, by coparenting and dating, by the sixty-hour workweeks and the five-hour-a-night sleeps. By just about everything.

"You got this," I'd push myself. If Grandma Gloria survived the loss of her daughter and succeeded in her academic career, if Auntie Lurma raised her son alone while juggling a career as a high-powered mayoral press secretary in Washington, then I had what it took to get the job done, too.

At the end of particularly exhausting days, I'd make lists of questions I wanted to ask my dad: "If you were me, Dad, how would you master this moment?"

I thought often of a conversation we'd had when I was about ten, Daddy in his favorite chair in our study while I sat on his lap. "Things happen when you're ready for them, Jodatha. At forty, I had bill collectors ringing my doorbell." No matter my age, Dad would always talk to me as if I were an adult. "I thought I was smarter than most people—definitely smarter than those white boys who had made millions. But my businesses had all flopped. One day a friend asked me, 'If you're so smart, John, why aren't you so rich?' That's when I got serious. If you want something, baby girl, you've got to study it, visualize it. Then grab it. It's yours."

All these years I'd been close to bosses and leaders and men at the center of things. I'd watched my father the Trailblazer, Dr. Cole the Motivator, my boss Carolyn the Ice Queen, Zac the Boy Wonder, Diddy the Dictator. I even hung Joseph Cinque on my wall because I admired his will to fight and wanted to feel close to that kind of power. But I never, not once, thought to be like those people or to grab the same things any of those people had. It took for the king to die, for everything to fall apart around me, for me to pick myself up and begin putting Jodie back together again, to realize that. Dad was never coming back. Truthfully, nothing external was ever going to rise up and fix me.

I went back to Daddy's words: "Study it." "Visualize it." I had done that, all my life. Since I was a little girl I had spent my time looking and absorbing. But what I hadn't done was grab the things I admired—fully and unapologetically.

"Grab it. It's yours." My father's words rang differently in my ears this time.

SEVEN

As It Were

"MAMA, YOUR BELLY IS SO BIG—Is there a *baby* in there?" I looked down at Georgia as we walked hand in hand down Lafayette Street in SoHo one afternoon, trying to give my best show of surprise. Four months into my second pregnancy, and I was obviously beginning to show.

"Wouldn't it be great if there were? You could have a little sister!"

"Nope," she said, shaking her head. "I want a brother. A sister would ruin my whole princess thing."

"Well, then—we should find out!"

"Is Papa the daddy?" Georgia's question was so innocent. Joe and I had been seeing each other seriously for a year now, and although we lived separately, we were spending most of our available time together.

"No, Ladybug." I smiled at her. "Joe would be this baby's daddy."

Her eyes got wide, still fixed on my belly, and mine went to my reflection in the window of the storefront beside us. I squeezed Georgia's hand and we continued walking down the street, excited by our "discovery." I wanted Georgia, now five years old, to feel in control of the life we were embarking on. There had been a lot of change for both us: a new job, a new boyfriend, a new coparenting schedule with her dad, and now this, a new baby. It seemed important to keep Georgia feeling central to everything. So I didn't tell her I was pregnant; I waited for her to tell me.

Well into my second trimester, I went in for a regular checkup with my OB/GYN, bringing Joe and Georgia with me to hear the baby's heartbeat. They all gathered around the table where I lay, and my doctor, who specialized in "at risk" births, began the ultrasound. Technically, my pregnancy was risky because of my age, an over-the-hill thirty-five.

He spread the jelly on my belly and searched for the heartbeat. Georgia, the eager big sister, stood close to Joe, beaming as soon as she heard the *thump-thump* of the baby's heart.

"My brother sounds so good, Mama. And I'm still the princess!"

While Georgia babbled away, excited as could be, I looked over at Dr. Wenschel, who was looking intently at the monitor. He was quiet, not saying a word, just looking at the screen.

"I think it's best if your daughter leaves the room now." Joe quickly walked Georgia, visibly annoyed that she had to leave the room, out into the waiting area, then came back in and held my hand.

"There is limited blood flow to your baby. He's not getting enough from you, Jodie." Dr. Wenschel's voice was clear and direct. "His growth rate is slow, well below the size he should be at this point." My mind raced back to all the extended hours I'd put in at work—not eating lunch until dinnertime, sitting in rooms full of cigarette smoke while designers and stylists and models frantically raced against the clock to meet the next day's deadlines. These past months with Zac, trying my best to conceal both my pregnancy and my fatigue, had been intense, to say the least. I scrambled to keep up with Sales Week, Fashion Week, Anna Wintour, the goddesses at *Vogue,* the socialites from Dubai, and the ever-growing list of "it" models and their agents. And I *really* scrambled to keep up with Zac, a zealous, demanding boss who could work fervently until midnight, partially because he had no kids waiting for him at home.

"You've got two options," my doctor went on. "You can continue with everything you're doing just the way you're doing it, and your baby will not make it. Or, you can rest."

"What do you mean by 'rest'?" I needed specifics. Was it shorter days, or shorter workweeks? Did it mean I'd take taxis everywhere and not carry another heavy bag for months? All of that sounded *great*. But Zac was going to need details—in fact, he needed me back in the office in less than an hour. My mind raced trying to imagine resting and working at the same time.

"Complete bed rest for the next three months, and your baby will survive. It's that simple."

When he put it that way—literally life or death, work or baby, one or the other—the answer seemed pretty clear. If keeping the job meant losing our son—"the next Ghartey king," as Joe's family constantly reminded me—I didn't need anything more to make the decision. I would stop working immediately. I returned to the offices on Laight Street later that week only to tell them I could no longer work, at least not until after the baby was born.

It was all a bit awkward and abrupt. There were lots of back-and-forth emails from my bed, trying to tie up loose ends. But it was also a relief, knowing that I was no longer responsible for editors or deadlines or fittings, or anything other than this very important, singular mission: making a healthy baby boy.

Week after week, propped up with pillows all around me, my laptop as my sole companion during the day, I realized that I'd have to be patient. The idea of having both a family and a career was important to me, and I knew it was possible. So I promised myself I'd return to my career as soon as our son was born.

To help me pass the time, my niece sent me a link to a five-part documentary on the Black beauty industry. I casually pressed Play, not knowing how important it would be for the next decade of my life. The doc started with Madam C. J.

Walker, a Black female entrepreneur who was raised in Southern cotton fields and went on to make millions creating and selling hair product to her community. These were products made
by a Black woman, for a Black woman. She focused her attention locally, yet had a massive impact on an industry—Black
hair care—that would eventually become a multi-billion-dollar
industry. An industry that is now dictated primarily by big
(white) corporate entities. I watched all five episodes, back to
back—and had a breakthrough.

What if I launched a beauty company? It was something I knew
well: the countless hours with Grandma Gloria, Mama, and
now Georgia in front of mirrors, brushing our hair behind
closed doors, loving each other and admiring ourselves. I could
turn what Mama had taught me, and what Walker had started
decades ago, into a business.

I tossed the idea around for hours that day, scribbling down
ideas and names for the business, even beauty retailers I could
intern with to gain some hands-on experience. It all seemed to
make sense, even in those first hours, tapping back into all the
good feelings and good times I had growing up, when hair was
love and brown skin was celebrated.

Immediately, I got to work with Joe's sister, Kiara, who like
Joe had an undergraduate degree and an MBA from Harvard. She
was just as enthusiastic about the idea as I was. Just a few months
after our son, Cassius, was born, Kiara and I opened the doors of
Georgia, a beauty boutique and salon in SoHo. I named the store
after my daughter, my golden-haired girl. This would be her legacy, and a bigger, more meaningful reason to go back to work.

My days at the boutique were long, and I embraced every
part of the business. Kiara and I lifted the gate and opened shop
in the early afternoons, then worked the register, greeted customers, researched new brands and product to stock the shelves
with, and even interviewed and supervised all the hairstylists.

There was always something new to learn, or something that desperately needed attention—like, say, a flood coming in from our upstairs neighbors who mistakenly left their water running. Only around midnight, when we'd crammed in all the work we could get in for the day, did we finally close the doors and lower the gate.

"Akwaaba! Akwaaba!"

Dr. G, Joe's father and the eldest patriarch of our newly formed family, welcomed our guests as they began to fill the room. It was a Saturday in springtime, and our home was flooded with sunlight. Joe and I had moved into a spacious loft on West Broadway, perfect for our family's growing size. We hadn't furnished it yet, the windows still bare and the rooms practically empty, but our two large couches and one dining room table were enough for what we needed.

Our family and friends were gathering to welcome baby Cassius into the world. Normally fussy, crying and fretting for hours at a time, on this day he was surprisingly calm. I looked down at Cassius in my arms, less than three months old. He was tiny, born only in the ninth percentile in weight, yet he had eyes the size of a grown man's. His hair was dark and curly, his skin brown and soft. I smoothed the long white christening gown we'd dressed him in and snuggled him closer in my arms, appreciative of his quiet.

Joe insisted that we have a traditional naming ceremony for Cassius, at which we would welcome our family—those still with us and those who had passed on—into the process of raising and protecting our child. I looked around the room, watching people filing in, waiting for the ceremony to start, and was proud of what I saw: our beautiful home, big enough for all forty of us—Joe, his two brothers and sister draped in Kente cloth, Dr. G speaking in Twi, laughing loudly with his older cousins, and my family comfortably mingling with our friends, who were taking it all in. Everyone at ease. I couldn't have asked for a better collaboration.

I felt a tug at my pant leg. "Mama, do I have to wear the African cloth thingy Jo-Jo and Auntie Kiara are wearing?" Georgia looked around at her new family, Joe's family, with worry in her eyes. "'Cause I don't want to." Almost everyone was wearing traditional African Kente cloth. I had wrapped a bright blue-and-orange swath around my waist as a skirt and paired it with a favorite white blouse.

"No, Ladybug, what you have on is perfect. Your pink tie-dyed outfit is beautiful." She looked up at me, lips beginning to form a smile.

Many of our folks had traveled from as far away as Ghana— or Atlanta, as my mom had—all to be a part of this day. Even without knowing ahead of time what the ceremony would be like, exactly, or what Dr. G would say, I understood enough to know how necessary this ritual was.

"It's not about what you're wearing, Ladybug. It's about what we're doing, together, as a family."

"We're celebrating Cassius, 'cause he's the first boy, Mama?" Georgia's question hit me hard. Did she see this as a celebration of maleness? Or Africanness?

I chose my words carefully, knowing how Georgia must feel being surrounded by new language and customs and new faces attentive to our new baby boy.

"This is for *all* of us, so we can celebrate our heritage and be reminded of what's most important in life." I pulled her closer to my hip. "You stay next to Mama while Grandpa G and Papa Joe speak."

With everyone formed in a loose circle around us, Joe's father and Joe led the ceremony, the oldest man in the room alongside

*Akwaaba! Grandpa G welcomes our
first son, Cassius.*

his firstborn son, uttering the same words spoken generation after generation by other men to their children. Our men, passing down the family wisdom.

"This is truth." Dr. G held a spoon to the baby's mouth, pouring in a drop of water. Cassius was still.

"This is false." He poured in another spoonful of liquid, only this time it was a bit of dark liquor. Cassius squirmed, moving his head from side to side, as the liquor touched his tongue. I, too, felt the reality of the words.

Joe took the baby from his father's arms and held him high, announcing his full name: "Cassius Kweku Kofi Joseph Patterson Ghartey—Cassius in honor of the world's greatest fighter, Cassius Clay, aka Muhammad Ali; Kweku for his grandfather, our oldest living patriarch; Kofi after the Ghanaian day of the week Jodie went into labor; Joseph after myself; and Patterson to carry on Jodie's father's name."

Our ancestors were all there in the circle, too, taking up just as much space as the living. I felt my dad and my great-grandmother Lurline, and so many others, standing shoulder to shoulder, spirit to spirit, with Joe's people, coming together to celebrate this new child.

Everyone cheered and laughed, the excitement reverberating in every corner of the room. Joe and I never took matrimonial vows during the hyperspeed that was our beginning. We didn't legalize our commitment to each other, never stood before our family and friends declaring our devotion—instead, we committed ourselves to the unit that was quickly springing up around us. This ceremony, filled with family and friends and love, was our first official gathering as Man and Woman.

The ceremony set a powerful tone for our young family, one of respect for tradition and male leadership, and I was okay with that. With a six-year-old, a newborn, two working parents, and our new love, Joe and I both agreed we needed a solution to get us through all the tasks and responsibilities that seemed to be piling up, month after month. We needed a strategy, one that would allow us to divide and conquer and not break under the pressure. So, in spite of my earlier vow to be different from the parents I grew up with, different from the roles I wanted to break away from with Serge, Joe and I gravitated toward what was familiar. We did what we'd seen our parents do, taking on the distinct roles we'd witnessed men and women play, roles from which they didn't stray. I became the moral compass of the family, and Joe became the provider. Although I worked at my store four days a week, sometimes putting in twelve hours a day, I saw myself best skilled at attending to the emotions of our family. Emotions and children became my territory, and Joe became our CFO. Every expense was his to cover: mortgages, babysitters, groceries, tuition, vacations, clothing—even the economic survival of my new and needy start-up business was on Joe's shoulders.

Although I wanted independence, a career, and self-determination, I wanted a family, too, maybe even more, if I were forced to choose. And with our backs up against the wall, the pressure of all of our responsibilities pushing down on me, it became clear that I couldn't do everything—at least not all at the same time. So with the reality of my growing family coming at me at a hundred miles an hour, I shifted into a familiar, old-fashioned gear, however flawed it was, to help me navigate so much new terrain.

The busier our lives became, the tighter we held on to those Man and Woman roles. I cooked all the family meals, made sure diapers were changed, noses were suctioned free of snot, doctors' appointments were kept, clothes were washed, and luggage was neatly packed for trips, in addition to running my business. Ms. Nancy, my longtime babysitter, helped out with the kids each week, but any "additions" I piled onto my plate, like working at the boutique or dinner with friends to maintain my sanity, were not to interfere with my main priority: making sure the children's needs were met. If our kids were emotionally sound, I was doing a good job, and if they weren't, by some mishap, I'd better hurry up and fix it.

On a certain level, there was a seduction to such clearly marked lines. When you're in charge of a specific set of responsibilities, there's an invitation to turn your brain off to the other things not meant for you to do. I tuned in to Georgia, Cassius, and my business and tuned out to the finances. Joe zeroed in on bills and our financial stability, taking a backseat on emotion.

Joe would often come home after a stressful day at work, giving me a kiss on the lips and a pat on the tush the way his father did to his mother, then plop himself down on the couch, still fully dressed in his suit and tie. While I was busy stirring something on the stove, Cassius swaddled and held tightly in my left arm, Joe would then wave his hands toward me, motioning for the baby.

"Does the king fancy his prince?" I'd smile.

"You're hysterical, Jodie. Our in-house comedian. But seriously, I've got one hour, max, to babysit. After that, I'm off-limits."

I'd bring Cassius over, privately a little annoyed but nonetheless relieved to have both arms free, and watch as Joe awkwardly held his son at arm's length, bouncing him on one knee and forcing a not-so-funny face. I'd turn back toward the stove, finishing up my chopping and stirring while Georgia sat nearby doing homework, and when the food was ready and set out on the table, I'd take Cassius back in my arms and we'd all sit down to eat. This was our typical routine.

It all looked very provincial, the woman cooking, juggling two kids, and serving a nice hot meal for the family, the man coming in from the outside world and putting in his precalculated quality time with the kids. But I knew Joe was only doing what he'd seen—molding himself into the image of what he'd been told a man should be. And during those days of too little sleep and too much to do—starting early and ending late— I just knew that I was doing my part to help us cross our daily marathon's finish line.

Although the roles Joe and I took on allowed us to feel productive, they also came with a catalog of restrictions. In exchange for the "perfect provider," I willingly agreed to give up the power and authority of my say—specifically where our finances were concerned.

"You're taking way too many taxis, Jodie. I've been looking over expenses and it's over the top." Joe was sitting at my marble desk looking at a pile of papers. According to Joe's rules, because I wasn't the person responsible for the money, I shouldn't be the person deciding about it, discussing it, or voicing my opinions on where it should go.

"Babe, there's no subway that works. In a cab, I can make my way across town to the store in ten minutes flat."

"Then leave earlier and walk. Or take the bus—like a real New Yorker."

I shot him a look. I *was* a real New Yorker—literally. He, on the other hand, was from the suburbs of Boston and preferred driving to and from work in his Aston Martin. I'd been taking subways all my life, but now, with a fifteen-pound baby strapped to my chest, yes, I needed a little assistance.

"Got it, Joe. I'll try walking next time. But it's going to take me three times longer to get to and from work."

"Take all the time you need. This is about my money."

So I did. The next day I walked home from work, slowly, comfortably, stopping for a slice of pizza and an iced tea, sitting on a park bench to talk with Amani, my best friend, when my legs started to swell. By the time we made it back to my place, Joe was enraged.

"Where the hell were you?" His loudness didn't bother me; I'd grown up with my father, after all, a man who was always making himself heard. It was what came next that took me aback.

"You are so selfish, Jodie. You knew we'd be here waiting for you—Kiara, my brothers, Mom. You're *late*. You're always *late*!" He slammed his hand down on the kitchen table for effect. Joe made a habit of putting on a show whenever his family was around. As the oldest son, he was supposed to always be in control. And control, apparently, always sounded angry.

Joe's mom, Penny, turned away from us, attempting to defuse the situation with her body language, drifting into the living room and sitting quietly on the couch, head buried in a magazine.

"This is what it looks like, Joe, when I walk home holding Cassius. Take a picture." I knew I sounded obnoxious, but I didn't care. "You can either sanction taxis," I said, taking a long pause for my own dramatic effect, "or see me when you see me."

I'd been doing my part for the family: nursing, cooking, then working, then coming home to start all over again. What else did he want? And what did the bus versus the taxi really matter anyway? We had enough money for me to take taxis for the rest of our lives if that's what it took to keep it all moving forward.

I had seen this before, this correlation between money and control, where control is in the hands of men, and women are often excluded, or minimized, from the conversation. This wasn't about taxis versus time, a few dollars spent here and there—it was about Joe waging a battle for absolute deference, maintaining the sole position at the head of the family table.

I deserved that head seat, too. Whether it was ten dollars or a thousand dollars, I wanted the authority to say how we would spend it.

We stared at each other from either end of our twelve-foot-long dark wood kitchen table—each of us seconds away from pouncing on the other. Joe's brothers and sister stayed quiet but close by. Amani took Georgia, who was already home from school, back to her bedroom, making themselves invisible. And I got very still. I whispered to myself, "Yeah, that's right. Taxis, damn it. Every damn day."

In that moment I knew that taxis, aka power, would be something we'd be battling over for years to come.

And then I smiled at Joe, choosing not to press the point further. I'd learned early on not to go directly up against him, challenging his opinion and demanding things, or I'd slam up against a brick wall. *Better not to say too much,* I thought as I made the first move to break the stare down. It wasn't over, not by any stretch of the imagination, but for now I'd just hush up and do what I needed to do—slowly, quietly, and consistently moving toward the things I wanted for our kids and myself. It would take that type of patience and reserve. "It's cool, babe. We're good," I said as I excused myself, walking down the hall and into the bathroom to pull myself together.

We ate the beautiful dinner that Joe cooked that night, all of us, laughing about this and that, choosing on the outside to move past the argument. But inside, Joe and I—and everyone there—understood just how serious and unresolved the issue was.

Later that night I found a quiet corner of the loft, in the kids' playroom, pretending to clean up the mess. I called my mom, trying to tell her about the things I hated in my relationship. About how controlling Joe was. I explained to her how small I felt when he cut me off or yelled at me in front of others, when he expected me always to do what he wanted. "If we're together as a couple, raising these babies, we should be making decisions together—money, parenting, all of it."

"Well, Jodie, that's how most men are. They like control, so give it to them. Your father was the same way. And Joe, he buys you so many beautiful things. Can't you just be a little nicer . . . easier with him? I don't know, maybe get some new lingerie? Men like lingerie."

I thought this was ridiculous, thinking lingerie could dissolve what I knew was sexism, plain and simple. But I tried taking my mother's approach of being less combative and more grateful with Joe. Sometimes it worked and I could hold my tongue, but as the disparities in our relationship grew, it became harder for me to defuse our fights. And often I was adding my own fuel to the fire.

Money and power—those issues alone could have broken us apart.

• • •

Meanwhile, as Cassius got older, the sheer physical energy he exhibited was starting to mystify me. Coming from a family of women, I often observed his actions like a tourist. He could spend half the day obsessing over his toys—separating the jungle animals from the trucks, the action figures from the building blocks, then lining up each grouping by size and color. He'd play with one set of toys before moving on to the next—never, ever mixing blocks with animals or Tonka trucks with action figures. Each toy was regarded separately, then set up for the main event: the crash. Houses were demolished and animals went head to head, then lay lifeless on their sides. One after the other, Cassius orchestrated each toy's destruction, and when he was done, he sat back and took in the fallout, smiling at his creation. Happy with his work, he'd start all over again—building and breaking, building and breaking. The louder the crash, the bigger his grin. Where Georgia was soft in her forcefulness, Cassius was brute force unadorned.

I wondered out loud to Joe one day if Cassius were sick.

"Like a cold?" he asked.

"No, no—like sick in the head." I just couldn't fathom why anyone would want to destroy all the time. But Joe insisted that Cassius acted the way that all boys did—that it was just "how we are." Cassius was a classic boy, I learned from Joe, and as a non-boy I didn't need to understand, I just needed to adapt to the male psyche better, needed to figure out how best to navigate this foreign terrain.

From what I was experiencing, it felt as though male energy was something to wrangle and contain—outmaneuver it before it outmaneuvered me. Whereas with Georgia, I was trying to help her explore and expand and dominate, Cassius—and even Joe these days—needed to be lassoed.

The story life kept telling me was this: The world is divided between two genders. My son and daughter were different, Joe and I were different—my own parents were night and day. All men and all women were meant to operate in silos, drawing from strengths unique to their sex. It sounded too absolute, but the supporting evidence was so overwhelming that I couldn't cogently argue against it. And when I looked back at what happened when men and women deviated from their assigned positions, it made me nervous even to question those roles.

My father used to tell me stories about his mother, who became the family's sole provider in 1920s America while her husband was repeatedly denied stable employment simply because he was a Black man. Domestic jobs were often the only steady source of income for Blacks during that time, and they were given to our women, mostly because our men were rarely allowed in white people's homes—or near white women and children.

So, while Pop-Pop stayed home with their three kids, Grandma Mildred went to work as a housekeeper, serving and cleaning for people to whom she was invisible. Then after work, before going home, she would take to the basketball court down the block, sweating out all the injustices she'd endured that day.

My father hated his mother working and his father at home cooking. He resented the imbalance of power—a woman in control, the breadwinner of the family, implied divine order askew. He spent his whole life, with his own family, trying to restore the balance, often bending my mother to his will.

He'd belittle her in front of us, often at the dinner table, where we all gathered at the end of each day. "Jamelle, why are we having steak again? We had it last night." Dad looked at her, leaning back in his chair.

"John, I asked you this morning what you wanted and you never answered. So I made steak."

My grandfather John Tollie Patterson Sr., or "Pop-Pop," as we called him (seated on the ground, second from left), dressed in his Sunday best.

"Wait one second." His laugh was hard, almost bitter. "So now I have to *decide* on the menu, too?"

Mama remained silent, gently resting her palms on the table—composing herself.

I jumped in for comic relief. "Yup, Dad, Mom's asking you to tell her what you want to eat, and then actually eat it." Everyone laughed, but I knew, even at twelve years old, that I had skirted the issue. What Daddy was implying was that Mama hadn't done her job, which consisted strictly of children, house, and food. And he was explicitly denying any involvement in her lane. My father had laid down the law.

I'd regarded these stories almost as a warning. In instances where people subverted tradition, like Grandma Mildred, or fell short of expectations, like Mama not handling dinner duty properly, the outcomes were never good. Sure, I knew gender roles could keep marriages together, families together—they could even keep a movement strong. But if they could not answer to me, if they couldn't put me at the center, how beneficial could they actually be? If these roles held me back when I wanted to go forward, made me ask permission when I wanted to steer, whom were they serving? And why were they there in the first place? When it came to my individual need for self-determination—or to take a taxi every damn day if I wanted to—these roles, these positions, were no longer, not even halfway, enough.

So many questions, chipping away at things as they were.

EIGHT

Faith Is Karma. Karma Is Faith.

———

I ALWAYS THOUGHT FAITH WAS LINKED to the unknown, like when you don't know, but you simply decide to believe. However, now I see it differently.

A cabdriver told me once that karma is faith, and faith is karma. At the time, I didn't fully understand, but I was open to learning. I had found myself in the backseat of his car, crying over an embossed black leather attaché folder that I'd lost earlier that afternoon. I needed a lesson that day.

I'd traveled to Boston to participate in a conference sponsored by Dell Computers. I was part of a think tank of techies, bloggers, and parents brainstorming better ways to engage in social media, ways that could unite people instead of polarizing them. On my way back to the airport I sat proudly in the backseat of my taxi, taking in our success. And then, without warning, like an alarm clock jolting me out of a glorious dream, my head slammed against the passenger window—hard and fast. Next I remember the screeching sound of rubber dragging against cement. We'd been hit. Directly after impact, my brain functioned erratically. I cursed. I cried. And then, as abruptly as it had all begun, I jumped out of my taxi and dashed into another conveniently located two cars behind. "Take me to the airport!" I yelled, dazed and confused. About ten minutes later, as my mind started to clear, I realized I'd left the folder behind. It had belonged to my dad—he had carried it with him while stomping all over Wall Street and the South Bronx during the sixties, seventies, eighties, and nineties; it represented so much dreaming, so much fearlessness and trailblazing. Of the few things I kept of his, this one was extremely important, maybe the most.

I asked the driver to circle back to the scene of the accident and I spent the next several hours walking all over the city, calling car companies and police stations, retracing my steps and ultimately missing my flight. But all roads led to dead ends. Eventually, I was forced to head back to the airport for fear of missing the last flight out of town. There were three taxis in front of me. The first driver was way too aggressive, waving his hands frantically for me to enter. The second one was way too messy, trash strewn about the front seat. The third one seemed just right, so I crawled inside, feeling and looking miserable.

In the rearview mirror, I could see my driver's eyes. They looked compassionate. He asked me what had made me so sad, and I told him my story.

"Have faith," Ahmir said then, peering at me through the mirror. He drove us around to search a bit more, pulling over whenever he saw a cabbie friend to ask after the folder, but with no luck. As a last-ditch effort, he made a call to Vinnie Z, "the man who knows everything about every cab in Boston." Ahmir told my story—for the twentieth time—to Vinnie, and this time, miraculously—karmically—the man responded with the words I thought I'd never hear: "Yep . . . I found the cabbie who says he has the folder."

After meeting up with the cabbie and collecting my prized possession, more accomplished than I ever thought I could feel, I climbed back into the car with Ahmir for the final trek to the Departures terminal. We spent the next twenty minutes together talking, praising the outcome of the day and believing in the goodness of life. It was then that he started talking about belief and faith and karma. "Karma is faith, and faith is karma," he said, looking up at the rearview mirror to see whether I understood. I didn't, but I wanted to hear it all—something about the day's bizarre string of events humbled me, opened me up.

Faith, he said, is an activity. Through rituals and acts and circumstances, we create situations that put God in front of our eyes. We create these moments—or sometimes they happen to us—and from those experiences we gain a stronger ability to believe in a higher force, something superhuman. Karma, similarly, is an action, or an event like the accident, that causes the entire cycle of cause and effect.

That accident was my karma, and the series of events that followed were my faith. Or something like that. "I still don't quite get it," I said from the backseat.

"That's okay—it takes us a lifetime," said Ahmir.

It was that kind of divine, cosmic happenstance—karma—and that same kind of strange and mysterious series of actions—faith—that led me to a young man called Nain.

"This song is bananas—I love Jodeci!" he proclaimed as he rolled into my store on his skateboard that very first night, bopping his head along to the song playing from the speakers set up around my shop. He looked like a modern-day Jean-Michel Basquiat, maybe nineteen years old, with bushy, almost dreaded hair, beautiful dark brown skin, and an air of confidence that all amounted to quite an impressive entrance.

The Georgia beauty boutique was positioned in a busy part of lower Manhattan on East Houston Street, just off the Bowery, a historic home to delinquents and artists alike. Houston was more like a thoroughfare, spanning the width of the city from the Hudson to the East River, transporting millions of people from west to east, borough to borough, and state to state. Most New Yorkers, at some point each week, crossed Houston Street.

I kept the store open late each night, hoping to capture any spillover business that might occur, from happy-hour drinking to last-minute grocery shopping in the neighborhood. Amani, who often kept me company at the shop on Friday nights, would pull up a stool next to mine at the front counter, and together we'd watch the action unfold: a wino scamming a tourist out of a few dollars, a belligerent banker stumbling around in his overpriced suit, a mom racing home with her three kids after school. We did this just about every Friday, until midnight, when I'd finally close shop. It was on one of those late nights that Nain rolled in.

He looked familiar, oddly handsome and vaguely like someone I knew. I couldn't put my finger on whom, exactly. I think he reminded me more of an era than an individual—a time when there was more personal interaction, less virtual living, and people carved out time each day to talk to one another—at the dinner table with family, to a stranger on a park bench, even in a dimly lit banquette in the West Village. He had a welcoming look on his face, like someone I'd have had a good time talking with downstairs at Nell's on a Saturday night until the sun came up.

Nain was tall, about six feet, lanky, no more than 145 pounds, and athletic. He wore black fitted jeans that revealed his bow legs, a worn black T-shirt that draped loosely around his neck, a stylish jacket that showed off his broad shoulders, and some sort of black sneakers without any logos or embellishments. His look was understated and monochromatic—a city-bohemian-grungy-high-low fashion vibe. Everything he was wearing was slightly worn, slightly androgynous, and slightly deceptive, each piece looking like nothing much but secretly costing a small fortune—like the Helmut Lang jeans he had on. I spotted those first. He was cool—cooler than I would have expected from someone his age. Beyond-his-years cool.

"What could you possibly know about Jodeci?" I teased him, a bit taken aback.

"Waaaay before your time!" Amani jumped in, trying to assess his age with her eyes.

"Whaaat? How you gonna play me like that?" He threw his arms up in the air for effect. "Just because I'm young? Eighties music is my thing!" He was gesticulating now with total abandon, rattling off all the songs and artists he loved from the era— Shalamar and Immature and Soul for Real. "Actually *music* is my thing. I got like a million songs in my head—all playing right now. As we speak." He tapped his forehead, pointing to the internal record player that was his brain, then leaned up against the counter, making himself more comfortable.

"Smell me!" He stretched his neck toward us. It was a strange request, and neither Amani nor I made a move. "It's Comme des Garçons, Anbar. Savory and manly—the only thing I'll ever wear." Curious, I leaned in a little and sniffed, surprised by the pleasant mix of citrus and something like incense.

"Yeah—nice, right!" It was a declaration more than a question. "So, I need a little decanter to carry around with me so I don't have to take this big bottle in my knapsack every day." He pulled out a bottle from the side pocket of his carryall and spritzed, refreshing himself. "Do you sell decanters?"

"Sorry, we don't have any." I hadn't met a teenager like Nain before, with so many peculiar identities all coexisting in one body: skater kid, eighties R&B aficionado, perfume connoisseur. He looked part hobo, too, as though he needed a nice warm bath and a good solid meal. I didn't want him to leave, so I asked, "What else do you have in that bag?" It was big and scuffed, bulging with things I could not see.

"Ha!" He seemed to like to start off sentences with a laugh. "Well, I got my computer and a toothbrush, my phone—oh, and this magazine I like, and the perfume, the Anbar . . . and a few other things that I might need tomorrow. Like, you never know, you just always want to be prepared." He smiled directly at me and winked, like we spoke the same language. I desperately wanted to understand him, but there were so many questions. My mind raced: *Where would he be tomorrow that would require such a random assortment of things?* Everything about this strange, magnetic young man was a puzzle I wanted to figure out.

We talked for hours that night, about music, skateboarding, and high school, and he shared bits and pieces of himself. That his name was Ernain, Nain for short; he was named after his father, whom he hadn't lived with for years—and nope, he had no idea where his name came from. He'd laughed off his senior year of high school but still managed to graduate, and he hadn't really considered applying to college. He talked about all the couches that he'd crashed on recently, illustrating in vivid detail the characters that flitted in and out of his life in the days and weeks before.

Between every other story, he returned to his love for music. He mentioned that he'd studied classical flute at Juilliard's pre-college division during grade school, and that he wanted to make music now, as a producer.

In all of Nain's stories, in all of his excitement about music and perfume and art, he didn't say much about his mom other than to offer her name, Beverly, and that she lived in Crown Heights, Brooklyn, with her mother, Nain's grandmother. I could tell, just from the brief time we'd spent together, that Nain was sensitive and caring and thoughtful—and it seemed reasonable enough to assume that he'd been raised well, with a lot of care and attention. So when he spoke very little of his mom, practically leaving her out of the conversation altogether, I noticed.

"How'd you end up at Juilliard?" I asked, trying to understand all of the moving parts.

"Ha! I've always gravitated toward music—in school, church, wherever. I find it somehow, or it finds me. If you want, go ahead and google me. You'll find mad articles . . . I was like, umm, a musical prodigy."

I probed a bit more, looking for clues, anything that would give me a better understanding of who he was and of the people who raised him.

"Did Beverly sign you up for Juilliard? What a great opportunity—to study with the best of the best."

"Nah, it wasn't Beverly. It was me . . . They came to my school and *I* auditioned. I don't want to brag or anything, but yeah, they chose me." There was that smile again, lighting up his entire face—the entire store, actually.

Everything about Nain's energy was on the verge of bubbling over. You felt it in the tilt of his head—how wide his eyes and mouth got when he smiled, his big, almost frantic hand gestures. Every single movement was charged, oversized and exciting—and there was so much joy in his voice. It was totally intoxicating. I could tell he was meant to leave a mark on this world. I couldn't help taking a series of pictures of him in action with my phone. In all of them, he's laughing, mouth wide open—his enthusiasm barely contained within the frame. It was his eyes, though—light brown, wide, expressive eyes—that revealed something else. A vulnerability, an unrootedness, a naïveté, that I recognized, very deeply.

After he left the store late that night, I couldn't stop thinking about him: Who he was. Where he came from. Where he was going.

Several days later, he rolled back in off the street, and again sat for hours laughing with me. It seemed like wherever the wind took him, that's where he'd be—just drifting through the streets on his skateboard. I would hope to see him again and he'd appear and reappear, night after night. On the few days he didn't show up, I'd notice his absence, hoping he'd drop in. I'd try to call him but his phone would be turned off. Those days, I worried. But then, he'd reemerge from wherever he was and roll into the shop again and we'd start just where we'd left off, talking, laughing, vibing off each other.

Over the course of a month, Nain visited with me at the store nearly every day. He'd stay until closing, helping me take out the garbage and pull the gate down over the glass storefront when it was time to lock up. Then I'd drive him to the train station on Canal Street, and we'd talk some more—sometimes about his music, sometimes about my kids—sitting together for a long time before he'd get out of the car. Almost stalling, making small talk, in order not to leave each other.

"Where will you sleep tonight, Nain?" I often asked him, sensing he never really knew. On most occasions, he'd be wearing the same clothing I'd seen him in the day before, and he looked tired.

I could tell Nain was running, as I'd been for so many years, from his past, and from people and their stories. It seemed as though he was trying to make new ones, maybe some with me, stories of his own, with new characters and new energy, something calmer than he'd known before. Something he could fully claim.

"I got this friend who's letting me crash," he'd always say. "And, umm—Ha! I got my computer in my backpack . . . so, maybe we'll make some music together." It frequently sounded as if he was piecing it all together in the moment, grabbing at ideas as they came. Night after night, I hoped I would hear something more concrete, like *I've got to rush home, my mom's ex-*

pecting me. Something I hoped my own kids would be saying at this time of night, if they were his age.

But Nain just sat there in the passenger seat, always fidgeting with his knapsack straps, looking lost. He made me think of myself in my senior year of high school, doing everything I could on a Saturday night not to go home. "Don't get distracted by the city, Nain," I'd say, as if he were one of my own. I wanted to tell him not to trust people too easily. Jacinda, the exotic dancer from years back, was right. People are crazy, and we need to keep our eyes open. But something about Nain wasn't jaded, he was still optimistic and bright in spite of life—and it was that specific something that kept pulling me toward him, like the sun.

Something had happened to Nain that separated him emotionally from his mother. Something bad, painful—too much to talk about, I assumed. He'd been drifting for a long time, just like me. I'd ask a few questions, about his family, very gently, careful not to be the one to cause any additional pain, and I'd hear the anxiety building in his voice and see the tears welling in his eyes. So I didn't push. If he wanted to share whatever was burdening him with me eventually, that would be fine. But if he couldn't put it into words, that was okay, too. I knew that if I were asked, I couldn't have said exactly what had separated me from my mom all these years. But that pain was real and it had stayed with me—perhaps it would for my entire life.

With Nain, I concerned myself only with the right now, the today, the face-to-faces we were having. What had happened before he stood in front of me and after he left were out of my control. But what I could put my hands and heart around were our moments together. We liked the same music, we both loved laughing, we welcomed more calm and love in our lives. And he liked my resolve: "You're such a strong woman. If you were my mama, I'd protect you. Not that you need my help. Ha! But I'd do it anyway." Nain, a little bit each day, was trying to make me his.

It was obvious that he was a little broken by life—but not entirely broken. Just fractured, sad, beneath his gregarious smile and big almond eyes. He was awkward in this life, dying a bit in this life, but joyful and optimistic still. My heart opened up to Nain—I wanted to pour in him all my love so he could make it through.

After that month of our talks in the car and his visits at the store, I knew that Nain was a part of me, he was mine—ours. Before it made any rational sense, before I said it out loud to others in the family, I knew, very deeply, that Nain was real, and the strength of our bond was beyond what I could put into words. I had no need for him, no obligation to him—rather, I adored him as if he were my own child. It wasn't about what he'd done in the past or what he was about to do with his future, or anything other than his right now. It was him, as is, unfiltered, who grabbed me. His place in our family was just waiting for him to fill. Little by little, night by night, that reality became more clear.

"What do we know about this kid? Who are his parents?" Joe challenged me whenever I brought up the idea of bringing Nain into our fold. All of his concerns made sense, in a logical kind of way. But something about Nain made more sense in a heart kind of way. Regardless of what Joe was expressing to me, I already knew that Nain was part of us. We were supposed to be family—that much was obvious. Joe, for his part, just needed to catch up and get to know him. And over time, through long conversations and hours spent playing basketball, he did, on his own terms. They'd talk about music, mostly, and sometimes about family. Between sharing laughs while shooting hoops on the West Side Pier, Nain also shared some of the sad memories he had of growing up—all with the grace and softness I knew him to have. During those afternoons, Joe witnessed what I'd seen whenever Nain came into the store, or sat in the car with me on Canal Street before jumping out into the night: someone special.

Eventually, I met Nain's birth mother and asked if it was okay that Nain join our family. I told her that we loved him, and that we were good people. Then, I asked if I could be another mother to her child. And without hesitation, she said yes. She could tell, she told me, how much Nain loved us. "He's been calling the kids his siblings for a while now," she mentioned. Although she didn't understand it completely, she was willing to embrace it fully if it made Nain happy. I was grateful for her blind faith.

It was then that Nain became our son, and we all became a family.

While Nain became a part of our family in the most surprising of ways, looking back, it's hard to imagine a time when he wasn't with us.

I call Nain the Gift. I'd always thought karma was the inevitable sum of your actions making their way back to you. Fate. But as I now understand it, karma *is* faith—when you believe in something even without reason. It is the exact moment when nothing is proven yet you still believe—and you keep moving with no specific purpose other than to find more love.

It was Nain, the one who seemed to fall out of the sky one night and land in my busy, hectic world, who reminded me with such gentle force to find love, follow love, be love.

Everything we do needs to be for love. I would lean, hard and deep, into that lesson in the years ahead.

NINE

Penelope

———————

WHEN JOE AND I FOUND OUT that we were pregnant for the second time, we were living in two different worlds. I was stationed in our loft in SoHo with Cassius and Georgia, and Joe was primarily living in a flat in London. His job in finance had taken him to England for three weeks out of each month, and to what felt like the other end of the universe. Our time zones were different, and our internal compasses were pointing in opposing directions. I was focused on motherhood to our children and on my store, while Joe was living in a world of numbers and decimal points, drilling down in his career, trying to keep up with the momentum he had set over the last ten years as a golden boy in his company of thousands.

"Can you get away for a weekend and come stay with me, Jodie? London is just so cold."

"Babe, I can't leave Georgia by herself with Ms. Nancy. You know how she gets. And Cassius was a nightmare on the plane last time. Plus, you know I've got the store . . . it's way too early for the sales team to run it without me."

There were real reasons for me to stay put. My life, everything that mattered, was in New York City. Everything minus Joe.

"Okay, babe. I get it . . . I'm fourth on the food chain, even after the store!" We laughed together because he was right, in a way.

"Then I'll see you in two weeks, babe. Love you."

We were moving in separate circles, experiencing life independently, and building up our careers from our own corners of the world. Consequently, oceans began to form between us. Our worlds were different, drastically different. Oftentimes a part of me wanted Joe to step inside my world and experience what I was feeling. In my world, children brought the most glorious revelations each day, and my new business felt just as alive as a new baby. At other times, I was so proud of Joe's corporate accomplishments that I wholeheartedly supported his going as far and wide as his career would take him, even if that meant being away from us for a bit. He was mastering a brutal industry, one that often didn't value or support Black men. Watching him succeed under those conditions made me love him that much more. And who was I to stop such a beautiful force of a man? We fought, but we also loved. Joe had successfully stabilized us as a family. I was less afraid. Before, I was a single mom with the notion of loss always swirling around in my head; now I was a mom several times over, an entrepreneur, and a partner to a man of action. I had so much respect for Joe, the man who brought me new life.

But I missed him all the time. I'd fall asleep thinking about what his bed in London looked like at that very moment—envisioning how the pillows might be tossed or how the sheets hung off the bed. In my head, I saw him getting dressed in those early hours, choosing the suit and tie he wanted to wear, while I watched him from the bed, smiling. He used to get himself together so fast in the mornings, it seemed almost superhuman. As I stumbled around with the kids, in all of five minutes Joe would be showered, shaved, dressed, and heading out the door, a determined look on his face. His focus was on another level. I missed seeing that force moving through the house at seven A.M.

The time apart had its advantages, though. I rarely had to get Joe's input before making family decisions. As the only adult in the house, I could do pretty much everything as I pleased. I lined up all our shoes neatly at the front door; drawers remained color-coordinated, kitchen counters spotless, and the couch pillows perfectly situated, just the way I liked them. The kids and I ate the foods I chose—even if they were overpriced—and we read the books I preferred, even if they wanted to watch movies all Saturday long. All the kid rules were mine to make up, and the order of the house was determined by me alone. I could sleep at night with my arms and legs spread wide across my bed if I wanted to.

And in London, Joe was at peace sleeping late on the weekends, working long hours Monday through Friday, grabbing dinner and as many beers afterward as he wanted. Being apart allowed us to unleash more of our particular, individual ways.

Those weeks in our own universes, going at life as we saw fit, allowed us to ease our way into a life together. Because this was all new for us: being partners, being parents to multiple children, and being the heads of a complex team. It had been only three years since we started seeing each other and our family had exploded in size, cutting the romance short in order to get right into the business of raising kids and building careers. With kids, there was no room for mistakes, or so it felt—so we moved fast and stayed focused on every area, except ourselves.

Whenever Joe was home from London, we'd organize family dinners at our loft where his siblings and their little ones would come over and hang out for hours. There'd be an African dish and a Southern dish, along with lots of wine and talk. Furniture would shift haphazardly, a couch to the left, a table in the center of the room, all to accommodate the family. Inevitably a glass or two would spill—"Oh! Cha-laaay!" a brother would yell out, yet no one would make a move to help clean except me—I was always trying to straighten up. "Relax, Jodie, it's pointless—my family is loud and messy. It's the Ghartey way!"

Often we'd take weekend trips to our house outside the city, sitting on the porch in the dark after we tucked the kids in, talking and laughing beneath the stars. Several years before I met Joe, he had bought the house with a dream of filling it with family and kids. There, we'd be reminded of everything we'd built together. We'd catch up not so much on anything in particular, but just listening to each other's voice, getting reacquainted with each other's rhythms. We'd go inside and Joe would wrap himself around me on a couch or a rug on the floor in the living room, and we would lie there, simply breathing together. In those quiet moments, it all made sense. We fit together perfectly. It was then that I'd relax into being his wife, no matter the lack of legal papers, no matter the distance, or the obstacles, or the frequent battles for control. Those moments reassured me that we were okay.

And then in a week's time he'd return to London, and I'd be reminded of another reality, one in which logistics dominated our conversations: How is Georgia doing in school? What did the pediatrician say? When should I book the next ticket for you to come to London?

Being so far apart and dealing mostly in logistics was not what I'd wished for in the early stages of our relationship. I thought we'd be together in a park pushing swings, or at home on the couch laughing about how tired we were. But twelve-hour days at the boutique on my end plus the kids, and flights back and forth from London to JFK a couple times a month on his end, kept our schedules borderline insane. Most of the time I was physically exhausted, operating solely on adrenaline and relying on a mere three hours of sleep each night.

I vacillated between loving my independence and missing my partner. Many a day, I felt like a single mom, wishing Joe nearer. But it was what it was, and at least we never wanted for anything. In fact, we had more than ever before. It was a time full of *things,* material comforts for our growing brood, but with not nearly enough tenderness between us.

With thousands of miles in the way, we grew further and further apart. The love and longing that fueled our London reunions in the beginning were replaced by anger and agitation when Joe would come home. We argued over sex, mostly, or the lack thereof. After hours of picking each other apart, sex became the last thing in the world I wanted to do. Eventually, we transformed into something I'd seen in other couples but never thought I'd become.

I constantly reminded myself: I could either have a busy husband who was tightly wound, or a deadbeat one. I preferred the first, so we'd just have to work around the complications and do our best to stay connected. If there were a few years when we were out of sync, so be it—we would have many years together to make up for lost time when the kids were older. Joe and I as individuals became the least important part of our equation.

Looking back, that was probably one of my biggest mistakes—not believing in romance, and not insisting on it. We very quickly started to feel like a machine, letting the hard parts just fall by the wayside—not learning how to love each other entirely, as we were. Some nights I'd lie in bed with Georgia and Cassius curled up next to me, Joe thousands of miles away, and ask myself, "Who is this man I'm with?" And I hoped somebody—anybody—would answer back, because I truly didn't know.

One night, Amani came over to take me out to dinner. She helped me get the little ones fed and in bed and Georgia situated with Ms. Nancy. With all the kids taken care of, I had several hours to be an unattached adult.

"All right, quick—let's sneak out before someone needs you,

Jodie." Amani knew it was only a matter of time before our plans would be totally derailed by the round-the-clock demands of Mama Duty.

"Okay, but wait, wait—I have this funny feeling . . . I think I might be pregnant."

"Noooo! You're officially crazy. What would you do with another kid? What would Joe say?"

She was right. Our hands were more than full. Adding anything else to the pile could very easily topple us over. We went into my bathroom, where I kept a stash of pregnancy tests under my sink. I peed. We waited. And as I had thought, I was indeed pregnant. Again.

"He's gonna lose it," I said, still sitting on the toilet. "This is not what we need."

Right away, I nervously dialed Joe in London from the bathroom. It was one in the morning his time, so I thought maybe he wouldn't answer the phone.

"Hullo?" His voice was thick with sleep.

"Oh! Umm, hey, babe. So, listen . . . We've got another one on the way. . . . I'm pregnant." I waited for the worst response. There was a momentary delay and then, "Cool, baby." I let out a sigh of relief.

"I mean, having another kid, this is crazy," he went on, "but I've always wanted a big family. Maybe this one's going to be a girl! I'd love a girl." He sounded happy and excited. Maybe this was what we needed.

Joe and I counted our blessings over the phone that night. We had so much to be thankful for, maybe it was time to start really seeing all the good we had. A new baby was coming. Despite all the difficulties, and all the miles between us, we both felt the shot of optimism coming from inside me. Suddenly, all the pressures weighing on us seemed small and surmountable.

This baby—any baby—was without a doubt the greatest gift we'd ever give each other.

Two months later, we learned from the doctor that Joe was right—we would be having a baby girl.

Not long after we heard the news, Joe and I stayed up late talking on the phone. I filled him in on my latest doctor's visit, which, for the first time in my last two pregnancies, was filled with nothing but good news. "She's growing perfectly, no complications. The doctor says she'll be much bigger than tiny baby Cassius, but nothing compared to chubby baby Georgia!" I laughed, thinking the idea of a round, healthy baby girl would make Joe smile. After bed rest with Cassius, we were both a bit nervous about this pregnancy.

"This is ridiculous, living in London while you're in New York. I'm coming home. I need to be there for our girl." It caused trouble at work for Joe, coming back when everyone wanted him to stay in London, but he didn't care, and neither did I.

We began tossing out different names to call her, maybe Gloria like my grandmother, or Maude or Zora or Madonna or Baldwin. I've always liked names that sound old—they come with history. Girls with those names know what they want. They like to kick around the dirt while wearing frilly dresses, and dig up worms after playing with their dolls. They're sly and mischievous. I wanted all those things and more for our new little girl. For the first time in a long time, Joe and I were both on the same page, excited and without anxiety for the future. Another pretty, opinionated girl would round out the family just right, and I could relax, knowing exactly what to expect.

I remember thinking, *This is going to be a piece of cake—I know girls like the back of my hand*. I had beautiful hand-me-down dresses from big sissy Georgia that I couldn't wait for the baby to wear. I was looking forward to endless girl chatter while we sat for hours detangling our curls in the bathroom—another "mini-me" to snuggle and giggle with.

When it was finally time, I felt our daughter's arrival before the doctors did. Normally active, doing somersaults inside me, in the days leading up to her birth this baby was unusually mellow, and it felt strange. I lay on my back in bed one morning and poked at my belly, trying my usual method of exciting her into action, but she barely responded, just slowly shifted her position.

"Joe, something's wrong. Baby's not moving." I demonstrated with more poking.

"That's because she's tired, babe. It's seven o'clock on a Saturday morning, let the poor girl sleep."

I knew this wasn't just a sleeping baby, so I followed my instincts, got dressed, and went to the hospital alone to figure out what was going on. I was quickly examined, told to calm down, and advised to come back again in the morning. So I did, and was told once again to go home. That night I lay rigid in bed waiting for the sun to come, and at the first signs of light I went to my personal doctor, who didn't work on weekends, determined to get some answers. Within minutes of being hooked up to a monitor, I learned that the reason for the baby's slowness was because she couldn't breathe. I was suffocating her with each contraction. "Go immediately to the emergency room. Your placenta doesn't have enough oxygen to support the baby." My doctor, normally full of jokes and smiles, was deadpan serious. "Don't stop to make a call, don't do anything else. Just get yourself checked in. You need to have her immediately."

I called Joe on the way, Joe called both of our moms. My mom hopped on a plane from Atlanta and brought Georgia to the hospital. Cassius stayed behind with our new nanny. They hooked me up to an IV and started pumping me with Pitocin to induce labor.

Three intense touch-and-go hours later, our baby girl arrived. If we hadn't responded quickly, she would have died inside me.

"Whoa!" Joe said when he finally saw her face squeeze out from between my legs, wide, open eyes and big, flaring nostrils. "You're definitely not a *pretty* girl!" He laughed clumsily. Everyone in the room turned to Joe in disbelief—were those really his first words to his kid, whose life had just been saved? Hadn't he any empathy? I looked down at my chest where our baby lay, exhausted from the birth, barely alive, apparently not that pretty, looking more like a wild fighter on the winning side of a boxing match than a cuddly, sweet baby. For a second I felt sorry for her. What would she become?

Feeling the tension, Joe filled in the awkward silence: "But that's okay, Daddy will always love you." His smile, broad across his entire face, was genuine, and we laughed then, all of us in the room—partly as a much-needed release. Partly for the strange love of a parent. And partly, too, because of the absurdity of the statement in the moment—Joe remarking on our daughter's beauty when just moments before, we'd thought we'd lose her. I thought, *Thank God we're not meant to be pretty. We're meant to be alive.*

The birth put things in perspective, serving as a reminder of just how fragile these situations are, how precious we are to each other. Holding our daughter between us, Joe and I both felt we needed to stick closer, to be nearer, as a family. She was tiny, just under seven pounds, and she was our precious, fragile gem.

I slept in the hospital room that night holding her in my arms, keeping one eye on her at all times to make sure she was okay. And when Joe returned early the next morning, he did the same. Even through our exhaustion, we never let her out of our sight or our reach—or alone with the hospital staff, not even to bathe. "No, thank you," I'd say to the nurse, who popped in every hour or so. "She's fine. I'll wash her when we get home tomorrow . . . Really, no, thank you."

If I could have looked into the future and seen whom I was holding, seen how strong this child was, how formidably strong, I would have understood that the one in my arms was the one who would push us, and break us, and reshape us. This baby would remake our entire universe. And for me, she would change my very purpose in life.

"Hello, Penelope," I whispered, watching her wiggle and kick, her big bright eyes on me. "Welcome to the world."

TEN

Tunnel Vision

In the beginning, things are simple. Tiring, but running on a predictable schedule. You leave the hospital on a Wednesday with Penelope in your arms and go back to work at the boutique on Monday, carrying her with you still. Sometimes you feel like a workhorse. That you can do anything—with new babies strapped to your chest, babies *you* birthed, with muscles still sore, with blood still pouring out of your body. Moving a little slower, maybe, but regardless of the obstacles or how physically grueling each day is, you just keep going and doing it all—one task at a time. You put in twelve-hour shifts while Penelope's happily snuggled close, nursing her in a chair near the front door of the store, greeting customers as they walk in.

At home, you make knee pads out of cloth and tape for her. Since she's learned to crawl, she's become an explorer—moving constantly and getting into things. You find her sitting on top of the open dishwasher hood, looking up at you with her big, gummy smile. You and Joe nickname her Baby. You watch her splashing around in the tub with her brother, making waves with the bathwater. You watch her at night, going down easily, sleeping soundly. You think, *I can do this*. You feel relief. Being Mom to four humans may not be as hard as they said it would be.

PENELOPE: YEAR I

Don't stop, don't slow down. Keep going. Keep pushing. Push a little more.

She can't run the show, Jodie. You hear your mother's advice replaying in your head as you attempt to change Baby. You grit your teeth and power through another diaper, and another and another and another. Sing a song this time to make it easier for her, make a funny face while you pry her legs apart. Try trickery, sorcery, alchemy, comedy—but every time, *every single time,* it's the same. She's sweating, screaming. Bearing down, lashing out, kicking hard, pushing back, turning red. You're sweating, insisting. Grabbing a foot, avoiding a kick. Calling for backup: "Joe! Help, please!" You hold down an arm, hold up a bottom, rush forward with the baby wipe. It's a frantic, frenzied dance—a battle of wills between you and your one-year-old. And the one-year-old is unbending, unbreakable. Her will is strong—so strong that it feels wrong for you to fight it.

Baby can't talk yet but her body language says it all. She frowns and pokes out her lips, she stiffens her back and makes it impossible to get a good snuggle in, she balls up her fist and swings at everything—at you, her dad, and sometimes even at her big brother Cassius while they sit on the floor playing. Cassius with his trucks neatly lined up in size order, and she with her dolls—paying no attention to them at all. She swings, knocking down Cassius's assembly of toys, and then she swings again, whomping him in the face. Baby is conveying, in every way possible, "No!" But you haven't a clue what she's refusing. Not a clue. You stay up for hours, thinking.

Don't stop, don't slow down. Keep going. Keep pushing. Push a little more.

Wake up, take Georgia and Cassius to school. Work till late, make your way home. Kiss the kids, kiss Joe. Work some more from your desk. Go to bed at three, set the alarm for six. Turn off the lights. Breathe deep. Get up and do it again.

You try your best not to be late. Georgia, especially, needs you to be on time. She stands out like a sore thumb at school, one of only three non-Chinese kids in her Gifted and Talented program. You walk to her third grade classroom each morning, holding her hand, and most parents avoid you both like the plague—staring suspiciously at you, two of only a scattered few Black people walking down the hallways. You raise your head higher and keep walking. You demonstrate resilience. But Georgia comes home each day with pee-soaked pants and tears in her eyes. You promise her you'll walk with her each and every morning until things get better. You fall asleep at night swearing never to be late again. You promise to do better, to be on time, the next morning.

PENELOPE: YEAR 2

Baby tells you about her wants, her likes. She likes olives and Brussels sprouts. She likes blocks and trains. She wants more juice, please. She likes her brother's T-shirts and jeans. His sneakers and boots. She wants to sleep on his pillow, use his toothbrush. "That one, over there." She points at the red-and-blue Spider-Man brush. She makes a face when you hand over her toothbrush instead, the pink-and-purple one covered in silver sparkles. "No," she whines. "*That* one. *There.*" She reaches out to take the Spider-Man toothbrush out of her brother's hand; he slaps her away, she slaps back. Crying and yelling ensue. You pull them apart: "All right, you two. Calm down." You put Baby's brush in her hand, put your hand over hers, and move it up and down together, brushing top and bottom teeth, tears still wet on her cheeks. She's not supposed to want those things, to wear what's not hers. Her brother doesn't like it, either. You determine that she must be confused.

The next day, you go to the store and buy pink and blue hangers. That weekend, you put Baby's clothes on the pink hangers and Cassius's on the blue ones. "The pink hangers are

*It seemed only right to dress
Penelope in head-to-toe pink.*

yours," you say to Baby, emphasizing the words "pink" and "yours." You reorganize their closet, separating out her clothes from his, putting hers on lower shelves so she can see them better. "*These* are your dresses, *these* are your shirts, *these* are your pants," you say, holding up pretty hand-me-down dresses, patterned shirts and pants.

You suggest trying something on: "How about the rainbow-striped dress? The one with the cute face of the brown girl with the Afro?" Georgia loved that one. But no, Baby doesn't want the rainbow-striped dress. She pushes it away. She wants her brother's bulky jeans. She wants his black-and-white Adidas T-shirt. She wants it so much that she starts to cry. *Here we go.* You pivot, picking up another shirt, another dress, another pair of socks, another pair of pants. She continues to cry; it's getting louder, fiercer.

Finally, you relent, letting her put on the bulky jeans and her brother's shirt. It's way too big in the shoulders and falls almost to her knees. The outfit is hideous, but she looks at you and beams—her once gummy grin now full of tiny teeth. No more tears. She struts around the house as if she's drenched in diamonds. You joke with friends about your kid's funny-horrible fashion sense, thinking about what kind of girl she'll turn out to be.

Maybe she's just jealous. Yes, probably jealous! That makes sense. Cassius *is* pretty amazing, the way he learns things with speed and does almost everything, big-boy things, with ease. Of course, that's it. She looks up to him, and wants to be him.

You watch your daughter watch your son. Baby observes her brother as though she's his understudy. It's like witnessing an intense game of Monkey See, Monkey Do. Cassius hurt his leg at the park one afternoon, and Baby limped around the entire day in phantom pain. "My leg hurt, Mama! My leg hurt, Mama!" she repeated, pointing to the same spot on her shin where her brother's bruise bloomed.

You see how Cassius and Penelope walk through life shoulder to shoulder. How she glances down at his footing to make sure she's got it right. How she watches you when you're disciplining him, reacting to his punishment as if it were her own. How she seems to look at the world through his eyes. Cassius sees it. He notices his sister watching his every move. Most of the time he's fine with her adoration. Until it becomes too much, until she smothers him with her presence—sometimes tripping over him to get as close to him as physically possible. "Give me space," Cassius says, placing a hand on Baby's chest, moving her back an inch.

"I am space," Penelope replies, leaning back in.

You try your best to be Penelope's everything, the way you were for Georgia. You look for the thing that maybe you haven't done enough of, and then try to do more of that thing.

Have you read enough books? Maybe she needs another story. Have you held her today? Touched her and showed her love? Have we sung songs like Mama did with you and Ramona? What's that song you used to sing, *Sippin' cider from a straw*?

"Baby, let's have some fun together. Just you and me." You try to lure her away from Cassius with the promise of some Mama and Penelope time.

"I not calking to you!" is her only response. You touch her shoulder but she brushes you away. She laughs when her brother hands her his Lego to play with.

PENELOPE: YEAR 3

Don't stop, don't slow down. Keep going. Keep pushing. Push a little more.

Work is difficult. You've fallen short every month on rent for the boutique. No matter how you rearrange the shelves with product, or how many hours you put in greeting customers, what comes out is always less than enough. "We just need a little more investment money and I'm sure we can make it work, babe." You've asked Joe to bail out the store more times than you're comfortable with. He's starting to doubt the business, maybe even doubt your abilities. So are you. After months of back-and-forth, you and Joe agree to close the shop, and if you're lucky, perhaps reopen it online. You admit to being afraid. "I don't have a clue how to run a digital company."

"Well, you'll have to learn," Joe commands. On the hottest day in August, you bring down the gate on the Georgia boutique for good—and on your current Manhattan hustle. Both have become too much.

WELCOME TO BROOKLYN the faded green sign reads as you drive your U-Haul down the freeway.

Another year, another move. There is another pregnancy, too. This time, a boy: Othello, who was in such a rush to come that you practically deliver him in the hallway of the hospital. You are now seven: Mama Bear, Papa Bear, and four little (and one not-so-little) cubs: girl, boy, girl, boy, boy. *Oh my God,* you think, panicking. *Five kids? When did that happen? How?* You and Joe move the crib out of storage and back into your bedroom—again.

Everything must have a schedule. Go to the park for thirty minutes. Toys for an hour. Bath time at six. Dinner at seven. Story time at eight. Children asleep by eight thirty. You fantasize about ways to streamline and professionalize the parenting process into an efficient system with the least effort and highest return on investment. If you can't get your business to be profitable, you damn sure won't screw up the family, too. Everyone needs to be on time and in their place, bathed and groomed, wearing the right clothes and the right attitude. Because late has become your new normal. Chaos constantly creeps into the routine.

It's Penelope. This three-year-old terror, breaking down your best-laid plans with all of her "no's." "No!" to certain colors (all the pinks and purples, too-light shades of blue); "No!" to the shape of her jeans. "No!" to the stitching on that button, "No, no, no!" to baths, to changing, to combing her hair. Since she's learned to talk, her favorite form of speech is protest.

You try your best. You know how important being on time is—Joe reminds you every day. Georgia in particular can't be late. She's the new girl at a fancy, highly competitive private school, and one of only a few Black girls in her class—again.

But there are twenty-four hours in a day, and you need twenty-five. You have lunches to make and hair to do, and new teachers to meet, and new house rules to establish for Nain, like no drinking directly from the containers of juice or devouring all the cereal late at night while stretched out on the couch. You have an eleven-year old, and a five-year-old, and a three-year-old, and baby Othello—and a young man who's come to you with his own undocumented peculiarities and habits. You have zero time for Penelope's antics. Her "no's" take you further and further away from routine, further from a schedule that's already *this* close to falling apart. There is an agitator in your midst, and her name is Penelope. She is the disrupter. A constant item on your list of to-dos.

Tonight's task: hide the stitching.

You hunch over a pile of clothes on your knees with a permanent marker, blacking out the pink stitching on a pair of Penelope's corduroys. She's boycotted all pink in any of her clothes. Although you've tried to duplicate her brother's wardrobe as best you can from the girls' section, she's spotted pink on the inside label of one of her shirts, and now she refuses to wear anything in her wardrobe. But you refuse to throw it all away. You look over at Joe, who's chuckling at the absurdity of the situation. "No one ever sees the stitching anyway," he says into a pair of khakis. "Why does she care so much?"

"I don't freakin' know, just do it!" you snap. Pause. Breathe. "Please." You can hear how mean you sound. Your nerves are shot. You're scared Penelope will walk in and discover the two of you trying to pacify her with a Magic Marker.

Joe somehow feels it's your fault, that perhaps you've indulged the kids too much and allowed them to express themselves too freely. Maybe they're feeling in control, and you need to take back the reins.

"You do too much talking, Jodie. You need to—"

"What, Joe? What haven't I done? What should I do more of? Tell me and I'll do it. I tried spanking for a month straight, but it didn't solve a thing." Silence. You shake your head. "Just color over the damn pink stitching, please."

Heads down, for hours the two of you go through Penelope's clothes, piece by piece, pulling everything out for examination with a ruthlessness that verges on maniacal. Hunting for suspect stitching, for that offending color. Running the ink over every single stitch, every single label, until all traces of pink are blotted out. *Handled,* you think.

You do this because you know what will happen if you don't. The tantrums that will rattle the whole house. You do this to make Penelope happy. And mostly, you do this just so you can make it out the damn door the next morning.

Today, after a week of begging us to "cut it into a Mohawk, like Papa's!" Joe takes clippers to Penelope's halo of blond curls.

Six months ago, Joe decided to leave his job—the office politics he'd been navigating had become ridiculous at best, insurmountable at worst. Plus, he now has other things on his mind. He's vowed to run a marathon, master woodworking, and get to know the philosophy of Eckhart Tolle. He moved all of his blue suits into an infrequently used closet, replaced them with jeans and T-shirts, and cut his hair into a drastic and defiant Mohawk. This is the Mohawk that Penelope wants, too.

She's been so restless these days, as though she's uncomfortable in every place she stands. Your closest friend from high school comes over for the day, visiting from Florida, and her oldest daughter, barely eight, relays to her after they leave, "Penelope doesn't like her skin."

When you first heard Penelope say "Cut off my hair," you froze. The prospect of cutting it short wasn't the issue. Remember your Spelman days. It also wasn't an issue for Joe. Growing up in Ghana, most young schoolgirls wear short Afros. No, it was the *way* of Penelope's declaration, the absolute clarity of it that stopped you short. She'd said it with so much determination in her voice that it caught you off guard. What could be so urgent that she's trying to say? She's only three years old, but she's willing to go against what everyone around her sees as "normal." It's as though she knows something, a truth that she's not willing to back down from.

You and Joe looked at each other when she first made her demand, searching for answers. But the answers didn't come, so you just walked away. Away from each other, away from Penelope. Away from the confusion you still feel.

You think Joe understands more now that he's home every day. He sees her unrest and tries to fix it. When *his* snuggles don't work—when nothing he tries works—his face starts to have the same look on it that yours has had for months. Defeat.

Baby's suffering has become your suffering. The tantrums, the tears, the constant disruptions. The tension in the moments leading up to picking out an outfit for the day, or preparing for a bath at night. The agitation with her body, as if she's ready to jump out of her skin. Clearly her hair, like so many other things, has been getting in the way of her joy.

So, after she asks you for the third time to cut it off, you and Joe both know what you have to do. It just feels right. In fact, you realize that it's the first good-feeling decision you've made together in a while. You don't do it for convenience, or for your needs. You tune in and do it, simply, for her.

Standing in the doorway, you watch as Joe leads Penelope into the bathroom and begins slowly cutting off row after row of her curls. In less than fifteen minutes the deed is done, and a smiling, glorious child emerges. She walks out of the bathroom with a lightness you've never seen before; it swirls around her, eventually spreading throughout the entire house like incense.

A lightness you want to bottle up and preserve for her so that she'd never be without it again.

Don't stop, don't slow down. Keep going. Keep pushing. Push a little more.

Amid your frenzied days, you start to notice things. Penelope's agitation rippling, deepening, expanding. Cutting the hair helped. Finally letting her wear clothes from the boys' department has helped, too. But these changes are not enough. You realize she will never be a pretty dress and Mary Janes kind of girl. The short rebellious hair and wide-legged jeans are part of the presentation—how she wants to be seen—but you know, at least you think you know, that these small changes are not telling the full truth.

Tiny differences—things you'd never noticed before—come into sharp focus when Penelope lays her eyes on them. She is a merciless judge, so attuned to what makes "girl" and what makes "boy" that you now analyze details that were once invisible to you: the sharpness of a collar, the size of a button, the hidden messages in the bedtime stories you tell her. The sweet, smiley tone in your voice when you talk to her and Georgia versus the matter-of-fact one you use with Cassius and Othello—even with Joe.

You see these things because Penelope reacts to them. How she frowns when Joe still calls her Baby, even after she's communicated to you both how much she hates that nickname. How much she hates being treated differently from her brothers—softly, delicately, with the extra care often reserved just for girls. And because you notice these things, you start to resent the blind spots of Joe's affections. You understand he is expressing his love in the only way he knows how, and you love him for that—but you still get mad. *Can't he just do whatever makes her happy?* you think. It's hard to watch the push and pull between them. You wonder when Joe's going to catch up.

The smiley voices, the feminine clothes, the expectations and assumptions for girls—they add up to a story your daughter doesn't see herself in. Present them to Penelope and her agitation builds, her anger bubbles up and spills onto anyone within reach. And it lingers, too—she is mad more than not. She's a bully on the playground, and a bully at home. This anger follows her around everywhere.

There is a bigger darkness looming, you know. Every night for months, Penelope wakes up screaming, her cries wild. You and Joe take turns rushing into her room to find out what's wrong. She tells you something about monsters, that they are chasing her, ready to gobble her up. You untangle her from sweat-soaked sheets, rubbing her back and touching her face so she can feel you next to her. You tell her something Mama used to tell you when you had nightmares: "Next time, say to the monster, 'This is *my* dream—go away!'"

But looking at your daughter's face, her eyes wide with fear and her voice a whisper, you know the monster is getting the best of her. You feel that something is very wrong. You feel it like a dull ache in your gut and in your chest. It reminds you of when the monster used to invade your dreams, chasing you for miles. You feel small again when you see how troubled your daughter is. You feel in danger again when you hear her crying at night. All you want is for the monster to go away. All you want for Penelope is peace.

ELEVEN

The Room

IT HAPPENED IN 2011 during Penelope's third year, late in the month of June. School had just let out for the summer and we'd begun spending long weekends at our house in Callicoon, a little mountain town on the New York–Pennsylvania border, near the Delaware River. The place is dewy and vibrant green—all the surrounding sounds made softer by the moss and thick trees encircling the property, and the rush of the stream that snakes around the back of the house. We have no neighbors up there, save for the black bears who stroll across the front yard at dawn during summertime, and all the little critters—the crickets and woodpeckers and frogs—who've made our backyard their own. The life we fall into when we walk through the house's big wooden door has become our haven. It's a space, I always think, that demands tranquillity. But on that particular afternoon, Penelope was fighting back against the calm, being especially difficult, displaying the usual outbursts on hyperdrive—throwing toys, provoking her siblings, refusing clothing, and falling on the floor in hysterics more than once.

"Baby, find something nice to do!" I remember ordering from my favorite spot on the couch.

She steamrolled through the living room, keen on taking down anything in her way. Then she zeroed in on Cassius, who, in his signature style, had just finished building an intricate tower of colorful wooden blocks that I knew Penelope had in her sights. She made her move, and with one deliberate push took down her brother's creation. He was devastated, shocked, and soon both kids were in tears. After all that yelling and screaming, I felt like joining in, too.

Exhausted from playing wrangler and referee, I decided to give both Penelope and myself a rare one-on-one time-out. I peeled her off the floor, scooped her up into my arms, and carried her into the kids' bedroom, shutting the door behind us.

I pulled her down onto the carpet with me and we sat face-to-face.

"What's the matter, love?" I exhaled, surrendering to whatever tirade was about to come. "Why are you so angry all the time?"

A pause, and then a flood of tears sprang from her eyes. And then came this:

"Because everyone thinks I'm a girl, Mama—and I'm not."

The stream passes right outside the kids' room on its way to join the Delaware. We hear the water most clearly in that room—it sounds urgent, galloping around the back of the house. Yet it is the kind of sound that doesn't quite register until it does—one minute it's background noise and the next it's all you can hear. Whenever I revisit this conversation with Penelope in my memory, the stream's presence is palpable—it was one of the most vivid parts of that day. Constant, strong, intruding, it was the soundtrack for everything soon to come.

In the seconds that followed Penelope's declaration, without hesitation, I pulled something from my Mom Rolodex of go-to references, words, and phrases that might fit the dilemma.

I remembered a book Mom read to Ramona and me when we were kids, *Free to Be You and Me*—the gender equality clarion call of the 1970s. I told Penelope then that she was free to act however she felt. She wanted to roughhouse with her brothers, have short hair, and be just like the boys? I was on board. "However you *feel* is fine," I encouraged. "It's what's *inside* that counts."

"You're perfect the way you are," I said. "I love you—and everything about you," I said.

But hearing this, Penelope's face crumpled. She jerked her body away from me, straining to put as much distance between us as she could.

We'd been here before—over and over and over. Penelope lying naked on the bathroom floor, her body in a tight coil while her tears made little pools on the tiles. Me lying next to her, trying to calm her. Every reassurance I gave was met with resistance and seemed to scratch her skin. Watching her in this room, I could finally recognize her expression for what it was—it was the look of deep disappointment. I had betrayed her. For Penelope, clearly the body had been the enemy. And if *I* didn't understand that—if *I* were siding with the body—then *I* was the enemy, too.

Picking her head up off the floor, Penelope tried again with me: "I don't *feel* like a boy, Mama. I *am* a boy."

The words shook me. I knew then that Penelope was talking about something deeper than what I knew.

Half the time as an adult, you already have the answer—or at least know what the shape of the answer looks like. We've done the job at work before, we've taken that route on the subway before. As parents, we've often dealt with the kid who doesn't want to brush his teeth or do her homework. These tasks may be difficult, but they're not necessarily surprising.

But this? "I don't *feel* like a boy, I *am* a boy"—this was a sentence I wasn't prepared for. It rolled around in my brain, pinging against the folders of my experiences looking for a match, an appropriate response, and came back with nothing. Blank, opaque, nothing. And in that moment I believed I failed my child for not knowing. Failed because I didn't see it coming, and could not offer up a plan.

"I love you, but I don't want to be you," Penelope cried, tears now starting to spill down my own cheeks. I listened carefully to Penelope tell me about hating her body—hating it so much that she wanted a doctor to make her a "peanut." She told me that her "tomorrow" would be worse than her "today" because tomorrow her body would look like mine. Penelope did not want tomorrow ever to come.

I watched Penelope watching me, waiting for a response, and I heard myself say that there were doctors who could help. I made this promise to Penelope without knowing what "help" even meant. I didn't know what being a boy looked like for my daughter, had no clue what truths "boy" held for her. But I did know the fear in her eyes. I know what it is like to feel small and alone, to feel afraid and weighed down, boxed in, constricted. And so when she told me "I'm not a girl, I am a boy," although I did not have an answer, I wasn't compelled to say "You're wrong."

But the guilt—the guilt seized me by the throat immediately. *What did I forget to do?* I thought. *What have I missed?* Had the tension between me and Joe, Penelope's difficult birth, my packed work schedule, manifested into something fundamentally imbalanced in my child? Or did it go deeper than that? Maybe I'd forgotten to tell Penelope the stories—of Toni Morrison and Maya Angelou and Nina Simone and Dr. Cole and her own grandmothers—all my sheroes who proved that I could be a woman and be more than one thing. Having been raised to cherish being female, I felt as if my child's rejection of that venerable symbol was my failure. The women in my family are proud of who we are, proud to be female. But my own daughter was ashamed.

My emotions were swinging wildly—between humiliation and protection. Between sadness and compassion. Between panic and relief. *How can this be happening on my watch? How has this moment made its way into my life?* But there were no explanations, no answers to the questions. Nothing but the silence, and that steady, galloping stream, filling up more and more space in the room.

The minutes continued to tick away. And in front of me Penelope sat there, still. My hows and whys were muffled by the sight of my three-year-old—this person I'd made a vow to be responsible for, to tune in to, from the moment I'd felt Penelope's presence inside me. This human, *my* human, was now suffering from a hurt rooted in something beyond the words immediately available to me.

But beyond my understanding is clearly where my child exists. And so, after words fail me, when my thoughts and explanations run up against the dark, I decide that the only way to walk through what I do not know is to shut off my questions. To honor the gaps in my understanding and let those huge holes just *be*—taking up the space between us.

We sat in that room together for hours, or days, or years, I don't know. Time blurred, the earth spun a little slower. And as my tears continued to fall, I gave myself over to my child, learning about how Penelope wanted to be seen by the world.

How . . . *he* wanted to be seen. How his heart beat.

I took Penelope at his word, and at his feeling. And for the first time in my life as a parent, I allowed my child to take the lead on what would come next.

I once saw an electric-pink sunset that hovered over the water in the most breathtaking way. It was so pure and vibrant and awesome that I needed to see it only that one time for it to be imprinted on me, deeply and profoundly, forever.

On that day with Penelope, late in the month of June, I felt something close to that electric-pink sunset. Together, in the room without time, while the stream galloped toward the Delaware River, a seismic shift began to rumble around us.

TWELVE

Ten Thousand Hours

MINUTES AFTER PENELOPE AND I EMERGED from the bedroom, I
delivered the news to Joe. I did it like any other debrief on a
typical kid meltdown, downplaying the major plot points in an
effort to hold on to the deeper meaning a little longer, to sort
things out on my own. I felt protective of the trust Penelope
had given me, of the belief that I would not betray him or his
secret, and of the hope that I was the person who could help.

I saw myself in Penelope—both of us smaller than our fear,
smaller than the world around us, and smaller than the answer.
I had felt myself die in that room when I saw how scared Penelope was. And then I was born again as we sat together, and I
realized that it would take my being present, with eyes and
heart wide open, for my child to stay alive. *Stay close to Penelope.*
I knew nothing more than that.

If someone could have done that for me—looked into
my pain and dissected it, thoughtfully, carefully, preciously—
I would have clung to that person and never let go. Dropping
the ball on Penelope, I felt, would have been like abandoning
myself. It was that primal. For those reasons, it was easier than I
expected to let the "she" next to Penelope's name fall away.
When we walked out of that room together, in my mind, Penelope became "he."

"So, Penelope just told me she's a boy," I said as I approached
Joe, who was resting on the living room couch. He looked at
me over the top of the cookbook he was reading and squinted,
cocking his head, trying to get a better read on what I'd just

said. "I got this, babe, don't worry," I told him, waving the words away as I said them—pretending our entire life hadn't just turned upside down.

"Penelope said she's a boy" could never sound the way it did when it came from Penelope's mouth. It was like a message in a game of telephone that was sure to get mangled. I knew that attempting a detailed explanation to Joe would dilute the meaning. It would leave it susceptible to being explained away with sensible answers and practical reasoning—reasoning that took the shape of statements like "She's confused" or "This is a phase" or "She's just our tomboy." Penelope's news went beyond all that. I knew in ways I couldn't yet articulate that this new information was vital—delicate, combustible—and needed to be treated with care. What it needed was time and protection, just as Penelope did. I wanted to keep it close to me, away from prying eyes, away from doubt and skepticism—and away from Joe, who would rationalize the information away with his practicality. I needed it to be just mine for a while.

Luckily, this wasn't hard to do. Raising children means there are always moments of total chaos in one corner while life goes on as normal in all the others. One kid falls out of bed, hits their head, and has to go to the hospital. Another kid gets rushed to the emergency room with a lung infection. Little crises pop up everywhere, but at the end of the day we've got to keep things moving. And so it was easy to pretend that this was another one of those times. I would handle the Penelope Event on my own while Joe kept the rest of the plates spinning.

The night of our conversation in the mountain house, and in the months that followed, while the rest of the house slept I lay awake attempting to make mental pictures with Penelope's declaration. Trying to reimagine body parts in bathing suits, summertime swimming, and first dates, reshuffling the pieces I knew until the image revealed a new assemblage of Penelope as "boy." I tried to transpose my predesigned "normal" with this other thing that was so unformed, all raw and jagged edges. This thing that I couldn't yet see clearly.

I needed new pictures, because the only ones I did have—like the *Silence of the Lambs* psychopath wiggling at the camera with his penis tucked between his legs, or the kids in *Paris Is Burning* whose narratives too often ended in body bags—were flooding the good spaces in my mind.

Cautiously, I started making my way onto the Internet in search of more. In the media landscape of 2011, "transgender" was still a word largely relegated to high art or carnival side-show. It manifested in exhibits that one might see in a gallery on the Lower East Side, a severe black-and-white photograph of a broken mom with her broken son, coupled with a sad caption revealing the bleak details around his transition: "After a life-time of pain, rejection, and confusion, Dylan's courageous decision to live life as he wants, as a man, comes with its own form of heartbreak."

Words that denoted fear and deviation were commonly used to define their experience—and the subjects in these exhibits were always people of color from "the wrong side of town." *What am I looking at here?* I often thought when I saw these images. Were these people broken because of something that had happened to them—a drug addiction, an alcohol problem—or because of some bigger systemic problem, like racism or poverty, outside their control? Why were things so bleak? Was transgender a form of divergence that led to a rough and troubled life? Or was there something hidden within these images that I had yet to understand?

Sometimes I'd see "transgender" appear in small print under flashy headlines: WORLD'S FIRST PREGNANT MAN—referring to the Thomas Beatie story that had dominated the talk show circuit just a few years before. I remember watching Thomas's interview on *Oprah* in 2008, a year after Penelope was born. Before bringing out her guest, Oprah prepared the audience, setting each word down like a trail that led to the mystery behind Door Number Three.

"Thomas, not Nancy, is the one who's pregnant . . . I'm gonna let you take that in."

Cut to mouths open, aghast, as studio monitors flashed photos of a shirtless Beatie, flat-chested and swollen-bellied at eight months pregnant, with short-cropped hair and a full beard. Oprah concluded the segment by saying that Thomas and his wife's story of love and family gave us "new definitions of what diversity means for everybody." But not before probing Thomas about his sex life and his hormonally altered body. The topic never seemed to be able to escape tabloid treatment, even from Oprah.

I didn't remember much of what Thomas said in this or any of the other interviews he gave during that initial media blitz. I only remember the aura that surrounded it. It was conjured as a bizarro world where women are men and up is down. It does sound freakish when you don't understand, and when the media serves it in such a sensational way.

Not much had changed since Thomas's *Oprah* interview took place. In those first months of my Penelope research frenzy, if I happened to run across the rare story of a person who was transgender, it still seemed that the media wasn't quite getting it. Transgender was still being presented as something that belonged in a documentary series alongside profiles of sex offenders and gay conversion therapy. And within all those conversations, never once did they include or discuss transgender children.

At night, while Joe lay next to me reading his book, I clicked from website to website, from article to article to article, searching for pictures—grasping for anything that could help me better understand.

In the midst of this relentless clicking I came across so many new words: androsexual; androphylic, aromantic, asexual; bi-curious, bigender, cisgender; demisexual; intersex; feminine of center, masculine of center; F2M, M2F; gender fluid; GNC—gender nonconforming; GSM—gender and sexual minorities; DSG—diverse genders and sexualities; gender straight, gender-queer, gender variant; gynesexual; pansexual; skoliosexual; same gender loving (SGL); mx, ze, hir. Third gender. Two-spirit.

I had no idea that the human experience could be sliced in so many ways. The words were dazzling, seductive, tongue-twisting, and so foreign to me—and for those reasons, they were intoxicating. It felt like being back at Spelman again freshman year, digging deep into a new world that opened up to me through stories told at Sisters Chapel, in the dormitories, and within the pages of *The Bluest Eye, I Know Why the Caged Bird Sings, Their Eyes Were Watching God*. These new words hinted at other universes—whole dimensions I had yet to explore. I wanted to know everything and understand it all.

Malcolm Gladwell says it takes ten thousand hours to master anything, and that became my guiding principle.

This learning exercise, though, had an ugly side. Doctors and clinicians categorized many of the identities I was discovering as disorders, the result of some kind of body chemistry gone wrong. I learned of doctors talking about transgender as a "condition" that might be caused by "hormone surges" in the mom. There was talk of trans people being "stuck in the wrong body." The phrase "gender dysphoria" crept into my new taxonomy, paralyzing me with the feeling that Penelope and the body were truly, medically, at war. That my child was inflicted with a condition that put his brain and his body at odds. According to this line of research, Penelope had a condition that no doctor seemed to know how to heal, and that often led to suicide or murder—death, so many mentions of death, in some form or another.

I've always had such faith in my children. Even before they were born I had a sense of their spirit. I could see their greatness like an aura around them. Georgia was wise, Cassius was receptive, Othello marched to his own rhythm, Nain had grace and a gentle way about him—and Penelope, I thought, *This one is tenacious. This one is lucky.* When I said I wanted children, I meant that I wanted to have healthy, beautiful, smart, capable children. But Penelope felt more like "broken." Someone who hated himself and couldn't be at peace with his own reflection—and I took on that angst. When my kids are thrilled, I'm over the moon right along with them. When they're low, it feels like my personal failure. I can't separate from them in these emotional moments. Seeing Penelope this way made me feel trapped in his sadness. Both of us trapped. And so I sank.

Penelope was not at all the child I'd imagined. Penelope would never grow up to become that brilliant, beautiful, witty woman the world needed more of. The type of woman I wished I were. No, he was never going to be that person, and I had to adjust to that. But even deeper, Penelope, with his mind saying one thing and his body saying another, was set up for disappointment, over and over again. He was, it seemed, the unluckiest kid in the world.

Such was the rhythm and force behind these late-night searches—full of incredible highs and soul-crushing lows. Although I was learning more, finding more, opening the door a little wider, what dominated my emotions was the sinking feeling that my kid was burdened. That the life I'd wished for all my children, and privately for myself, would never be possible for this one, and freedom—uncomplicated freedom—was out of Penelope's reach.

. . .

"Joe, babe, have you seen the book I've been reading? I can't find it." We were in bed one night, about to turn off the lights.

"Which book? There's one right there at the foot of the bed. Are you reading *Goodnight Moon,* babe?" Joe cut a smile at me.

"I wish," I joked back. "It would probably put me to sleep much faster. No, I'm looking for the book I've been reading for the last month. I think it's called *Transgender Basics* or something like that, I can't remember."

"Yeah, I took it with me to Ghana on my last trip. *Transgender 101,* by Nicholas Teich."

"Umm, yeah! I didn't know you were reading it." I turned toward him so he could see the smile on my face. We hadn't genuinely smiled at each other in a while, and I wanted him to notice.

"I'm *so* happy you picked it up! What do you think? It brought up so many questions for me . . . Did you see how much I underlined? And all the stuff I wrote in the margins?" I was about to explode. Maybe Joe and I could do this together.

He had been slow to read the signs around Penelope, but even slower to define anything that we were witnessing. He wrote off the coloring over of pink stitching as typical mom indulgence of a daughter. The boy jeans as a bad but comical style preference of a child who didn't know any better. The moody disposition as part of the typical middle-kid syndrome. I'd yet to hear Joe say out loud any form of recognition that we were in deep over our heads—looking at something we'd never seen before, something completely new. What a beautiful surprise to see him trying to *learn* about Penelope.

"You know, I started it. But I never finished. Actually, I think I left it in Ghana . . . I'll call Dad and ask him to hold it for me."

He was short on words, even a bit dismissive. I did an about-face on my enthusiasm, pulling it back into my chest.

"Oh. Got it. Well if you could just remember to return it to me . . . I want to keep those notes I wrote in the book for future reference."

"Yup, I'll grab it when I go back next time. Night." Joe rolled over to sleep, completely unaware of the tightness on my face, or the restraint in my breath, or the disappointment that suddenly took over me.

I read more books and clicked away on the Internet thousands more times, alone. To take away my growing anxiety, I'd wash it all away with a glass of red wine. Sometimes that glass would become a bottle, maybe more. It was that bottle that loosened me up and made me think good thoughts. It gave me a warm feeling of peace and alignment, that everything would eventually work itself out. Sometimes I even felt euphoric. I would drink until my brow relaxed and my lips were no longer tight. Until my bedroom walls started to flicker with golden lights, my eyelids getting heavy while I watched the dancing glow. Eventually, I'd fall asleep.

That's how I got through those ten thousand hours.

THIRTEEN

Shifting

———

WHAT CAME NEXT WAS CHANGE—the slow shifts, the profound moments, the lessons learned that come along with navigating so much unknown.

There were no big announcements from us, no formal family meetings—no memorable shouting-from-the-rooftop declarations. Instead, I wanted us to move like water—changing incrementally in the flow of our days. I wanted to teach our children about transgender the same way my parents taught Ramona and me about Blackness, infusing it into our lived reality, moment to moment, interaction to interaction. When we were growing up, Mama and Daddy never made us chant or march or announce our allegiance to the race, as they often had to during segregation. For Ramona and for me, our Blackness, that key component of our identity, became more defined over time with each experience my parents created for us.

Identifying with our Blackness couldn't be pinpointed to a single moment. No one ever sat us down and said, "You. Are. Black." We simply *were* Black. It wasn't just explained to us in a picture of the Great Migration hanging on a wall, although it did include that. Nor was it singularly defined by Uncle Gil and his revolutionary lyrics. Our culture had infinite manifestations—and that's just how I wanted our family to feel about gender. I wanted it to be normal and pervasive and beautiful. For it to be that powerful, it needed to be inseparable from who we were, indivisible from ourselves. Like coffee from its water.

Fluidity was my goal—and it was a tough one to achieve considering how green I was in my own understanding. At home, I'd try my best to call Penelope "he," succeeding most of the time but sometimes slipping up. Embracing new pronouns, again, wasn't the hard part—I found that compared to the nightmares I had about Penelope's safety, ones that jolted me out of my sleep, quibbling over "she" versus "he" felt silly. It was my brain's default system that kept getting in the way. "She" rolled off my tongue so automatically, while "he" took an awareness and consciousness that required me to be connected to each moment. If I wasn't focused, if I was tired from the day, or preoccupied cooking dinner, maybe, I'd slip up, sliding back into "she." "Sorry, Pleppy," I'd say, feeling guilty of betrayal—a sin no parent wants any part of. "It's going to take Mama a while before I get this. You know I see you as a boy, right?" He'd nod, giving me a forgiving smile. "Yup, it's okay. I know you're not doing it on purpose, Mama." I was glad Penelope took it in stride, knowing exactly which side my heart was on. It was just my brain that needed to catch up.

In public, I fell short, too. As much as I supported Penelope in my heart, I also felt a strange obligation to the rules. In school and out in the world, Joe and I had a need to keep to the formalities. For teachers, administrators, doctors—or any official person or document—we'd revert back to "she," as if we were answering to a higher authority. As if Penelope's authority weren't enough. Report cards would come back from teachers: "Penelope is an outstanding member of the classroom community. I am so impressed with the effort she puts forth and the perseverance she shows every day in her work." And we'd leave the pronouns alone, glaring at us from the page. In those moments, it never felt one hundred percent right to stay silent, but it was what we thought we should do, so we did.

There was also a third reality we lived, which complicated

things even more. We'd started having small conversations about Penelope's preferred pronouns, with my mom and some close family and friends—a next step from the "she's just a tomboy" conversation we'd been having with them for the last two years. But when we were around certain people—folks we thought would resist too fiercely or take too long to adapt—we removed gender altogether. To simplify things for those people, Joe and I would stumble through sentences, zigzagging around pronouns, adding in unnecessary words just to steer clear of gendering. "Please make sure Penelope goes to sleep at eight o'clock sharp, Mormor" (our nickname for Joe's mom). "Penelope needs a lot of rest. And if Penelope has a nightmare, try rubbing Penelope's back." In those awkward moments, it took more time to convey a simple bedtime routine about Penelope than it did with any other kid. More than once, I caught Penelope watching us with a look on his face as if to ask, *Why am I such a big deal?*

But I was determined to get it right.

"Don't you think it's strange, Joe," I offered one night, cleaning up dishes in the sink after dinner, "that we don't know any transgender people other than Penelope?" It was the first time I'd used the words "transgender" and "Penelope" in the same sentence.

It felt as if we'd been containing ourselves in a bubble, not valiant enough to explore this new world we were learning about. But I was ready to start blending in new vocabulary, like transgender, cisgender, and gender nonconforming, into our everyday talk, and even incorporating transgender characters into our bedtime stories. In a year's time, I wanted the immediate family to look and sound different and to think differently. That was my plan.

"Whoa, babe—slow down a second with that word," Joe jumped in, making me sound hasty and irrational, minimizing me. "We're not going to just follow all those books you're reading, Jodie." He was making this into a fight, I could feel it coming.

Joe, I knew, understood Penelope to be different, with unique needs unlike his brothers'. Over the last few months, he'd accepted that. But hard plans, definitive pronouns, prescribed language, were just not his way. He preferred to let things unfold on their own, never wanting to corrupt or taint what was organically happening. He remained firm in his approach to let things just be—with as little interference as we could get away with.

"Labels are the last thing Penelope needs." I hadn't expected that response, actually. I assumed he'd say that I needed to stop indulging Penelope, be tougher, worry less. But the idea that *I* was restricting Penelope by using the word "transgender"—it shocked me. From where I stood, saying the word out loud was the first step toward tuning in to and supporting Penelope, not restricting him. Never that. I felt that using "transgender" made me, and everyone else, pay more attention to his specific needs. I wanted to defend myself, show Joe how defining things, making deliberate and perhaps uncomfortable changes in our lives, was the right thing to do. But I thought better of it when I saw the look on his face, as if he was processing something he'd been working on for a very long time.

"When I was a kid living in Boston, they'd call me 'nigger.' Then when my mom moved us to Ghana they called me *abroni*— 'white boy.' It's too much, Jodie. Labels imply that we're not enough—not white enough, or not Black enough, not girl or boy enough. Transgender is just one more narrow box to put Penelope in. And I can't. I won't do it."

Joe had told me these childhood stories before, but never like this, in this context. They struck me in a different place. Maybe it was just a matter of learning a new and more delicate language, together—one that would make us both feel good about using it.

"I get limitations, Joe, I do. That's not at all what we want." I turned off the faucet, placed the sponge on the counter, and turned to face him, trying to show with my body language that this was not a fight. "But what should we do when your dad comes from Ghana and stays with us for two months? We're going to need to address it somehow."

Joe's seventy-two-year-old father was arriving from Ghana in a few weeks for a long visit, and we both knew he would pose a challenge when it came to Penelope. He was the family elder—bold, unwavering, religious, and very traditional. The last time Dr. G visited, Penelope had been much younger, and a lot had changed since then. We could both see him disapproving of a girl wearing shorts and sneakers, possessing a "non-girly" attitude. Penelope definitely wasn't going to sit by his side, patiently serving him food upon command or handing him his newspaper and his notebook, as he might have expected—things his daughter, Kiara, had done for him when she was young.

"Have da chil' bring me dat glass of cold wa-ta!" Joe was great at imitating his dad's accent and the Ghanaian way. We laughed and imagined what it would be like if we dared to bring up the esoteric conversation of body versus soul, something I'd been recently thinking so much about.

"So I shouldn't explain to Grandpa G as soon as he walks through the door that form follows feeling and we exist as spirit first?" We both chuckled over the scenario, knowing damn well that that wouldn't do.

"I have an idea." Joe winked at me—problem solving had always been his thing. "It's not brilliant," he teased, "but it's very, very, very good. Why don't we just ask my dad to change his wording, just say 'he' instead of 'she'? Keep it simple."

"Yup!" We high-fived. It was decided: We would stick to what was most pressing—asking Dr. G for his most basic level of acceptance: to simply refer to Penelope as "he."

Joe and I were often at odds when it came to Penelope, but that night we found some common ground.

Two weeks later, when Dr. G arrived, we sat him down at the kitchen table to deploy Operation Pronouns. I poured him a tall glass of water and placed a proper Ghanaian meal of hot lentil soup and rice in front of him to set the tone. Never mind that Joe had actually cooked the meal earlier. I made sure to be the one serving and smiling, enthusiastically giving our family patriarch every bit of my attention in order to keep his defenses down. It would only make our case worse if he thought the family had abandoned tradition entirely.

We slowed our normally frantic pace way down that afternoon, letting Dr. G taste the soup and savor the spices. Seeing his father's obvious pleasure, Joe went in for the ask: "Dad, would it be okay if you used male pronouns for Penelope? . . . It's just what he likes." He was staying on script, keeping the explanation sparse. Joe and I took a seat on either side of Dr. G, crossing our fingers under the table. We smiled and waited, then smiled some more. We were nervous. Very nervous.

I remember once, during a family discussion, Dr. G told me never to speak after Joe. "Because men always conclude important conversations," he'd said. It startled me, such blatant sexism. And then I recovered and quickly spoke up, trying politely to revoke what he'd said.

"Dr. G," I started off, "although that might be your way, in our house Joe and I are—"

He cut me off right before the most important word, "equals." "It's not *my* way," he said with a laugh. "It's the way." He turned toward Joe, done with me, and I, too, looked over at Joe—for backup.

Joe, just as stunned as I, had a guilty look on his face that read *Sorry, babe, for my father and his ways. Let's just move on without any extra drama.*

Today, under these circumstances, Dr. G could easily have told us how disappointed he was in our parenting, how bad a woman I was to teach a girl to act like a boy, how weak a man Joe was, unable to keep order in his own home. Gender roles—male as lead and female as subordinate—were inflexible. A boy was only one thing: strong and dominant. And a girl was the opposite of that. End of story. These roles were not to be subverted, mangled, or messed with in any way. So we braced ourselves for the worst.

Dr. G ate a bit more of his soup, wiped his mouth with his napkin—then slammed his hand down on the table, letting out a big, booming laugh.

"*Ayyy!* It's no problem at all! In my language of Twi, Jodie, we don't use gender pronouns. I never remember them anyway! He, she . . . It's all the same to me!"

I wanted to thank God and praise Jesus all at the same time, but instead I leaned back in my seat, making eye contact with Joe. I winked at him, showing how grateful I was for his idea. We couldn't have asked for a better response. I don't know why Dr. G didn't probe us on the whys—but he didn't. He never asked why Penelope preferred to be called he or him, or why we felt it so important to do as Penelope preferred. Blessedly, thankfully, he only said, "Sure."

We sat together at the table for another hour feeling grateful, listening to Dr. G tell us good-time stories of his childhood in Accra, bringing us into his world. Many of the stories we'd heard before, and others sounded familiar but with just a touch of added drama. Dr. G was a showman, and on that day we threw attention his way as a thank-you for making a potential conflict almost undetectable.

Maybe it didn't have to be ugly after all. Maybe we could get through this. Maybe with a little change here and a little shift there, the impossible was actually feasible. That day, eating lentil soup with the oldest and most traditional man of the family, Joe and I felt in control. If we could set the stage for Penelope's happiness, as we'd just done with Joe's dad, Penelope and the family—and perhaps the world—could all coexist without much upheaval. The future felt manageable.

Next up, Penelope's fourth birthday. I had grown up with birthdays being big, creative celebrations. Some years Ramona and I had a baseball theme and all the guests would meet us at Riverside Park for a day of games and pizza. Other years Mama would hire a clown who balanced me in a chair on his chin. We had fancy dinner parties at the house for our ten closest friends, or more low-key gatherings on the Vineyard to celebrate a sweet sixteen. However they were done, birthdays were always a big deal, and I carried on that tradition with my kids.

But with Penelope, birthdays had become a bit more calculated. As things like dolls and hair bows and books about sassy little girls revealed themselves to be the worst possible gifts for Penelope, I decided we should forewarn relatives about his "preferences"—just in case they hadn't caught on yet.

"Let's get ahead of the situation with the family, Joe, like we did with your dad—without getting into the pronouns thing. Maybe we could just politely ask that they not gift anything 'girly.'"

"Sounds like a plan, babe." Joe and I believed it would be that simple—we'd remind the aunts and uncles, cousins and friends, to cater to Penelope's tomboy side—sports attire, sports equipment, sports tickets, anything sporty—and steer clear of anything pink or feminine. That would have to do for now.

We had moved into a beautiful Brooklyn brownstone a year ago, and on the first of October, we invited everyone over to celebrate Penelope's big day. We gathered on the grand staircase that spiraled through the house to open gifts. I sat at the top of the steps just above Penelope as he ripped open his presents. We watched him grab each present, eagerly waiting for the squeals and smiles. Scooter! *Yes,* I thought. Signed basketball! *Great, so far so good.* Soccer jersey! Stickers! *Perfect and perfect.* There was one last gift to open, and as Penelope tore through the wrapping paper, I could tell from the box that it was a pair of sneakers. I did a mental fist-pump. *We're in the clear! Sneakers! Penelope loves sneakers!* I was beaming, knowing how terrible the "wrong things" made Penelope feel. And how the "right things" made him smile. On his birthday, more than any other day, I wanted Penelope to be happy.

He rushed to open the shoe box, throwing paper wildly into the air, eager to see what was beneath. But just as soon as he peeked inside, the vibe in the room quickly changed from euphoric to awkward. Out from under the tissue paper emerged sparkly, shiny bedazzled sneakers. Jewels upon jewels decorating the front and sides flickered and gleamed in the light. They were the very *definition* of girly—most definitely the "wrong things."

I watched as Penelope's face went flat and expressionless, as though the wind had been knocked out of him. He looked embarrassed, as though he'd done something wrong. I think because everyone was watching, including the big-boy cousins Penelope idolized, he was determined not to cry. But I could see the disappointment on his face, along with the wall that rose up right in front of him. "It's okay," I whispered, putting an arm around his shoulders when he looked up at me. "Just put them back in the box and say 'Thank you.'"

Those damn sneakers never made it out of the box again.

Later on that night, I let all my frustration bleed. "Joe, tell your family to show some respect for Penelope. Don't they know by now that they're not going to break his will with a pair of sparkly pink sneakers?" Did they think he would change his mind about being a girl because of some present? Were they trying to massage girlhood back into Penelope by way of not-so-subliminal gifts?

Just a week earlier my mother had made a similar mistake and I'd sent her an email, politely trying to explain why it was so wrong:

Hi Mom,

Thanks so much for thinking about Penelope and the cute gift. I know it was out of love!

The flowers and the color really are not his style. It would be like buying a floral pink-and-orange tote bag for Joe. It would be very strange and it would reflect a disconnect between you and him.

It's the same for Penelope. The bag is totally inappropriate for him. When he opened up the box and saw the gift his face told it all. It hurt his feelings a bit and made him very uncomfortable.

He said he wants to tell you if you ever want to get him a gift, to please buy him something more "rock n roll." But he also said it looked like "love" and "we could hang it on the wall."

When he calls please don't try to convince him to like the bag or that the bag is OK.

Colors and symbols mean more to him than you may understand.

Love,
Jodie

I was able to use a bit more decorum with my mother, but by the time Joe's family struck, I had lost my reserve. I was mad that our preemptive warnings hadn't worked this time around, and that our efforts had failed. Mad at the family for not giving Penelope what he wanted. And I was mad at Joe, most of all, for not noticing Penelope's face when those sneakers invalidated everything our son had made so very, very clear.

"What part of 'no girly things' did they not understand, Joe?"

My anger was valid, but the approach—all wrong. When you come between a man and his mama—his family—it never ends well.

"Tell them yourself if it bothers you so damn much," Joe said as he turned away from me, walking into our study and plopping himself down on the couch. "Everyone's fine but you, Jodie. You're the one who's always angry." He was dismissive, choosing the wide-screen television over us, not giving us a chance to talk it out.

Joe was right, I *was* angry. Fuming. Penelope as boy was complicated and intrusive and awkward for everyone—even me. But I wasn't turning away from it, slinking into an overused couch, pretending it didn't exist. The study had become Joe's den, his go-to spot when his max had been reached, when he'd had enough of me. He stayed there on that couch watching movies until the next day.

There we were again, Joe and I on opposite sides of the battlefield.

A few days passed and I was back in the mindset of figuring this out on my own. I happened to google "transgender child" on my laptop and Jazz popped up, a pretty, petite, brown-haired, bubbly girl no older than six whom the Internet was buzzing about. I clicked on a video and watched Barbara Walters interview her, asking direct, hard-hitting questions without stumping or embarrassing the little girl once. The interview prompted me to dive into Jazz's YouTube series, where I witnessed her speak words of wisdom far beyond her age: "If someone asked me why I was a boy before and a girl now, I'd say that I have a girl brain and a boy body. I think like a girl." *Whoa.* Jazz had nailed it. She had put this thing in crystal-clear perspective and broadcast it for the world to hear. *She's right,* I thought. The brain and the body are distinct, not always doing the exact same thing. Jazz had clarified my thoughts in a way I hadn't been able to do. I was smitten—maybe my kids would fall in love with Jazz just as I had.

Early the next evening, I called a family movie night. Georgia and Nain happened to be out for a bit and Joe would be behind his computer for the next several hours working—giving me the space to choose, without much challenge, the movie we'd watch. I piled the boys into our living room—Cassius perched on the arm of the couch, Othello curled up in my lap, and Penelope beside me. For hours, we were a captive audience to Jazz and her family, watching them proudly. I thought: *This is us. We are proud. We don't hide.* Up to that point, we hadn't been living anywhere close to how I knew we should.

"What does transgender *actually* mean?" Cassius probed, trying to understand this on a cerebral level. "Boy *and* girl, Mama?" Othello asked, a look of wonder on his face. And then Penelope jumped in, "Was she born that way?" The kids had a ton of questions and didn't hesitate to fire them off. What I loved most was that they weren't interrogating Jazz, they were genuinely curious. I tried my best to answer all of their queries, and when I got stumped—which was often—I started a conversation. "Well, what do *you* think?" "What does it look like to you?" "How do you think Jazz feels?"

By the end of movie night, Penelope snuggled up to me closer than we'd started, and for the first time ever, he said the words out loud: "I'm transgender like Jazz, Mama."

It was with such calm and pleasure that Penelope identified himself for all of us to hear. The simplicity of it jarred me to my senses. We needed to fully acknowledge him—completely and absolutely—as boy, without half-stepping around his truth. Jazz's words, "I think like a girl," felt so real to me, because this was about Penelope's brain, not his parts. This was about how his heart beat. Penelope was a boy through and through, from his most thoughtful and intuitive place—his mind—to his most open and loving place—his heart. And we had to believe it with passion, the way Jazz's mom had done. I was starting to get it now.

I'd been guilty, we all had, of fragmenting Penelope, allowing only bits and pieces of "boy" to be the reality. We'd agreed to half boy, or a boy spirit, or boy haircut—and even boy pronouns. But still, we were, *I* was, stumbling over how to let "boy" just be.

Watching Jazz was a hard slap on the hand. Their family was accepting and communicative around their child—making us look almost shameful in comparison. I never wanted Penelope to be fragmented. He, his siblings, all of us, we needed to be complete. I knew this intellectually, that humans need acceptance, but I hadn't been able to see what that looked like when it came to transgender, until Jazz.

Yes, Joe and I had been able to let go of the hair, allowing Penelope to shave it down the sides and grow it high on the top, to have just what he really wanted all along: a Mohawk—not some watered-down baby 'fro. We eventually tossed the cute, frilly bathing suits, slowly letting go of the physical manifestations of "girl," one little thing at a time. Sometimes we let go because of Penelope's sheer force, or because of the urgency of

Penelope changed the game.

his unhappiness, or because something else that day took precedence, like the brilliance of his smile. But even in those moments of release, I was still only partially acknowledging who Penelope was.

But that night, watching Jazz speak about growing up trans, hearing Penelope claim that word for himself, something clicked. His dignity was—and is—more important to me than gender. In fact, it became *the* most important thing. It became everything. I needed Penelope, like Jazz, to be comfortable enough to talk about himself, and own himself, in front of everyone and anyone. If he couldn't do that, he wouldn't survive. And so I let go.

Had I invited Joe to sit with us, had I been less afraid of the confrontation my decision to watch Jazz might have evoked, perhaps Joe would have opened up completely that night, too.

Once you can clearly see the urgency in front of you, you let go of that which is less important. You let it go because it no longer needs to be held so tightly—because it no longer serves you. You let go because something else, something bigger, more vital, takes your attention, like living. And when you do finally let go—fully let go—you realize that you were holding on to a thing, a myth. For me, that thing was the clothing, the hair, the words—those details we assign stories to. But the true energy, I discovered—that which wholeheartedly needs our protection—is called Penelope. And Penelope doesn't live in the hair, or in the clothing. I can put those stories away, knowing that Penelope will never disappear, because Penelope is spirit. We all are. This is about Penelope, his soul, nothing else.

Jazz, at all of five or six years old, became my spirit adviser, the one who reconnected me so fiercely to my own child. Wherever Penelope was, I would shift—over and over again.

FOURTEEN

What Breaks

Dear [Insert Name],

We have some big news to announce. As you may know by now, Penelope has asked to be recognized by family, friends, and the world as a boy. Although born physically a girl, Penelope has expressed through actions, body language, and words a self-identity that is very different from the way the world sees Penelope.

This has been very hard for us to fully understand, and even more difficult for Penelope to bear.

Through careful self-exploration, family talks, and analysis, we've come to understand more. We're now supporting Penelope's request and embracing Penelope as a boy. First and foremost, we love Penelope unconditionally and will offer support on his journey.

Clearly, we've never restricted our kids from doing things based on gender, so essentially, Penelope's life remains the same. He will continue at the same school with the same friends and doing the same activities. The biggest change will be seen in our words. We are now consciously changing our language to support Penelope's sense of self. We are very proud of Penelope. As you are an important part of our lives, we want to be able to share this with you as well.

We know this may be confusing for you. It remains very complex for us. There is so much information available about transgender people that may help to clarify some of your questions. Easy places to start might be the specials on Oprah and 20/20.

*You can find them online. (Those were the places I started with,
and while not perfect, they provided an introduction, a starting
point to deeper conversation.)*

*We ask that you support Penelope's request to be seen as a boy.
Please refer to him only by male pronouns or by his name (which
he has asked not to change). Despite any personal feelings you
may have about our decision, we expect that you will be respectful
of Penelope and of our decision.*

*Our love and respect for Penelope are complete. We hope yours
will be, too.*

This is a version of the letter I sent out to dozens of people,
both family and friends, formally announcing Penelope as boy.
I'd found a sample letter in a book I was reading that could be
used by parents of transgender kids to publicly state their child's
preferred gender. The letter was so direct, and at the same time
so loving and poignant, that I decided to use it for our loved
ones. The time was right, I felt, for each of them to meet us
exactly where we were, with more clarity than we'd ever been
able to offer.

We don't hide. There's no time to hide. Those words, something
Grandmother Gloria might have said during the civil rights
movement, replayed in my head as I constructed the letter—
addressing it to each person, putting together an opening, list-
ing details, crafting a conclusion. With each sentence, each
thought, I clarified the importance of my decision to support
Penelope, for myself and for the reader. The letter didn't ask for
approval; it didn't waste time explaining or justifying. Its only
goal was to command respect. Respect for Penelope, for me,
and for Joe (that is, if I could get him to support my idea).

After reading and rereading the letter several times, making
sure each word was perfectly placed and my points were clear, I
nervously shared it with Joe. With all the respect he was ac-

corded in his family by his siblings and his parents, I knew Joe's cosign would be like the supreme judge's gavel slamming down once and for all.

"Babe, I wrote this letter. Can you come over here and take a look at it? If you sign it, we could even send it out tonight." I could see him shifting—assuming his standard argument posture.

He read the letter, chuckling when he finished. "You want me to sign *this* letter, love?"

"Yup," I answered dryly, moving papers around on the desk without looking up.

"Well, if I sign *this* letter—*your letter*—it'll be obvious to my family that I didn't write it."

"Why?"

"Because it just isn't what I'd say."

"Okay. Well, what would you say, then?"

He pulled my keyboard toward him and began editing what I'd written, typing in a new line: *We are also aware that Penelope's self-identity may or may not change over time; however, from what we have read, the most important thing is that we support Penelope in his wishes.*

"May or may not change"? He was giving Penelope an out, a way to be fluid in his decisions about himself. *You are fundamentally missing the point of what's going on,* I thought as I read over his words. Penelope's identity was not a decision. It was a fact. The assumption that Penelope could change his mind eventually was ridiculous to me. But Joe's intentions were genuine, and his heart for Penelope was in the right place. We were collaborating on a big family decision, and ultimately—thankfully—this time we were fighting on the same side. Progress.

Rather than sending it out via mass email, I wanted people to receive the letter individually, and really feel the weight of the words. I pulled Penelope into the process as my editor and assistant, "approving" language, stuffing envelopes, and hand-delivering letters to those who lived nearby. For those who weren't as close, Penelope added a stamp and dropped them in the mailbox. He sent each one out as if it were an invitation to his wedding—he was absolutely jubilant.

My entire family responded with a flood of supportive, loving, and wordy emails, congratulating me as an "understanding mom" and Penel as a "courageous young man."

My niece Naeemah wrote to me:

> *Jodie, I support self-determination (and mama-determination!).*
> *And I look forward to conversing with and experiencing Penel*
> *for myself, so I can 'officially' get her as a him. I am curious to*
> *see where/how he continues to develop (on all levels, in all as-*
> *pects), as I am with them all. We are fortunate to know that we*
> *(Pattersons) are free to stand in whatever we choose and be loved,*
> *accepted, respected regardless.*
>
> *Generally speaking, I am of the notion that none of it matters*
> *anyway . . . that the only reason it matters is because people*
> *make it matter.*
>
> *So, lucky us for being the stand-out, stand-up family we*
> *are—who can show people how to beautifully Be with such a*
> *seemingly complex situation. Thus being a vessel for the transfor-*
> *mation of the world. :)*

I was proud to know my family was willing to accept Penelope in whatever form and energy he showed up in. In contrast, Joe's family remained silent—not responding at all to what we wrote. Well, at least not to me.

In seeing Penelope as spirit, I saw the physical world—the one that gendered everything in either pink or blue—as the enemy.

Anyone or anything that couldn't be comfortable around Boy Penelope was on the opposing side of my fight. This was a turning point for me: When I had something beyond my own fears to fight for. When I loved more than I was scared. When I felt there was only one move to make: choose Penelope or choose the world.

I was carrying a weight on my back—Penelope's truth. And that weight would stay there, I vowed, until the world knelt for my child. Forever if necessary. It was the least I could do.

Boy Penelope was happening—and would continue to happen—with or without us. Our job was not to question, it was to pick a side: either be with him, or be against him.

The letter we sent out to family and friends was my first line in the sand.

I started to weave what I was experiencing with Penelope into every part of my existence, speaking transgender like a familiar cadence, loud and clear, rather than like something that snagged and disrupted the flow. I added this big new thing into our everyday, then worked to smooth it out, quickly sanding the corners and polishing the rough spots so that when Penelope walked into a room, he'd feel at ease. Like a street sweeper, I brushed dust off the roads before Penelope stepped onto them. I moved debris out of the way just before he arrived. I cleared the air before Penelope had a chance to breathe it in, waving away anything doubtful or alarming so that my boy could just strut. If I didn't like the way a room felt, if the eyes of the people looked mean or suspicious, I grabbed my kid's hands and went in the opposite direction.

Moving through a radical change—really embracing it—makes you want to break the rules. Abiding by protocol, being polite, looking for the "appropriate time"—those were at the core of the very problem. I spoke about transgender everywhere, at dinner tables and cocktail parties, business meetings and girls' nights. Ask what I'd been up to in casual conversation, and prepare to hear the unadulterated and unprettied truth:

"So, how've you been? How are the kids?"

"Oh, you know, Penelope told me the other day he really wanted to start peeing standing up—so I let him. The first attempt was hilarious. I mean, pee just in every direction—on the wall, on the floor, on the both of us. We fell *out,* it was so funny. I was like, 'Okay, Okay, this isn't going to work.' So then I went to the kitchen and brought back our cooking funnel for him to use. Problem solved!"

I started telling my friends these anecdotes as though they were something to brag about, or at least laugh about, so they would stop looking at us with such pity.

They'd half-smile at me suspiciously across the table, as if they thought I were exaggerating, and then reveling in the apparent absurdity of it all. Then they'd look away and start an entirely new conversation. "Anyone up for a glass of rosé?"—burying my comments about Penelope under banal topics like wine.

Making things worse was the fact that we didn't live in a bubble—we were with our extended family and friends all the time. Big holiday celebrations, weekend road trips—we never stopped our family rituals during this time of transition. And our family was full of opinions, traditions, and rules—specific to the South, to Ghana, to Black people in general. Because of that, we had eyes on us, always. Loving eyes from the "village," but eyes that sometimes judged the decisions that I, Penelope's *mother,* was making on behalf of my own child. Eyes that questioned my motives, as if my motive could be anything other than Penelope's best interest. If they only knew how much I didn't want to make these tough decisions, how much it nearly broke me to put on a smile and send my baby out to school, to karate, on playdates, fearing how people might look at him. But they did not know how hard it was for me. Behind closed doors, I quietly raged at what I saw as the judgment in their eyes. And then I got back up again the next morning, prepared to fight another day.

Soon, I found an LGBT national events calendar on the Internet, then started attending panels and workshops, some a six-hour drive from our home. Sometimes bringing Joe, sometimes going on my own. I'd sit quietly in rooms with people much more knowledgeable than I was, weaving together complex thoughts about gender that sent my mind in a million different new directions. But I kept quiet in these forums. Adding my own voice to the conversation was an authority I felt I hadn't yet earned.

Every day my head spun with big ideas of what life could be like for Penelope. I looked for people who could teach me more about my son and about a world where gender didn't define a person. Through my work I discovered Janet Mock, a well-known transgender woman of color, writer, and advocate.

After shutting down the Georgia store, I continued writing the Georgia blog, focusing on inner beauty and the modern lifestyle of women. The blog grew in popularity, and within a year I attracted the attention of a successful beauty executive. Together we launched an even larger-scale blog and beauty retail site called Doobop. As my voice was being heard throughout the country and beyond, my views on beauty were leaning toward the radical. I could no longer just talk about it from a surface perspective—going on and on about product ingredients and makeup techniques. How could I, the mother of a kid who had been refusing to conform all his life, promote shallow vanity and follow-the-leader standards of beauty? Standards that left everyone, including myself, feeling "not good enough"? Each blog post I wrote became a deeper look into a woman— her emotions, her way of thinking, and her culture—and less about what was in her medicine cabinet.

Ms. Mock, a luminary as far as I was concerned, and one of the most famous transgender people in America, would make an ideal interview subject for the blog. I spent an hour on the phone with her one afternoon, listening to her stories of growing up in Hawaii.

"I grew up in a place and time where there were other spaces beyond male and female—'in between' spaces. Growing up in Hawaii enabled me to avoid internalizing the shame that a lot of transgender people take on. I found myself in Hawaii. I found my best friend in Hawaii. I found a community of trans women and LGBT people. That's the kind of space I grew up in."

From what I was learning, in Hawaii, among other places, trans people have always been normal parts of society—and even considered special, transcendent, and two-spirited—a term I was growing to love.

After our conversation, I wrote this about Janet:

If you were to take a snapshot of what we would hope our beloved granddaughters and grandnieces to be like in 3014, Janet Mock would be it. She's "free, boundless, and unapologetically fly." Those strong words are the very ones Janet uses to describe the ideal girl she's dreamed up: someone unconstructed by gender, class, stereotypes, and societal assumptions. Upon meeting Janet I quickly understand this: She is that futuristic hybrid of all things wonderful.

I wrote these words to all women, and I didn't care what it sounded like: me saying that Janet Mock, a transgender person, was the ideal. I wanted for Penelope what Janet had: a life in which he made sense.

I became even more urgently committed to Penelope, more

insistent on establishing his dignity. I did it because I had read that over 50 percent of transgender teens attempt suicide, and because violence against trans people had become an epidemic. I did it because I knew the decision to love and support Penelope would be a decision that could make the difference between his life and his death. So I continued to bring up transgender as often as possible, on beauty sites and at tech conferences. Any time I was interviewed for anything and every time I was given a microphone, I'd find a way to get around to gender, how complex it was and how we hadn't even begun to scratch the surface of it.

And I started to walk away from anyone who showed signs of rejecting Boy Penelope. Standing still while someone is transforming can make the bystander feel uncomfortable, I know. Some people, who just a year before saw Penelope dressed in pink skirts and Mary Janes, were genuinely taken aback when they saw him now. But if they couldn't recover from that initial moment of surprise, if they stiffened upon hearing me use these "strange" new words in association with Penelope—"transgender," "boy," "nephew"—that became their problem, not mine. I would drop folks like a bad habit, and think about it another day.

But coming home at night, when I'd put to rest my boxer's stance and my zero-F's attitude, I'd break down, losing all my bravado. The relentless demand for "proof"—to "explain" and "justify" and "defend"—became a dead thing chained to my ankles, threatening to take me under.

Proving and explaining ourselves, even dodging mean bullets, was something we all did on occasion, but I was doing it day in and day out. A few people close to me suggested I pull back on being so visible, so outspoken, for the safety of our family. Apparently, showing off our differences and being proud of them could put us in harm's way. This possibility of being hurt, even attacked, made my sleep erratic, sometimes impossible. I hated for Joe to leave me alone at home with the kids—checking and double-checking the locks on doors and windows several times throughout the night. By being transgender, Penelope lost the privilege of simple and safe existence, where you just go about your day, unbothered by others, and I gave away mine when I stood by his side. I hadn't stopped to think what that would mean for us. I hadn't calculated the stress it would rain down.

Every single day I came home from work, or from a relative's house, the dead thing got heavier and heavier. Every single day, I wept.

"You know—real women, Jodie—we cry and type at the same time." Letting out a deep sigh, my sister-friend Johnica delivered this gem of harsh wisdom while she watched me in the throes of a particularly bad episode one afternoon, curled up in a ball on the couch.

It's an old Southern saying meant to tell us that those who are about the business of change will work through their sorrow without ever stopping. They aren't immobilized by emotions, but emboldened by them. Her words lodged deep in my heart, and stayed there.

Chin up. Eyes up. Fists up, I thought. *We are revolutionaries like our grandparents.*

I would press on.

If the letter we sent out about Penelope was my first line in the sand, the second was where I spent my time. I began to circle around Penelope—protecting him—at the expense of the other people living in my own home.

Too many times to count, I chose Penelope—over Joe, over Georgia, over Cassius and Othello and Nain. I chose to show my love for him more, to touch his face more, tell him more than the others how beautiful he was.

I chose to sit through each of his karate classes, never missing a single one, often skipping his brothers' tennis and gymnastics classes so that on the car ride home, Penelope and I could talk about the new kata he just learned. I chose to sleep next to him more than the others so I could push back his nightmares. I chose to walk with him into every new space he ever entered, two steps ahead, so he would never feel alone.

"It's cool. Everyone knows I'm always last on your list." Joe half-smiled at me whenever I forgot to pick up a coffee for him when I got one for myself, or greeted the kids with a hug and a kiss and forgot to show him any love. There were countless other instances that reinforced what we both knew was true but couldn't honestly, fully admit.

Most times he blew it off with a sarcastic comment and a pat on my butt, as he'd done for years. But other times, it really got to him, knowing without a doubt that his needs, sometimes physical, sometimes intellectual, sometimes emotional, would most likely not be met by his wife. But my hands were full and my brain was taxed. Catering to Joe felt like coddling a grown-ass man. My empathy reserves were gone by the time I turned my attention to Joe. I couldn't see past Penelope and me.

My choices had taken a toll beyond my marriage. Cassius began spending more time with Joe, preferring him to me, brushing me off with a scowl and a cold shoulder. Othello still clung to my leg most of the day, but he was slow to speak, the only one of my kids who wasn't using complex sentences by age two. He'd rely mostly on his brothers to talk for him, or to him. He'd nod and smile, understanding everything but responding mostly by pointing, or using only one or two words. "His vocabulary is smaller than it should be," relayed a mildly interested therapist we'd hired to assess the situation. "I'm sure you have your hands full, but try *reeeading* to him." She was patronizing, but I couldn't argue the point. Othello, the baby, wasn't getting enough from me.

I was falling short on giving Nain what he needed, too. He was complicated—some moments he acted like the young adult he was, craving long, thoughtful conversations with me about college applications or part-time jobs he wanted to take on for a little extra money. But he also needed me to hold his hand while he learned daily routines, like eating nutritious meals that included vegetables (freeze-dried didn't count) and soups (the canned kind didn't count, either). Whenever I had a few extra seconds to focus, I'd try to coach him on social interactions he sometimes struggled with: *Look people in the eye when you speak. Don't turn away when they're talking to you.* But I could zero in on Nain only briefly before I got pulled in another direction—then he'd be left to figure things out on his own.

And then there was Georgia, my Ladybug, my everything, who'd always made a beeline for me no matter where we were, happy to be close to her mama. Now fourteen and in full-on teenager mode, she could barely stand my touch. She'd cringe whenever I tried to hug her, relegating me to the "dummy" corner in every conversation we had—as if I didn't know her inside and out, as if I hadn't been the one to birth her, or lived all these years on this earth.

"I don't have time to talk, Mom, I'm late for school." Georgia had stopped calling me "Mama" recently, and this new, formal "Mom" title irked me like nobody's business.

"We need to talk, Georgia. I'm not interested in how late you are. You should have woken up earlier." Every day for a month, I watched her walk directly into her room after school, slamming the door behind her. She spent most of her time in her room or with her friends. And any time I tried to breach that invisible boundary line, she'd snap back with an eye roll.

One morning during this routine, I cornered her near the front door. "I expect you home by four today, no excuses, Georgia."

Stepping to the side of me, away from my direct gaze, she responded, "I can't predict the train schedule, *Mother*." An *even more* formal "M" word that she knew would set me off. I was tired—mentally freaking exhausted—and Georgia was testing me. I hated her for it.

I snatched her arm, pulling her back in line. "I'm not playing."

"I don't even know what that means," she fired back, unafraid.

"It means, Georgia, what the hell is going on? You come home late every day. I have no idea why. You say the library, but then your grades . . . And your attitude. And all you say to me is 'Close my door behind you!'" I took a long breath in. "Who are you?" My head started spinning. "In fact: Sit. Your. Butt. Down. You're not going to school today."

I wasn't making any sense, clearly, but I didn't care.

"You can't stop me from going to school," she taunted.

"Watch me."

Georgia turned her eyes toward the front door and lifted her foot to walk. My arm, with a mind of its own, flew back and then whipped forward—landing a hard smack across her face. It was the first time I'd ever hit my daughter. Ever. As a baby, she never needed much of a reprimand, a slight raise of the eyebrow and she'd pull herself together. But that day, she took me there. Life had taken me there.

We both looked at each other, stunned by what had just happened. I was back in Ramona's bedroom on Riverside Drive, watching the power dynamic shift in our household all over again. Except this time, I was the one who sent the household reeling.

A stream of emails from my mother in the days leading up to the slap had taken me to the edge.

Hi Jodie,

I hope you will take Penelope to someone, be it a cranial sacral therapist or someone else you choose, who can truly help him totally release the trauma . . .

She was referring to the catheter the doctors had inserted in Penelope's urethra when he was a baby, after suspecting a urinary tract infection. Though supportive, my mother was still under the impression that something had *happened* to Penelope to cause him to be like this. She was still searching, as I once had been, for a concrete reason, because if we could find a cause, she seemed to think, then surely we could find a solution. With a little adjustment here and a little wiggle there, life could return, she hoped, to the way it used to be. When the email popped up, as with all of her emails of late on Joe, on Penelope, on my general attitude toward life, I read it with only half my attention, rolled my eyes, and then moved it to the Mom folder. I just didn't have the time.

There was too much to keep hold of—and so much to undo. One part of my brain was continuing to take apart everything I'd learned about boys and girls and how we should behave. The other half was just trying to remember the necessities of each day, of each kid. I'd make pages-long to-do lists and get through them all in two days, crossing each and every item off with a vengeance. Pay taxes. Upload blog post. Schedule Georgia's hair appointment. Find a chess coach. Locate trans book. Done. Done. Done. And done.

But then I'd get a ringing between my ears, and that's when

the migraines would start. They were debilitating, like a thin needle being dragged in and out of the space between my eyes. Sometimes I'd crawl back into bed and bury myself under the covers for hours, trying to manage the pain through slow, shallow breathing. I'd tell Joe I couldn't pick up the kids from school or make dinner, and he'd jump in, doing parent overtime.

Once, after spending a late afternoon with Georgia and Nain, taking them around the city to the different places they needed to go—listening to their chatter for *hours*—I felt it coming. My squinting made driving our SUV difficult.

"Is everyone's seat buckle fastened?" I asked as we hopped back into the car after our fourth stop in Manhattan.

"Yo, Mama!" Nain let out a hearty laugh. "We're not babies! I'm like twenty-two—a *man*—and GeeGee . . . Well, I can't say what she is . . ."

"Don't even start, Ernain!" Georgia used his full name whenever she was trying to be funny. Laughing rowdily in my backseats, they were about to start, I could tell, a long banter of trash-talking.

"Hey, Georgia?" my tone was soft and strained, noticeably different from theirs. "Do you think you guys could take a taxi from here? I have to go farther uptown for a meeting. I can't make it downtown to drop you off at your dad's."

"You okay, Mama?" Nain leaned over toward the front seat, sensing the struggle in my voice.

"I'm fine. Just have a lot on my plate. You guys go on." I pulled over to the corner.

"Hop out. Grab that cab. Text me when you're with Dad." It sounded normal enough to them—Mom giving orders—so they obeyed.

I watched them make their way into a Yellow Cab—Nain opening the cab door, trying to be the big brother, Georgia laughing at his gesture—and I pulled off, knowing they were safe. I made my way one block closer to home before the pain took over.

It was Forty-Second Street and Broadway, in the heart of Times Square—a no-parking zone as crowded as a concert stadium—but I pulled over anyway, turning off the engine. I dialed Joe for help, found the darkest, quietest nook in the car, and curled up there, down between the steering wheel and the floor. I stayed on the floor of my car with my eyes closed tight for an hour, until Joe came and drove me home.

We carry weights on our back until we can't go any farther. Truths are weights, and I carried Penelope's truth on my body—which was buckling, fast, under the pressure. I could feel that breaking was inevitable. The tensions were too taut. The rub between Joe and me, between me and the rest of the family, between Penelope and the rest of the world—everything was wearing me down. It wasn't a question of when, but rather of what.

What will break first? I asked myself, over and over again. *The family? The woman? Or the construct?*

By 2014, I was in over my head. I had become Penelope's personal advocate and our family's official bad guy, all the while working twelve-hour days. By the end of each day all I craved was sleep, but there was little time for that.

And there would be even less time for sleep in a few months—I was pregnant again, with our sixth child.

I continued on full force as if my body were made of steel, racing from obligation to obligation, borough to borough, person to person, meeting to meeting. A typical day went something like this: Up at six, check email, hop on social media and look at what's trending in the LGBTQIA community, wake kids, eat breakfast, school drop-off, grab coffee, exercise, clean house, tend to business, hop on the A train, pop over to the Doobop office, meet with team over lunch, find a quiet corner to do a phone interview, brainstorm on company expansion, touch base with interns, hop back on the train to pick up the kids, karate class, then finally back home for homework, dinner, nightly prayers, and good night kisses.

Wasn't that what a "modern woman" was supposed to do? Get everything done on the to-do list no matter what? My body could take it—it had never failed me before. I could push it, and then push it even more, if that's what my life demanded of me. *Don't stop, don't slow down. Keep going. Keep pushing. Push a little more.*

But six months into the pregnancy, I realized just how human I was.

It was Easter, and as difficult as it was to get everyone up and out on a Sunday morning, I insisted we attend Reverend Calvin Butts's service at the Abyssinian Baptist Church in Harlem. I wanted the kids to experience Black church on Easter and understand the relevance it's had to our lives. I got all the kids dressed and, miraculously, we made it to church on time. We sat up close to the pulpit while Reverend Butts gave a moving sermon—about what, I can't now recall, but it was of the moment and very political, as Butts is known to be. I remember Georgia, normally a church skeptic, nodding in approval. I sat back in the pew, looking to both my right and my left, seeing all my children and my husband peaceably together, and I felt proud of us as a family for making it there. It was a simple pleasure and I reveled in it.

After the service ended, normally we'd make our way over to Sylvia's for fish and grits, cornbread and iced tea. For the kids, this was the big payoff for a long morning spent behaving well. But that day I was exhausted and my belly was starting to feel heavy, so we decided to go directly home. I made brunch for the family and our neighbors came over to celebrate the new baby.

After everyone had eaten, I plopped down on our couch, looked around the room, and smiled. *How could I be so lucky?* Despite all the tribulations, we were expecting more life, more joy into our family.

As soon as our friends left, I sank deeper into the couch cushions, preparing to take a good long nap. About an hour later my temperature spiked, and halfway through the night Joe and I rushed to the emergency room. The baby's heart had stopped. There was no more life inside me.

Somewhere along the road, I messed up. I wasn't superwoman after all. Apparently there was a limit—and I'd just reached it.

Two months later, I continued to spin.

"Jodie-love, you're *really* skinny," Joe said to me one evening while I hunched over the kitchen counter, struggling to keep my thoughts together to plan for the next day's marathon. After losing the baby, there'd been no time to slow down, to catch my breath, to take stock. Instead, I leaned more into everything, harder, fiercer, afraid the sadness would consume me if I changed my pace.

I walked away from Joe, pretending to let his concerns slide off—it was something I'd gotten used to doing with most people lately. But in truth, they hung there, bringing me back to my small, insecure ten-year-old self.

I hadn't played Mama's "I love myself" game in at least twenty years, but that night, I found myself needing to see what would happen if I did.

I stood in front of our tall living room mirror and stared at the woman in front of me. I recognized the same upside-down-banana lips, now with deep creases framing the edges. The Peter Pan ears looked familiar, too, though my hair was thinning all around. The gymnastics-made muscular thighs were now hollow where my legs met. Long, thin fingers fell limp against bony hips. My eyes were lined with worry, my reddish-brown skin had turned sallow. All the visible signs of chaos and stress were there for everyone to see. I stared at her—at me—running my eyes over her face, her hair, her body—and I couldn't bring myself to say the words.

My body, the thing that had nurtured my strength since Georgia, that showed me that I was indeed powerful, was now betraying me. I asked myself once again, *What will break first? The family? The woman? Or the construct?*

My body answered. I was looking at a broken woman.

FIFTEEN

I, Woman (The South, Revisited)

RETURNING HOME IS WHAT I KNOW—it's what the Blackwell women have always done to treat their heartaches. After my parents' divorce in the late 1980s, my mother left New York, to eventually move in with Grandma Gloria. Grandma Gloria had done the same a long time ago, packing up her three girls in her convertible to escape a bad marriage and driving straight to her parents' home in the middle of the night. Even my sister Ramona came back down south to live with Grandma for a stint during her adult years when life became too overwhelming. Home is safety in the most basic way: food, shelter, and rest.

I need the South now—it owns something in me, and I need to touch that place it owns. Let it revive me, hold me, until I come back to life.

The cul-de-sac my mother lives on in Peachtree City is quiet. I rarely see much action in her neighborhood, just a few people driving by during their regular commutes—to and from work, the grocery store, or the mall. As we pull onto her road on the way back from the airport, every face we see is a familiar one: a church friend, a teacher from the nearby elementary school. We both wave as we pass them, putting on a smile. Mom's is wide and warm, filled with the kind of genuinely happy surprise you wouldn't expect to see from someone who likely runs into these same neighbors every day. Mine is tight and strained, a little too polite, a little sad. The neighborhoods of Peachtree City go on for miles, and it's the back roads that connect them all—long and meandering streets canopied by weeping willows on either side. The suburb is expansive, though it feels more like a village. Folks either know each other or make it their business to.

Soon after I arrive at Mama's house the doorbell rings. I peek through the curtains at the side window, and I don't recognize the man standing there. "What do you want?" I ask cautiously from behind the front door.

Hearing the commotion from the other room, Mama rushes over, looking at me funny, before pushing me aside so she can tend to the man at the door. Turns out he's just Mr. So-and-So from down the way—stopping by to say hi and to share some of the mac and cheese his wife had made earlier that afternoon. They sit on the screened-in porch and talk, my mother's tinkling laughter echoing through the rest of the house. Later, after the man leaves, I remind Mama that that type of behavior is cause for concern back in New York. "Showing up unannounced like that? I mean, come on. You sure he's not trying to case your house?" She looks at me funny again, then makes her way into the kitchen to fix a late lunch.

It's not easy for me to be here. This trip doesn't come as a vacation. There's real pain and awkwardness in each moment between us.

For years, it's felt like what I need has been way bigger than what Mom knows or can do. I can't talk to her about my company, my investors, or the looming debt that I'd stacked up while running the store because money makes her uncomfortable. I also can't tell her any more about the battle for power between me and Joe—her solutions, like lingerie and a little gratitude, they never work. She's been unable to fix my crises, time and time again. And honestly, I'd love for my problems to just be "handled"—not managed or lessened, but obliterated altogether.

But Mama is neutralizing; she never aggravates the fire. Growing up, whenever Daddy belittled her, I'd watch her get quieter, more still, defusing his outbursts. Every time he raised his voice, I wanted more than anything for her to ball him up in her fist like a piece of paper and hurl him far away. I came to realize that big problems, mean people, can't be offset. They need to be grabbed, swung around twice, and then hurled into the sky, letting the sun burn them to ashes. But Mama isn't aggressive—it's just not who she is. And the slow realization over the years that she will *never* be the one to obliterate a problem has grown an anger in me that I can't release. It sits there between us, year after year, stifling conversation, making it hard to even hug her—deeply, warmly. That is why I don't tell her why I'm here.

But what Mama can give me is stillness, and slowness. In her house, I can hide away for hours, or watch her clean the kitchen, or climb into bed at six o'clock as the day darkens outside my window, without bringing in the baggage of my past or the weight of the future. There, I can just show up and surrender, giving in to the things I can't change.

In Peachtree City, we typically take long, quiet drives in Mama's golf cart along the dirt paths behind the houses, encouraging her little putt-putt-mobile over the hills and around the bends. Sometimes we'll take a different path than we're used to—getting lost on the other side of the miniature bridge, turning right at the duck pond instead of scooting around its perimeter. It's these winding pathways that take you everywhere you need to go in the neighborhood—to the movie theater, a neighbor's house, the corner store, or nowhere in particular. Those roads are like veins moving blood back and forth through a giant communal body.

I need *my* blood to move. To feel my limbs again.

The day after we arrive, I wake up before the sun. Georgia has come with me on this trip—given all the recent drama be-

tween us, I thought we could take a break from the city together. While she sleeps soundly next to me, I find my sneakers,
put on some leggings and an old T-shirt, and make my way to
the kitchen. Mama's already awake, sitting at the table in her
bathrobe, cradling a cup of hot water in both hands.

"Good morning, lovely!" she says, blowing on the steam. I
ask if she feels like tackling the paths on foot—her golf cart is
broken, so walking is our only option. She smiles, nods, and
goes into her room to change.

There's a steep hill at the foot of the property you have to
climb to reach the paths we're after. As soon as we approach the
hill I attack the pavement, pumping my arms aggressively, digging into each stride. I want this to be a workout. I want to
sweat, to plow through it. I even want to beat my own sixty-
three-year-old mother to the top of the hill. (Yes, I'm that competitive.) If it had been up to me, we would have kept up that
pace—going all out on our nature walk—but when my mother
eventually makes her way to the top of the hill, she's panting.
"Can we slow down, please?" she breathes, putting both hands
on her waist.

"Oh, right—sure, Mama," I mutter, marching in place to
keep my heart rate up.

We cross the main street, cutting into the next subdivision,
and then look for signs pointing us in the right direction. Following the arrows, we take a sharp left down the side lawn of a
neighbor's house. The pebbled path behind the house's back
garden marks our entryway. Immediately upon crossing over
into the wooded area, the feel changes—from suburban sprawl
with pretty houses and two-car garages to something more natural. More beautiful.

But on our first day out, I'm really not interested in beauty.
I'm annoyed. My body is tense, my jaw is clenched. Silence

is the one thing I want to hold on to. I keep my head down, my posture leaning forward. *Left, right, left, right, left, right.* Commanding the sweat to form. Even in the middle of this walk, where there's all the time in the world to chat, to catch up—to explain the reason for my frantic late-night phone call to my mother, my last-minute flight to get here—I'm saying, without saying, that I don't want to engage, or talk—or even take it all in. I just want to sweat.

But Mama is persistent, in her way. "Well, isn't that a nice house? Don't we just *love* that house?" she muses as we pass a ranch-style house with a wraparound veranda. She insists on breaking my pace, slowing me down to pause, or stop, for a little while, just to notice what's happening all around us.

No, I think. *We do not love that house.* But we must stop and discuss that house anyway.

"Yes, Mama—the peach awning does remind me of a Caribbean sunset." "No, Mama, I did not know the Robinsons sold the house to the new owners." "No, Mama, I don't remember you telling me that the new husband works for Delta."

When you talk to someone Southern, they don't just give you a quick brief on a person, they give you the whole history—the entire family tree. She tells me everything that's happening or has ever happened in this ranch house—much more information than I would ever want to know.

"And anyway, enough about that. How *is* your friend Dara, Jodie? Is she still with that man she was with in college? Remember she had that great jacket with the shoulders?"

My mother never gets grumpy. She's never *not* in the mood to chat. And this irritates me. The last thing I want right now is conversation. But she keeps talking—talking about her friends, about strangers, about the nature—the *beauty*—around us. I concentrate on my breathing instead, on the movement of my feet. My mind, my heart, they can't handle much more. I tune

Mama out and keep on, hearing the soft crunch of her footsteps next to me.

On the second day, we wake up and meet at the door. In silence, we make the trek up the paved hill just outside the property, cross the main road, look for the pebbled path. Mama's rhythm is similar to the trees'—she moves but she is rooted, she feels no need to rush.

This time, instead of letting her struggle behind me, I slow down so we can fall in step. She's meeting me where I am—granting me this walk without her commentary—so I return the favor, meeting her at her pace. There's no sense in continuing the push and pull between us. I might as well give in.

At Mama's step, the environment comes into focus. I see chipmunks scurry up tree trunks and red birds perch on branches; the grass and dirt feel soft beneath my feet. The scent of gardenia, sweet and musky, starts to fill me up in the spaces where I feel hollow. Once in a while a few teenagers whiz by in their golf carts, forcing us to jump to the side of the road. We use this as an opportunity to tie our shoelaces. Bent close to the earth, I see plump, sandy worms wiggling through the dirt. The ground is teeming with them.

Each day the walks extend a bit more than the day before. We keep moving without much talk. We take new back roads and get lost. And then we double back and retrace our steps as best we can, using intuition and each other to navigate our way back home. We don't ever move fast, and the effort in the slowness feels good. My heart is awake. My body is tingling. And the sweat on my skin is clean. Clean like rain, like moss, like dew. I realize it's the most pure and unburdened I've felt in months, maybe even years.

The walks make my body feel that it can be strong again. That it can be useful and capable again.

Thinking about the baby I thought I was going to have, I

allow the sorrow to take leave for a while. It slips out from around my heart and escapes through my skin, through my sweat.

I forget about the fierceness and confusion that Penelope has brought on. Instead, I loosen my grip. And for the first time in a long time, I don't feel the world bearing down on me.

Something in me begins to swell and open up.

After our morning sojourns, back at the house Mama pours water for us both and puts the pot on the stove to make grits. She measures and mixes, and it feels a little like witchcraft—this nourishing elixir made with water, grains, butter, salt, and pepper.

As she cooks, I think about the time we've lost. So many years have divided us since the days when I would watch her cooking in her underwear, shaking chicken in a brown paper bag.

The space between my mom and me is the same space I now see rising up between Georgia and me—and I hate it. I hate the way it makes me afraid of time moving forward, and the unavoidable separation that occurs between people.

I think—or maybe I hope—that people sometimes drift apart because we all need to find our own individual way. But there's also something else at work between my daughter and me, a built-in distance that comes along with city living and modern life. A life in which kids spend more time outside the house than at home with family. A life in which a subway ride can take a teen halfway across the world—or so it seems. I worry about Georgia's friends. I don't know these new friends the way I did the ones from her grade school days, the ones who'd sit in our kitchen and laugh at my jokes for hours. These friends don't come over as often, and when they do they go directly to her room and shut the door, whispering under their breath. "We can always call an Uber if your mom doesn't want to drive us." These kids are more like adults than I'm comfortable with.

So on this trip I hold Georgia closer, tighter, keeping a constant eye on her. I don't want to make the same mistake my parents did of assuming. Assuming that all was fine with me, that I needed less than Ramona, that I could handle everything on my own. I now know, two times over, what happens when one child in a family demands something so urgent that it takes up all the attention, requiring everything else to be put on hold: tasks, chores, laundry—people, too.

Ramona was urgent, just as Penelope has been. Everything else in my life has been shelved as blurred pictures in my periphery. But now I'm seeing clearly, facing the consequences of what happens when you hold tight to one thing and let the rest slip away.

Georgia never wakes up early enough to join Mama and me on our walks. When she does eventually make her way to the kitchen after we get back, the three of us—daughter, mother, and grandmother—gather around the oval wooden table to eat, and I notice the walls between us. In fact, I'm sure we all notice them. Teenage Georgia is brooding. She takes a seat in the chair closest to the bay window, leaning over her grits, chin in hand, and complains about the homework I asked her to finish three days ago. I sit at the head of the table absently cracking my knuckles, quietly making my way through the depression that's crept up on me. And through all of this, my sixtysomething mother is calm. She's cleared her own hurdles at this point in her life, especially the ones that look like teenage melodrama and grown-woman weariness. She finds her way to the opposite end of the table, where she can take us in. I think she's content just to have us both there in her kitchen.

We sit and eat together just as Ramona and I used to do when we were little girls spending summers with Grandma Gloria in Atlanta. Grandma wasn't the best cook—her meals usually consisted of a hodgepodge of whatever she had around: a can of tomato soup, a bit of turkey, grits, and always a warm biscuit. But it wasn't the food that mattered, or even the presentation of it. It was about the company—the proximity to one another, sitting side by side, and the way time hovered above us, suspended.

Grandma Gloria's home always meant sunshine and warmth, and an easy, slow-paced love for me. The house she lived in years ago, when I was a kid, was surrounded by hundred-year-old trees and bordered with cobblestone walkways, and it had a little turtle pond just off the front yard. Entering the house at the start of each summer was like being greeted by an old friend. I often walked from room to room, returning to hidden spots and favorite corners to take in their secrets anew.

Our daily ritual began at the kitchen table—we'd gather there in the mornings while a procession of friends and relatives drifted in and out of the house well into most afternoons. Mother-Dear and Sissy, Aunt Gigi and my cousin Vicky were always the first to greet us at the start of our stay. They promised to take us shopping, marveled over how long our legs had gotten and how grown and city-sophisticated we were. They wrapped their strong arms around us and laughed loudly at our Northern ways. When I was very little, I thought my grandmother must have sent out formal invitations to family members announcing our visit (it was that much of a to-do), but I soon discovered that all meals were treated that way. Each one was an opportunity for communing, a chance to come together and discuss the day.

Our lives revolved around the table—no one ever ate alone. And this house—the one we're in now, the one my mother still lives in after Grandma Gloria passed away—is no exception. For generations we've gathered at the table by habit, to socialize, even when we're not eating. The table is a place to connect with one another.

There are just three of us women here now—Georgia, Mama, and me. And even with the spaces between us, this trilogy makes sense to me in this moment. Three generations of women. No wild boys running around arguing. No cell phones buzzing to announce meetings. No deadlines looming. No big, ominous questions filling up my head. If nothing else, here in this stillness, I know who I am.

We may not like it sometimes, and it may not be fair. But we are women. We are Black. And we have the South running through our veins. There are no questions about identity here at this table. In this moment. Right now, who we are is easy. Easy is how I feel when I go back down south and sit among my women. With them I feel comfortable—being a woman who is Black and Southern at her core.

In the afternoons I make my way to the sitting room, where I'm surrounded by all the mighty women in our family, both the living and those who have long since passed. On the walls, on top of cabinets, and crammed inside drawers are striking pictures of the Blackwell women in tarnished frames and time-worn albums, along with old portrait photos and warped Polaroids. Photos of Mama Mabel, Great-Grandmother Lurline, Grandma Gloria, Aunt Gigi, Aunt Lurma, and Ramona, the baby sister my mother lost in that terrible car crash, the daughter my grandmother grieved for.

I used to page through these old photographs as a child, look-

My women: Mama, standing far left; Grandmother Gloria standing in the middle; Aunt Lurma standing far right; and Great-Grandmother Lurline, seated.

ing at the grown women who shared my name, my nose, my lips, and I'd imagine what it would be like to step into their skin and *be* them. I wondered if I could see my own future by looking through their eyes.

The poet Rilke wrote,

> *I know that nothing has ever been real*
> *without my beholding it.*
> *All becoming has needed me.*
> *My looking ripens things*
> *and they come toward me, to meet and be met.*

It's true. Nothing exists until you see it. It's hard to be something you've never seen before, for me at least. I've always done better with a visual guide. The photos of my women told me so many stories. I learned womanhood, femaleness, feminism, through them. Just from their pictures. Preserved in time, they were composed, but not complacent. And they were fierce.

Poring over the same photos now I try to remember, hoping they will serve as my trigger to tap into what's perhaps always been there, buried deep—my mojo, my own special well of magic. I look into their faces, asking them to remind me how to dig deep and push forward at the same time. I also ask them to help me remember the ways in which we care for and strengthen ourselves, so we can weather whatever tries to tear us down. Whatever tries to test us.

My grandmother, for one, was tested many times. From the many conversations I had with Grandma Gloria cuddled up in her bed over the years, I knew she transformed sadness and fear into empowerment. She made it through the Jim Crow South, the death of her firstborn, five marriages, one master's degree, one Ph.D., and more than a dozen arrests for her civil rights work, with prayer, journaling, and her beloved books. She was a busy woman, with a million people who counted on her, but she was never too busy to stop and notice. She found moments, or moments found her, and she would write down her thoughts wherever she was. Notating in the pages of her books and journals how she saw the world. I think writing and reading, for her, were a way to push back—to challenge herself to see the world in the widest sense possible, despite whatever narrow reality was in front of her.

My aunt Lurma became a passionate practitioner of transformation, too—willing her fear and anxiety into calm to cope with the challenges that any working mom, married or not, is often plagued with. Those anxieties manifested in unsettling dreams in which she'd be extremely late picking up her son from nursery school and have to run frantically down some street or highway, often barefoot, many miles from where she needed to be. Lurma learned to fight for control of those nightmares, casting out negative thoughts with affirmations, often pasting little sayings all over her house: "I am love." "My feet are kept in the perfect path." "God is within me and for me." She made a practice of smiling to get through the anxiety.

Meditation and mantras were my mother's methods of pushing the sadness away, too. While it's always frustrated me that she's never taken a different approach—never lashed out or yelled or hurled her problems away—there is something undeniable about going inward: It often reveals both the problem and the answer. Meditation tells us that life can change when you shift your perspective. It allows us to be both powerful and peaceful in the same moment.

Belief in the power of the self, that comes from Mama.

As I was growing up, whenever our house got too tense— when Dad got too bossy, or Ramona got too difficult—Mom turned to meditation. She found a quiet chair, closed her eyes, and tuned out the noise. She visualized light beams, or ocean waves, or calming reverberations, and she focused all of her energy on them. Sometimes she paid attention to her breath for an hour. Sometimes she paid attention to her muscles, flexing and then relaxing different parts of her body for as long as she could.

My body needs that attention right now.

Mama would meditate every day, and whenever we saw her, eyes closed as she sat in her chair, we knew we were not to bother her. If we got too loud, she'd raise an eyebrow or open one eyelid and shoot us a sharp glance, and we'd know, then, that by no means should we continue whatever it was we were doing. As hard as it was for us, we understood that she was taking her time. And that time was not to be disturbed—it was for her, and if she didn't get it, *we* would be the worse for wear. So Ramona and I found something else to do for an hour. And after her hour was up, she returned to us renewed.

It's time to do for myself what Mama did for herself all those years.

When we got older, before we went to bed, Mama would teach us to relax our bodies and focus on our breathing. Deep breaths in, long and slow breaths out. Over and over again. We'd start at the top of our head, acknowledging every area on the body, and work our way down to our toes—clenching and releasing, clenching and releasing—so that we could understand the difference between tense and relaxed. Mama put us to sleep like this many nights when we were kids. Meditating us into a deep calm.

Gloria, Mama, Lurma—all the women in my line—I think about them now. I think perhaps we are only as strong as those who teach us; only as capable as the tools we learn to employ. Maybe we are only as committed as the time we spend in meditation and prayer. Only as prolific with our spoken words as we are in our silence.

"Nurture the roots, Jodie," I heard my grandmother say, our hair-brushing ritual on my mind. "If you don't nurture the roots, nothing will grow."

Every night in her room, Grandma untied her dark hair and led Ramona and me in the exercise. We would sit on the edge of her bed in our nightgowns while she leaned against her headboard, facing us. "Start at your scalp, and brush in long, gentle strokes," she'd say as she placed her fingers over mine, guiding my brush. "Hold it *this* way. You have to nurture the roots." Together, we'd slowly make our way from brushstroke one to one hundred. By the last few strokes, my arms were weak, but I understood the lesson.

During those childhood summers in the South I learned about caring. How to nurture things and take my time. And although the years had caused me to forget, at Mama's house, sitting among my family's things, I now know what I need to do.

I need to call on what makes me happy—recognize that there *are* things that make me happy: My children. My wellness. Spirituality. Travel. My work. My Joe. If I make time every day for each of the many parts of me, if I touch each element, in no particular order, in no particular amount, maybe I can get back to myself. If I welcome all of the parts of me into each day, maybe I can return.

Listening to my mother and Georgia chatting happily in the next room the day before we leave for New York, I think about what I've gone through this past year. At Mama's house, there is so much time to remember. I know now that it is dangerous to fall apart alone, without tools, without support—and how vital it is to let go. Letting go, I'm coming to learn, teaches us to know how best to put ourselves back together again.

A few months back, a girlfriend of mine told me a story. She confided that she once fell into a manhole in the middle of the night on a quiet road. She was trying to get away from someone who had scared her, and as she was running fast through the dark, she fell into a manhole, tumbling deep down inside. Scared out of her mind and with no one to come to her rescue, my friend channeled her fear into one urgent directive: *Out*. She scratched and pulled at the dirt walls. Climbed and fell and climbed again. Inch by inch, hour by hour, she clawed herself upward. With her body bruised and bloody, her nails broken and skin torn, she finally made it out into the fresh air.

Whenever I replay this story in my mind, I can't help feeling that I was her—that I'd been clawing my way out of a manhole ever since Penelope and I walked out of that bedroom in the mountain house. In the beginning, acting on impulse and adrenaline alone, I hoisted myself into action and climbed frantically up, knowing that up there was the only chance we had. Not caring how we got there, or who I had to get rid of to make myself lighter for the climb.

For myself, for Penelope, for my relationships with my family, with Joe, I know that I have to change. I need to relax my muscles and breathe deeply. I need to be steady, not frantic. I need to go inward and find my light. I need to be the woman *my* women taught me to be.

PART II
Woke

I'll grow back like a starfish.
—

ANTONY AND THE JOHNSONS

SIXTEEN

This Body. This Boy. This Magic.

―――――

RETURNING HOME FROM MY MOTHER'S HOUSE in Atlanta, I felt renewed. The end of the school year was approaching and summertime was just around the corner, which meant Joe and I and the kids would be spending more time at the house in the mountains. I was glad that we would all soon be surrounded by nature.

In the mountains, I know what freedom feels like. There's something about our home in Pennsylvania that makes me feel right: central, capable, and whole. I think it's the crisp, good air—it moves through my lungs like fuel, energizing me. Maybe it's the sky, too. The sky in the country is big and open, and nothing—not a building or billboard or power line—obstructs my view. From our porch at night I can see straight to the moon. All the twinkling stars blink back at me and I'm certain that not a single thing stands between me and the solar system. It's just the stars and the sky and the dark, and me. I know, then, that I'm part of it all.

During the day, I watch the eagles making their rounds, taking lazy circles around the tops of the trees—"my trees," as I call them. I say they are "my trees" because I've watched them curiously ever since Joe first brought me up to this land seven years ago. I know they've watched me, too, from where they are. Tall and dense, they envelop the house and shield us— keeping out the crazy, shooing away the bad. Sometimes it feels as if no one even knows we're here, except for maybe the black bears and wild turkeys we share the land with.

Joe and I try to spend as much time in the mountains as possible. We know how important this place is to our survival and our soul. When we're here, at this house, however we envision the world, it just is—all we have to do is name it and it becomes. If we want to be frog catchers for an entire day, we are. If we prefer to see ourselves as artists, we sit on the floor and create until dinnertime. If we're dreamers, we lie down on the daybed on the screened-in porch and think or sleep for hours. Anything and everything is within our reach.

"Come run with us, Pleppy!" I tugged at his arm, urging him to trust me and get up from his little corner on the porch. "Sitting is for babies. Let's be Wild Things!" I started to wave my arms and spin around like a tornado. Making a scene, hoping to elicit some laughter.

It's Saturday and we have an entire day to let loose. Spring is here, and with it my favorite ritual as the weather gets warmer. I insist that we strip off all of our clothes and run from the porch to the edge of the forest, yelling "Freeeee like a bird! Freeeee like a bird!" at the top of our lungs. The first time to tell ourselves, the second time to tell the trees. Cassius, Penelope, and Othello have been doing this since they were very young—it's a silly game I play with them, and they've always liked it. But truthfully, I think I like it most. Running across the grass naked, my toes pressing into the earth, is a reminder of what my freedom feels like.

"Can we take off all our clothes, Mama? Everything?" Othello likes being naked most. Cassius is somewhere in the middle. But Penelope now refuses the game altogether. He remains unmoved, hands stuffed into his mouth, nervously chewing on his fingernails—eyeing his brothers while they frantically peel off their shirts and shorts.

"Yes, that's the entire point, babycakes! Let's get this party started!"

Whenever I run wild or dance, or take a spontaneous dive into our pond, the kids all crack up. "Look at Mama!" they screech, doubling over. "Go, Mama, go!" They rarely see me letting loose like that. If I'm not cleaning or organizing homework, I'm usually reading a book from my favorite spot on the daybed, or scribbling in my journal on the couch. But on the rare occasion when they're watching *me* sprinting, being the first one to jump into the water, or doing a cartwheel on the grass, I think it lets them know that Mama has it in her, too, that desire to be limitless.

For me, freedom means protection. It means a safe space to run wild without prying eyes. It means family close enough to touch, a warm meal, a cozy home. But freedom is not the same for everyone. What makes me feel liberated doesn't necessarily do it for the next person—not exactly and not profoundly. And what's more, even if I have access to freedoms—like family and safety and love—if there's just one thing oppressing me, I feel I'm being choked.

I'm continuing to find that out with Penelope. Although he has those freedoms, lots of love and a caring family, he is still fighting. Fighting for his identity, warring with his body. And in this moment, on our front lawn, with our mountains and eagles and sunshine surrounding us, that fight, for him, is overshadowing everything else.

"Take off your shorts, Pleppy. Feel the grass on your tush!" I prodded him, smiling. But Penelope continued to pull back, retreating a little more into his seat on the porch.

"I got this." Joe, reluctant to participate in my game, seized the opportunity to tend to Penelope. "P and I'll watch you Wild Things from the hammock. Let's go swing in the hammock, P."

Penelope grabbed his dad's hand and in unison they took several steps toward the edge of the porch, plopping themselves into our white hammock while the rest of us streaked across the lawn. While we screamed and laughed and ran back and forth, Penelope watched, cuddled up close to Joe with his face drawn, gnawing on his fingernails.

Even after all the conversations we had, after all that Penelope revealed to me about being "boy," I know he's far from free.

The battle with the body is a long, ultimately solo journey. One that starts as soon as we're born. In the beginning, our bodies serve a clear purpose: to breathe and eat, move and think, grow and refuel. The soul, I believe, is at peace with the body during this stage. But the trouble starts as we accumulate more filters— more ways of labeling ourselves: Black, female, older, ethnic, metropolitan. All those filters start elbowing their way in, vying for dominance, creating a division between our bodies and our authentic selves. The body then becomes vain—caring more about the size, shape, and color of it than about what the soul has to say. This is when the soul and the body start their battle. From my experience, no one escapes this struggle; there are no free passes.

It's only with wisdom and experience that we can make it through, releasing the vanity and returning, over time, to the *purposeful*. I think about this often from our front porch as I look out at nature: *What are we humans meant for?*

Since having Penelope, I'd been thinking a lot about the body—what it was made for versus what we force it to do. And what kinds of stories it tells. My own body tells me that I birthed four children, that I've smiled a lot over the years, and that I am strong.

Penelope's body, I knew, told a different story, as all bodies do. For Penelope, the body reminded him that people saw him differently from the way he saw himself. They saw Girl, he understood Boy. Seeing him hanging back from the rest of us while we laughed on the grass, I was reminded of just how much Penelope hated his form. How much he hated the assumptions his particular body stirred up—assumptions about who he was and what he should or shouldn't be doing.

A few weeks later, back in Brooklyn, an old friend I hadn't seen in a long time was passing through town and asked to stop by our place in Brooklyn. She wanted to catch up with me and see the kids. I had first met her through Serge some twenty years ago, just after I'd graduated from Spelman and was living downtown. Maripol was a photographer and fashion stylist from France who clothed the likes of Madonna and Basquiat. She hung out at Nell's, my favorite nightclub from my high school years, snapping Polaroids of her eccentric friends—creative outsiders, just like herself.

I was always impressed by the fact that she knew all the trendsetters, a mix of people who refused to conform: artists and singers, models and muses, all with wild spirits. They surpassed their gender, their race, and their class. Maripol was my friend but I looked up to her; she was an example of the type of human I wanted to be: free. The passing years had made her a bit more mellow, but she still buzzed with the same electricity that had drawn me to her all those years ago.

"Your three boys are so handsome!" she'd said while she rolled with us throughout our day, tagging along during the regular routine. "But didn't you have a little girl, too, no?" The question lingered in the air as she looked from Cassius to Penelope to Othello. I smiled, moving my head vaguely, but otherwise revealed nothing.

"Strange, I guess I must be remembering Georgia when she

was small! . . . But no, I could have sworn you had a little girl . . . ?" Her voice trailed. She laughed it off as older-woman memory failure, and I didn't disagree with her. I thought, *The right time will come. Wait for it, Jodie. No need to force it.*

When it was time for the boys' bath later that night, Maripol followed me and the kids into the bathroom. Leaning on the archway of the door, she casually watched me undress the boys while we chatted and laughed. First socks, then shirts, then jeans got tossed onto the floor. But when, finally, the kids dropped their underwear and Penelope was naked, legs spread apart as he started climbing into the oversized tub, my friend's mouth dropped open. Suddenly, there was a break in her laughter as she struggled to catch up. There was no disgust or anger on her face, but clearly she was attempting to do some mental math, adding up the scene in front of her.

Maripol tugged on my shirtsleeve, and her eyes begged me for an explanation. With my own eyes, I asked her to be kind, to wait until later when I could explain. I turned away from her, continuing to splash water around, distracting the boys with bubbles. I looked over at Penelope, hoping to relay a sense of calm. But it was too late; his shoulders had started to slump, his eyes darting between my startled friend and his brothers, then down at himself as he compared notes and connected the dots. With only my smile, I tried to tell him that everything was fine, that this was just another bath time. Just another evening. That my friend wasn't staring at him. That he was perfect and complete.

All day Penelope *had* been a normal boy. All day Maripol had witnessed Penelope as "he." All day Penelope had made sense—until his body was exposed, telling a different story.

Here it goes again, I thought. *The body stirring up trouble, making a mess and confusing the truth.*

. . .

The story of trans people, to me, was shaping up to be very similar to the story of Black people, of women, of people of color all over the world. Of all oppressed people throughout history. Stories in which some have tried to rewrite people's identities to serve their own needs.

I saw people trying to rewrite Penelope all the time, into a tomboy, or a misguided girl. And of course, he was none of those things. Penelope is a boy—with a vagina. That's just how he was born. We are who we are not because of the body, but because of the soul.

If I can work on that truth with Penelope, if I can deemphasize the body parts just enough to disentangle them from gender so that they can do the things Penelope actually enjoys, like throwing balls fast and furiously and one-arm push-ups, then, I think, I can help Penelope be free.

He's never been a gloomy kid. In fact, his natural disposition is joyful—he is bubbly and determined, eager to learn and be and do it all. But those emotions come out only when his armor is on. If Penelope's hair is cut in the exact Mohawk he likes, if his underwear is decorated with superheroes, if he's wearing his favorite wide-leg Wranglers. When all of these things are laid over his body just so, Penelope feels protected and safe. That's when you see the dynamic kid, the chatty kid, the front-of-the-line kid. That's when the straight-up rock star emerges.

But take those things away, and the light vanishes—he retreats further and further from us.

I knew that if I allowed Penelope's visuals to take the lead, he might forever be in doubt of himself. Forever stuck in those defeating bath time moments, like the one witnessed by Maripol that left him feeling inadequate. I'd rather help Penelope—

help all of my kids, in fact—nurture their emotions. Build the fortress from within. Make them see that, yes, the body is a beautiful thing, sometimes a peculiar thing, but not the *only* thing. And certainly not the thing we rely on to tell us fundamentally who we are. In order to push us all a little closer toward true freedom when it came to the body, I knew we had to go deep.

Every household has a belief system. Every mama sets a tone with her kids, whether she wants to or not. Intentionally or otherwise, we teach our children values, a certain code of ethics that remains with them throughout their lives. We spend years trying to sort out what we believe in, then we share those beliefs with our children, infusing them with our ideas of right and wrong.

At the top of my list was knowing that everything good, everything real and true, comes from deep inside, beneath the surface.

The culture I was now interested in cultivating with my kids was one of depth, and of purpose. Of training the mind to listen to what it really has to say. If there is one thing I've learned over the years, through relationships, career experiences, and the many years I've spent reconsidering myself, it's that we are who we know ourselves to be, not how others perceive us. We are strong, we are wise, we are capable. Regardless of what people see or assume when they look at us. Not the most revelatory of messages, I know, but one that I've stumbled over and kept coming back to; a message that has kept me going time and time again.

And so it became my mission to steadily undo all the stereotypes we'd learned about the body—all the stories that tell us who we're supposed to be and what we're expected to do.

We are not a shy family. I often cook in my underwear, as my mother did when I was growing up. And the kids regularly hang around the house in little more than their boxers all day, reading books, doing homework, cleaning up, doing chores. More and more, I encouraged the body to be exposed; I wanted to remove the mystery. Put the body out into the open so we could see it for what it is: a house of endless possibilities, varied and unique—no two ever exactly the same. I wanted to dismantle any notions of an ideal body, and to show my kids that what's most important is that it is *theirs*—to admire and adorn and perhaps contemplate, but never, ever to compare.

The body is overanalyzed and micromanaged as far as I'm concerned. Women, myself included, seem to talk more about the outside—about the length of our eyelashes or the size of our lips—than we do about what we're feeling and thinking. I rarely hear people talking about beauty in the purposeful way, the way my grandmother taught me to think about it, where you "nurture the roots" so something strong and healthy can grow.

Picking apart the body piece by piece—that's not what it's made for. What's important is the fluidity and the connection of the different parts. We dissect our bodies, but when we put it in motion, when it either does or does not perform, we understand why it was made—to be useful, purposeful, powerful. The body is not to be obsessed over or dwelled upon, inch by inch. What's always been most fascinating to me about it is what it can *do*. I'm into the doing part. My women taught me that.

I thought Penelope's body was amazing. Whenever he was jumping on our trampoline, or splashing in the pond, or flipping around with his brothers, or hugging me—at those times Penelope's body was magical, and I wanted to tell him that all the time. Affirmations have always been big in my family. "Your body is awesome! Your body is beautiful! Whoa, look at those legs!" were my go-tos with the kids. My parents used to do the same with Ramona and me, complimenting us all the time on our physicality.

But with Penelope, those kinds of affirmations went only so far. When the body is the enemy, it's not to be trusted. So Joe and I began to switch tactics. Instead of praising the form, we started encouraging Penelope to *do* things—things that needed the body, pushed the body, relied upon the body.

At night, I taught him meditation so he could learn to still his muscles and control his breathing; his heartbeat would slow, and his emotions would shift. Joe encouraged sports, and I signed him up for karate (which proved to be a total game changer). These were activities that actually *needed* the body, required Penelope to work in conjunction with his body, to trust it. Each time Penelope learned something new, like dribbling the ball between his legs, swimming without floaties, or staying up on a skateboard, he beamed with pride.

I was amazed by what he'd accomplish, seemingly stronger and grittier than his brothers. When Cassius would eventually leave the basketball court, exhausted and ready to relax on the couch with a book, Penelope remained for another hour, shooting free shot after free shot—eventually making one out of thirty attempts. Where Othello would shrink if anyone ever raised a voice near him, Penelope rose up in those moments. Whether it was when Master Bill belted out karate commands, or when Joe reprimanded him at home, or when his brother told him he would always be "better" because he was "older," Penelope never buckled under pressure, never shied away from a taunt. He'd get more focused, more determined, push himself further.

Penelope's body defied every one of those stereotypes that said girls are less than boys. So I stopped talking about "boys'" or "girls'" bodies, stopped comparing and contrasting them altogether. I took up a human-centered approach instead, using phrases like "some humans" and "this human" and "your body."

"Some of us develop, carry, and feed babies," I'd say, "while other bodies carry the 'seeds' to help *make* babies. Both abilities are equally incredible." The kids would nod, giggle, and then look at themselves and one another as if they'd just discovered their superpowers.

Getting past physical bias is difficult, even now—it is so ingrained in us to believe that men and women are not physically equal. Clearly, the key was retraining the mind, putting the body to work and letting the soul lead. And that meant thoroughly separating gender from body parts, activities, and behaviors. It meant placing gender in the brain, as part of the identity process we all experience. So regardless of Penelope's body, or how he looked, I repeated to myself all day, every day, like a mantra: *Penelope-Boy. Penelope-Boy. Penelope-Boy.* Slowly, consistently, I would rewire my brain.

At night, I started throwing all the kids into the bathtub in the same rough-and-tumble style. I adjusted my voice so it never sounded as if I were favoring one over the other. And when the kids fought, which was often, I held myself back from jumping in too quickly and coddling, especially not Penelope. In fact, I started intentionally allowing for a couple of shin kicks to connect before I broke them apart.

Watching Penelope play basketball all day in the country with his brothers, cousins, and uncles, I held myself back from correcting him when he got in someone's face. *It's okay, P—Get dirty. Be smelly. Be entitled. Get rough.* "I know!" I blurted out one afternoon when I'd had enough of his sad-face routine during bath time. "Let's call your vagina a tiny penis!" More and more, I was diving into unconventional approaches, just so I could really make the point to Penelope, to myself, and to the world: This here is a boy, *my* boy—full stop. I pushed for hyper-boy, tough-boy, assertive-boy—and I encouraged Penelope to step right in and get comfortable, to grab what was rightfully his. Each one of these changes took another bit of mental power, another level of conviction.

"I'm not that type of boy, Mama, one who just likes to crash cars," Penelope said to me one day when I asked him if he wanted to play with Cassius, who was doing exactly that on the living room floor in the mountain house. "I want to draw. Can you color with me, Mama?" He caught me off guard with that one—"I'm not the type of boy who just likes to crash cars." In fact, he often caught me off guard with the things he knew and saw that I did not. He shared those things with me, gently, patiently, until eventually I understood.

Clearly, Penelope was telling me there was still so much more for me to learn. So instead of veering him—and really, all the kids—in any one direction, I started looking for signs to reveal each of their particulars—the unique things that made them happy. In the mountain house, I sometimes spent twenty minutes at my sink, washing, exfoliating, pampering my skin. All the kids gravitate toward me when I'm in the bathroom at night. Georgia, Cassius, Othello, and Penelope all huddle in my one bathroom, elbowing each other while we reach across for the toothpaste, holding our noses while one uses the toilet, complaining when another leaves the lid off a jar of very expensive French face cream.

I started noticing that Penelope always reached for my lotions and potions first. He loved to slather my creams all over his face. Then he'd spritz himself with a toner and rinse everything off with a scrub. No concern for order or economy, he simply indulged in the smells and textures, in this me-time in front of the mirror that made him feel so loved. During those nighttime bathroom rituals, he got all into his reflection, appreciating what he saw. We all brushed or picked or twisted our hair, smiling at the new styles we'd come up with. This private, cozy place is where I began to see another side of Penelope, different from the athlete, the competitor, the kid who destroys one-arm push-ups. In the bathroom, his soft side, his creative side, emerged.

Form follows function. I stumble upon on those words one day while sitting on our screened-in porch in the mountains. It's a principle in architecture that means the shape of something should be based primarily on its intended function or purpose. I think again that we aren't meant to be pretty—we're meant to be capable, strong, and alive.

When my sister and I were little, my mother trained us to be strong in her own way. During car trips, she'd climb into the backseat, squeezing herself between us, and start telling us stories—about Afro'd princesses named Jodie and Ramona, revered in all the lands for their beauty, their brilliance, and their bravery. These princesses could do anything. We'd often interject during Mama's stories with burning questions like "So Rapunzel has cornrows, Mama, just like ours?" I loved those stories because they made me feel as if the entire world, from east to west, north to south, was familiar with *me*. As if I were not foreign, or strange, or an anomaly. As if I were the prototype.

I've done the same thing with my kids—making up stories for Georgia when she was younger, and doing it with Penelope, Cassius, and Othello now. In my stories for the boys, three brothers named Penel, Cash, and O lie very still in their beds at night, waiting for their unsuspecting parents to fall asleep. As soon as they do, the magical brothers climb out of their beds, unfolding gorgeous black wings from underneath their pajamas.

Out the bedroom window they soar, *swoosh!*, into the brisk night. On their special wings, Penel, Cash, and O take flight, soaring into the night air, skimming the stars with the tips of their fingers as they whiz past them, circling a big yellow moon before continuing into the dark. With great speed, they fly across the earth, touching down in Ghana, in Vietnam—wherever they please—visiting family and new friends, tasting delicacies, simply for the adventure and the excitement of it all. After roaming the world all night, thoroughly spent from all the fun they've had, they soar back across the ocean against an approaching sun, climb through the window and into their warm beds, then tuck themselves under the covers just before Mama comes in to wake them with morning kisses.

In my stories, the children are brave and undaunted, flying thousands of miles without tiring, getting by on the strength of their wits, the capability of their bodies, and of course the bond they share with one another. *They* are their own idols. They are the masters of whatever universes they create. This is how I see all of my children, free and powerful.

I tell these stories for all three of my boys; there are lessons in them they all need to hear. But I know Penelope pays particular attention. He drifts off to sleep visualizing himself as a hero—a brave, strong boy who can soar confidently beside his brothers and explore the world. And when he wakes up the next day, my hope is that he carries that grace with him—that feeling that tells him, I am not a weird boy or a pretend boy, I am *this* boy. A boy made of magic.

Soon after I started telling this story to the boys, Penelope left a story he'd written in school under my pillow. It began like this: "Once upon a time, there was a boy named Penelope . . ."

SEVENTEEN

The Highest Vibration

*One of our problems has been that we have had no mechanism,
except the black church, for transmitting our struggle or our tradition of excellence and hard work from generation to generation.*

—

DR. JAMES P. COMER,
*Associate Dean of the Yale Medical School,
on the state of Black America*

IN 1976 MY PARENTS FOUNDED a small, private after-school program in the historic community of Sugar Hill—a beautiful,
mostly Black, and relatively quiet part of Harlem. It opened
during a time when my "uncle," Gil Scott-Heron, Aunt Lurma's longtime lover, was singing songs like "Save the Children,"
and the conscious world was quite aware of a serious divide between the lives of white families and those that were Black.
Mama and Daddy named their progressive institution the Patterson School, and they built it around (and for) a community
that had largely been counted out: Black families. People who
had historically been alienated from good schools, good neighborhoods, good jobs, and a good life. The state of affairs of
Black people in America—and particularly how Black kids
were faring—was the impetus for the Patterson School's found-
ing.

Around the time when Ramona and I were in grade school,
my mother started seeing that we were the "tokens," often two

Gil Scott-Heron, with his longtime love Aunt
Lurma, taught us the revolution will never be
televised. It will happen live and direct.

of only a few Black kids in our classes. It was a narrative she'd
heard from many other Black parents with children in mainstream schools—that their kids were also "the few" and "the
only"—and Mama saw that as a critical danger. Dangerous because, rather than being grounded in our heritage, celebrated in
our Blackness, we were being conditioned to see the world
through a white lens, and to see ourselves as a minority. Typically, *our* backgrounds were left out of those mainstream school
environments, and *our* history was often relegated only to stories of slavery. In the books we read and on the posters we saw
on our classroom walls, only a sprinkling of Blacks were
mentioned—Martin Luther King Jr., Rosa Parks, and Frederick
Douglass were standard favorites.

When explaining to people curious to know how their
school was different, Mama went back to her own academic ex-

periences. "In learning how to compute averages, for instance, we had to figure out Babe Ruth's batting average. Here at the Patterson School, we'll use Hank Aaron's as the example." She stressed that the point of a school like theirs was not to push a radical agenda. "It's not about being militant or separatist, it's about being aware. The more you know about *your* culture and heritage, the more productive you are and the more confidence you have in dealing with others." She meant that a child's understanding of self is primary, and until that feels right, everything else takes second place.

Mama grew up with Grandmother Gloria and Great-Grandmother Lurline, women who felt that education and the church were the lifeblood of the family and the foundation of the individual. The church was the one place where our information could be shared and recorded—passed on from person to person, generation to generation. The Black church preserved our history and exalted our traditions. In contrast, the outside world attempted to erase us. Education was how we counted ourselves back in. It was about gaining back the information that was kept from us. The mechanism of slavery was to take—our labor, our religion, our families, our customs and language, our food, our heirlooms, and our bodies. And even after slavery was abolished, that theft continued. Going to school was activism—our middle finger to those who had denied us for years.

For my mother, education was, without question, her weapon. She earned her Master of Arts degree in teaching at Wesleyan University, and later did postgraduate work at Harvard and the University of Strasbourg, in France. She wanted to make sure good schooling had a place in her children's lives. My parents' school, located on a quiet street behind a small and unassuming church, became a kind of surrogate family, injecting not only heritage and history into Black lives but pride.

The Patterson School was a collective of civic-minded and community-oriented people. The parents were a close-knit team—they often socialized together, staying up late in their living rooms talking politics, music, and business while we kids piled into sleeping bags, giggling together in back rooms. Some of us lived in communities outside Harlem, mostly on the Upper West Side, while the majority were local families rooted in the surrounding neighborhood. If any parent couldn't manage the monthly tuition, which was often the case, my parents found a way to cover the cost. No one was ever dropped; every committed family was kept inside the fold.

The school was for the entire community, regardless of economic background. We didn't buy into the division of Black people along economic lines. Race was our rallying point; the hard issues that we were fighting against affected us all. We came together and used what we had. Those who had more, gave more—of their time, their skills, their networks. The film director Stan Latham taught us storytelling. The journalist Charlayne Hunter-Gault sat with us and talked current events, and the jazz musician Ron Carter gave us our fundamentals in music—their own children learning alongside the rest of us.

Our parents took it into their own hands to create the exact environment that was missing from mainstream schools: a reflection of self, the Black self. When the images, language, and customs of an entire community are not acknowledged, it can break an individual and break apart an entire community. The conscious world understood this dilemma, yet the mainstream world was in denial of racism and its widespread impact. But the Patterson School didn't hide behind the notion of race. It supported the child by putting Black culture at the center of learning. Enabling each child to be secure, happy, and bold in the world.

During our childhood, Ramona and I were able to leave our

"otherness" behind whenever we walked through the doors of our parents' school. Along with our daily doses of math, history, science, and the fine arts, we learned even stronger lessons in community—in what it means to belong.

School, for us at least, was the mechanism of transmitting our struggle, our traditions, and our excellence that Dr. James P. Comer thought missing. I grew up believing that in the hands of the right people, people who truly cared, school was much more than good grades and report cards—it was a place to learn about yourself, and what you could become.

Thirty years later, with children of my own, and in constant need of community support, Joe and I gravitated toward a school in Brooklyn for our kids that mirrored the environment my parents designed in Harlem. Our kids attended a small private school in the heart of Crown Heights. Established inside two converted brownstones, the Miriam Ann Carr Academy for the Development and Education for Multicultural Youth or MACADEMY as it's commonly called, sits unassumingly on a residential street. Most of the families and the administration are of West Indian descent—Black, religious, and conservative. The administration are predominantly women who come from backgrounds that place tradition—no-nonsense parenting and old-school markers of respect—as the cornerstone of their personal ethos.

Adults are addressed by their last name, always: "Hello, Ms. Patterson!" "Good day, Mr. Ghartey!"—less for formality's sake than as a sign of deep respect. And the kids aren't regarded at arm's length the way kids are in many schools these days. The students at MACADEMY are hugged tightly and loved passionately, just as they might be at home, by their own family. The women of MACADEMY (and the handful of men who teach there, too) model tough love at its best: stern in their discipline, exacting with their expectations, but always free with their affection.

The captain of this academic ship is Bishop Sylveta Hamilton-Gonzales, the founder of our school. Fondly known as Bishop, she is a tall woman in her sixties with long dreadlocks that are always beautifully coiled into a bun. Bishop usually strides into work each day wearing real "ready-for-action" clothing. Often that looks like a Bob Marley T-shirt, sandals with thick woolen socks, and a long, beautiful African print skirt. In fact, each staff member wears clothing that best expresses who they are. There's no uniformity about the way people are put together at MACADEMY, but it's always meticulous and full of self-pride. Some have naturals, some have weaves, some have long, decaled nails with ornate designs and rhinestones. It's refreshing to see the school's commitment to individuality. Under Bishop's leadership, that message is pervasive—it's reflected not only in the African artifacts that line the school's shelves and the many Black faces that appear on the walls, but also in the presentation of its people. The adults that these kids see every day are a reflection of themselves, multiplied in a beautiful variety.

Bishop is a dynamic woman, moving around the classroom as though it's her stage, punctuating her teaching with the occasional curse word to drive her point home. She is funny: getting down on the dance floor with the kids at the school's annual disco. She is smart: graduating from Princeton's Seminary School, where she founded the Seminarians for Justice Coalition. And she's incredibly committed: often boarding kids from school in her own home when needed, and providing counsel to parents after hours in her office. Bishop reminds me of the preachers I've seen in Black churches: super sharp, a little unpredictable, a lot respected, and regarded, always, with just the right amount of fear.

From the time we first met Bishop and her team in 2011, they embraced our complex family as if we were no big deal. And that was saying a lot, because we brought a lot to the table. I remember the day before we started school, I boldly stated to Bishop that we had great kids who were soon to be great students—I was betting on top of the class. But they came with a few particularities I needed her to understand.

Cassius, I explained, was an extremely sensitive child; he had been since he was a baby. Physical touch—hand-holding, hugging—didn't make him feel comfortable. In the past, I'd seen people thrown by Cassius's particulars, making assumptions about his intellect and social ability. I received a lot of carefully worded suggestions from friends and relatives that maybe Cassius was "slow," or "on the spectrum." But in reality, he was just shy. Whenever new people came around, he'd often avoid making eye contact or hide behind my body, clinging to my leg. I just wanted Bishop to see Cassius for what he was: a kid with quirks—quirks we all have.

Penelope, only three years old at the time, would be entering school with a few particulars, too. I tried to state the gist of it to Bishop as simply as possible, without getting into what I'd just learned from Penelope that summer in the mountain house: *Everyone thinks I'm a girl and I'm not.*

"Penelope will never, ever wear a dress or a skirt," I said to Bishop. "Not to school, or in a class play, or anywhere else for that matter. She's just not that type of girl." I let Bishop know that the girls' uniform would be out of the question, and asked if Penelope could wear the boys' uniform instead. I knew I wasn't telling the whole truth, but the bigger topic, the one that acknowledged Penelope's spirit, felt too complicated for that moment. These were still early days—the ten-thousand-hours period—and Joe and I were still trying to figure things out privately, between ourselves. Even more, I wasn't sure how Bishop, a woman of faith, would take to knowing that my "daughter" was actually my son.

"As long as Penelope's in *a* uniform—either the boys' or the girls'—and she does the work that's required of her, she'll be just fine," Bishop said after I'd finished all my explanations. "And Cassius will be just fine, too. Don't worry, we got this." These were small acceptances from our new school, but hearing them from Bishop at the time made me feel at ease. From that first interaction with the school's founder, I had a strong feeling that we would get along. She, like me, seemed less concerned with outside appearance than with the inner workings of a person.

It was this tone of acceptance set by Bishop and her simple, reassuring words that gave me confidence in the school, enough confidence to entrust them with my children, quirks and all. But I questioned whether the entire truth about Penelope would be something the school could digest and stand by when the time came. Until I could be sure, I knew we would have to speak in half-truths, inching our way out into the open one day at a time.

And for the next two years, that's just what we did.

Penelope went to school on his very first day, and every day thereafter, wearing the same uniform as Cassius: blue front-pleated trousers, white button-front shirt, navy blue tie. And, to our surprise, there wasn't a teacher or student who ever asked why. In fact, some even complimented Penelope's style. "Love it!" they'd say as he walked up the school stairs in the morning. As time went by, other students picked up on Penelope's confidence, and a few girls started wearing pants, too. Each day he walked inside the school I saw his confidence grow.

I learned over the years that at MACADEMY, whatever your particulars, they celebrated you. You could see the love poured into each child, and the high expectations set—expectations that all of the kids at the school, mine included, were eager to meet. "How do you do it, Bishop?" I often asked. "How do you get all these kids to love school and work so hard?" Bishop's answer still lingers with me: "I assume only the best of each child."

I've seen it with my own two eyes, children rise—they rise to the highest vibration around them. If there is goodness, a child will find it. If there is strength, that's what they become. And when there is love, there is always an anchor. Bishop is that highest vibration.

And the children of MACADEMY responded to Bishop's love with their own form of acceptance. With no formal announcement from us, Penelope's classmates, over time, began referring to Penelope as "he," "him," and "boy." These three-, four-, and five-year-olds clearly understood more than what we

Penelope (left), proud as a peacock, outside school with his brothers, Cassius and Othello.

were saying. They read past my half-truths and tapped into something deeper—working out gender as they experienced it firsthand with Penelope, normalizing what they felt, and swiftly moving on.

I knew this was happening because the news trickled up—moving beyond the circle of kids to the adults in the school, and then eventually to me. One morning during Penelope's second year at MACADEMY, I was in the middle of my typical hundred-yard dash to get the boys to school on time when I spotted another mom out of the corner of my eye waving to me. With only three minutes to spare before Cassius, Othello, and Penelope would officially be marked absent, I put up my hand, motioning for her to give me a minute. With my other hand, I swatted each of their behinds up the stone steps and through the front entrance.

"Let's go, let's go! Double time, boys. Hustle, *hustle!*"

The mom watched this whole scene from a distance, waiting with an even smile on her face until the last of three backpacks disappeared behind the door. With the mad dash finally over, she made her approach.

"Ms. Patterson, hi there—I've been wanting to talk to you." She looked happy, if a little nervous. "So, it's the weirdest thing. My daughter, she keeps insisting that Penelope is a boy. For whatever reason, she keeps calling Penelope 'he.'" Hearing this, I planted my feet firmly on the pavement, fastened a smile on my face, and took a deep breath.

"And you know, I keep telling her that girls can wear pants and have short hair, too." She said this last part with an air of solidarity. She wasn't mad or rude—actually, it was an incredibly caring gesture, this expression of girl power. "But she keeps insisting, '*No,* Mom! Penelope *is* a boy!'"

I waited for her to finish, then smiled again, gave her a reassuring laugh, and left it at "It's complicated." Sure, I knew something more was happening. And maybe she did, too. But at that moment, with her standing in front of me waiting for an explanation, I just didn't have the words.

A short while later during that same year, the conversation came up again at parent-teacher conferences. Penelope's teacher, Ms. Rice, explained to us that she repeatedly attempted to quell the classroom chatter whenever the kids brought up Penelope being a boy. " 'Girls come in all varieties!' I always tell them." Ms. Rice recounted the story to Joe and me with that same sense of feminist good intention I received from Morning Drop-off Mom a few months prior. Her long, bedazzled nails glimmered as she dismissed the issue with one confident motion of her hands. "Don't worry—Penelope is fine. I got this."

It was a testament to the school's greatness that these teachers and parents were so quick to come to Penelope's defense— advocating for femininity, for individuality, and for the right to be your own version of you. But the irony of those efforts, of course, was that Penelope wasn't a tomboy, and feminism wasn't at stake. Penelope was in fact a boy. His classmates knew it— they'd figured it out a long time ago—and they were not about to let the adults confuse what they so fiercely knew to be true.

Bishop's love, the kids' intuition, the parents' and teachers' surprising advocacy—these were signs that gave me hope. If the school could champion the individual in such a full and comprehensive way, maybe, I thought, we could finally come out with Penelope's whole truth.

Those continuous half-truths I'd been dishing out at school— "It's complicated" and "It's just her style," the tight-lipped smiles and vague responses—had been steadily building up an anxiety that lingered over my body. It was taking shelter in the corners of my subconscious, coming out at night as nightmares, or during the day as defensive reflexes, my not realizing until a conversation was over that I'd been clenching the whole time. It

wasn't until later that I'd start to feel it: the exhaustion of waiting, the nagging obligation to keep up the story, a ridiculous
story that I knew would eventually come apart. Penelope as
tomboy? It was ludicrous. All the while, the waiting. Waiting
for the moment that would finally bring out everything that
hadn't been said, all the words we were saving for another day,
another time.

And so, when Penelope entered his third year at MACAD-
EMY, after a million baby steps, I decided it was time for our
family to let the school in on the whole truth.

As Joe and I walked through the tree-lined streets of Crown
Heights to meet with Bishop about Penelope, we held hands in
solidarity. As much as we loved MACADEMY—respected the
staff, the kids, and the administration—we were prepared to remove our children from the school if the next few minutes
didn't go as we hoped they would.

We walked silently as I gathered my thoughts. Truthfully, I
had never felt comfortable talking about trans in large Black
circles, circles I'd been in all my life. If we were reading the
subtext right, transgender was a topic frowned upon in our
communities, discussed only in whispers and behind closed
doors—frivolous at best, shameful at worst. It was not something we Black folk talked openly about, rallied around, or
championed. And it most certainly wasn't considered a Black
issue, like poverty or gun control or racism. From what I'd experienced, much of Black culture—and West Indian and Latino
cultures—were steeped in traditions that see gender variance
and homosexuality as sacrilegious and immoral.

Though MACADEMY had never given us any reason to
question their support, I knew we were venturing into un-

charted territory. Since we first walked through their doors, they had demonstrated their devotion to our kids, nurturing their minds and their spirits, making them feel pride in their history and culture. But how deep did that devotion go? Would it stop at transgender? At what point might some religious or moral filter get in the way?

"A woman shall not wear a man's garment, nor shall a man put on a woman's cloak, for whoever does these things is an abomination to the Lord your God"—Deuteronomy 22:5. We had heard statements like this before, and they stung like hell.

The knot in my stomach tightened as Joe and I joined Bishop in her office, taking seats at her desk. Wearing her characteristic coiled bun and a new Barack Obama T-shirt I'd never seen before, she looked across at Joe and me serenely, with her hands clasped casually on top of some papers.

A couple of days before the meeting, Joe and I had sent her a version of the letter we'd given to friends and family announcing Penelope as a boy. We figured it wise to give her some time to process the news on her own before we discussed it face-to-face.

"Bishop," I began, mustering my strongest authoritative voice. "I know this might go against what you believe, but Penelope has asked to be recognized as a boy." I figured I'd get straight to the point. "We respect everything you've done for our kids. But we need more. Going forward, we're asking everyone at school to refer to Penelope as 'he.'"

Bishop blinked back at us, shifting her weight in her chair. Then she unclasped her hands, placing her palms on the desk, and leaned forward.

"I read your letter," she said softly. "And I was very moved."

Bishop smiled then, warmth radiating from her kind eyes. "Penelope is a prophet. And I'm with him on this journey."

After that, the knot in my stomach released, along with all the tension that filled the room. I thought Bishop might quote the Bible, as many had done. We thought she might say something like "I'm sorry, Ms. Patterson and Mr. Ghartey. Although we'd like to help you, we are a God-abiding community and we cannot, in the name of God, support such views." But instead, Bishop sided with humanity. She placed herself next to the child and a family in need—and by doing just that, she aligned herself with the highest force of all—the God of Love. "I am with him"—the words every parent hopes to hear. That afternoon we understood, definitively, that Bishop would accept the whole person, and would go with her students wherever they were journeying.

"If Penelope had asked us to call him Love, we would have called him that," Bishop said months later to a news crew working on a story about the early acceptance of transgender. The fact that Bishop had chosen the word "love" in relation to transgender, and to Penelope, told me how purely she saw people.

The first step, for all of us, was breaking the silence. Once that's done, you can begin to fill the space with something good— good information, good dialogue, good feeling, good progress. Soon after our conversation, Bishop organized a staff meeting to discuss the very new topic of transgender to her very eager team of teachers and administrators. And she and her staff started learning together, speaking collectively about what transgender meant for their school. Addressing Penelope's identity was at the core of the school's values: not counting out one single child. Letting nothing—not race, gender, economics, or anything else—deter a child's potential.

In the days and weeks that followed our conversation in Bishop's office, teachers came up to me with tears in their eyes relaying their support and reconfirming their love—for all of us, and most deeply for Penelope.

Issues continued to spring up from time to time, there were classroom scuffles and the occasional playground upset. At one point, it even came to my attention that a family had decided to take their child out of MACADEMY because Penelope was there. I knew that scenarios like that might play out again—in a school of a hundred families, it's impossible for everyone to think the same way. With such a polarizing topic, I knew there were bound to be people who didn't agree.

But even in those extreme circumstances when others backed away from us, we had our community holding tight. MACADEMY had proven itself to be the greatest example of what acceptance could look like. It continues to be for Penelope and his classmates, what my parents' school had been for all the little Black boys and girls who walked through its doors: a haven, a safe space, a place for them to rise to the highest vibration.

I often replay our journey with MACADEMY whenever I need a reminder. A reminder of the abundance of good in the world, even when there is so much that is ugly—particularly for a family that looks like ours. The school, from the very beginning, illustrated what's possible. It showed us all the wonderful things that can happen when we push past our fears and assumptions and speak—even in the most unlikely places, and even when there is so much to lose.

MACADEMY surprised us, protected us, loved us, and through it all, always allowed Penelope to carry on happily oblivious, free to concentrate on the more important things. Things like the stories and lyrics he so liked to compose:

> *I might be a ninja*
> *But I got a heart*
> *I might be tough*

But I got a heart
I'm like that
From the start
My legs are hard as steel
But I'm not despicable

—PENELOPE GHARTEY, *age six*

EIGHTEEN

The Widest Sense of We

Had I not created my own world,
I would have certainly died in other people's.

—

ANAÏS NIN

ON THE EVE OF 2015, I told my family that going into the new year, we were trying something new. We were going on a mission to find others who looked and lived like us—who embodied the world we wanted to create. Humans were not meant to survive on their own; we needed each other, I thought, to recognize ourselves. Because although I was showing Penelope as best I could that he was good enough, I knew that "we can't *be* what we can't *see*," as the wise Marian Wright Edelman once said. My *showing* Penelope was different from his seeing it first-hand.

"Listen up, family!" I said to a row of skeptical faces that New Year's Eve in our mountain house. "This year we need to find transgender friends. Period!" I knew it sounded forced and maybe a little awkward, but we would never go back to that old world, the one in which there were only two ways to be: male or female. What we needed was to move ourselves forward.

We all need community, people who reflect who we are and who we want to be. And we needed a village to raise Penelope as boy—a queer community of believers who understood where we were coming from, who understood the nuances. I wanted to be surrounded by folks who embodied our new understanding, immersed in their stories and experiences, so that Penelope could truly feel what it was like to be placed at the center. So he could feel the joy of being of the majority—the things that made him "different" in the other world rendered blissfully boring in a new one.

We, the family, needed this community just as much as Penelope did. Despite the blips of team unity—glimmers of being on the same page—the truth was that Joe and I were struggling. We'd been operating in silos for so long it was hard to remember a time when we weren't. Our years together had shown me that we were so caught up in our *own* ways of providing for and supporting our kids—supporting Penelope—that we'd each fallen into viewing the other's style as an attack on our own parenting. A power play for "the right way." We needed to see—I needed to see—how other parents did it. I needed to feel that I wasn't alone. And I knew that Joe needed to feel that he wasn't alone, either.

And the kids, they needed to see that gender in practice was what I was preaching—that people didn't come in two forms, but limitless ones. They needed to know that their brother wasn't just an exception, Penelopes existed everywhere. I wanted all of us to reimagine "I" into the widest sense of "we." To understand that *we* are trans, *we* are cis, *we* are human. This wasn't just about Penelope or "those people over there." It was about the transitioning of every single one of us into a better, more open and loving mindset.

And so that summer we did what millions of Americans do when they're in search of a place where they belong: We went to camp.

I signed everyone up for a four-day overnight experience at Aranu'tiq, a camp specifically for transgender and gender-nonconforming kids and their families. No one complained—

but no one was ecstatic about it, either. Joe questioned the type of adults who did this kind of thing. "Jodie, we'll probably be the only Black family there. We'll probably be surrounded by hippies in Birkenstocks. We'll probably have nothing in common with them." I could see the anxiety all over his face. Privately, I held similar doubts, but I wasn't about to show my cards. We needed this too much. "Let's just try it, babe," I said. "We've got nothing to lose.

"And by the way, Joe-Joe," I added, "allow me to remind you of the three pairs of Birks between us, currently sitting in our closet."

It was a six-hour drive to New Hampshire. The long roads and monotonous hours gave the two of us plenty of time to cast even more assumptions about what might happen over the next few days. Joe's eyebrows remained furrowed for most of the car ride, his hands clenching and unclenching around the steering wheel. The book on tape he'd been listening to (Eckhart Tolle, I think, for the tenth time) did little to help the situation. He blamed it on the traffic, but I was sure his mind was calculating what we were about to experience, and how uncomfortable it was going to feel to be submerged in a world he wasn't even sure he wanted any part of.

We intentionally downplayed our anxiety for the kids, knowing it was probably best for them to enter the weekend without apprehension or a "gender agenda." We sold them on the idea of a fun camp experience, filled with games, cabins, nature, and opportunities to make new friends. We made the drive there like any of the hundred other road trips we'd ever taken: loading up on junk food, charging all the gadgets, bringing our favorite blankets, and engaging in just about every road-travel pastime we know: Find the Alphabet, Word Association, Hangman, Pokémon, Storytime, and Sing-along.

When we finally arrived at the campgrounds that night, it was dark; all the other families had gone to bed. We were late (as usual), we were exhausted, and we were nervous. All of us needed to unwind. After doing a little exploring, Joe and I found a hula hoop in a back room off the main hall, and we all took turns twisting and twirling and laughing, closing out the night with our kind of perfect family activity. With a little more calm than before, we made our way to our cozy cabin. I made the beds with a stack of mismatched blankets, sheets, and pillowcases I'd brought from home, and we climbed in and fell asleep.

The next morning, we woke up early to a gorgeous scene. The camp was situated deep in the woods, and at its center was a huge clear lake. Rolling hills dotted the background, and thick stands of beautiful pine, oak, and birch trees surrounded the buildings. Wooden signs were nailed to the tree trunks, directing us around the camp—bathrooms this way, archery that way, rock climbing around the hill, the mess hall at the center of the grounds.

Breakfast began at seven, and all six of us—Joe and I, Penelope, Othello, Cassius, and Georgia (Nain was working in the city)—made our way toward the mess hall, past the clusters of rugged log cabins, where everyone gathered at the beginning of the day. Before pushing open the doors, Joe and I instinctively took long, deep breaths, fixing our faces into smiles, preparing ourselves. Preparing to be awkwardly Black—the standout family, the one and only. Preparing for the racial divide to get in the way of what we came to camp to do.

The buzz of chatter in the hall hit us at full volume when we opened the doors. Families sat together at long wooden tables, digging into bowls of oatmeal and plates of eggs. With Penelope and Othello tugging on my arms, and Cassius close to his dad, I did a quick scan of the scene—and the very first thing I spotted was a family of four across the hall. *Do my eyes deceive me?* I thought. *Are they . . . ? Yes! Black folks!*

"Well, well, well—would you look at *that*?" I turned to Joe, slapping him playfully on the arm.

We made our way toward them, and as we did, Joe started to smile. We got a little closer and he broke into a grin. "No Shit!" he said under his breath. "That's Yaa." I recalled the name because it was unusual—Yaa was his high school girlfriend from back in Boston. Sitting across the mess hall at our transgender family camp was Joe's teenage sweetheart. His first serious girlfriend, whom he hadn't seen in decades.

In the thirty seconds or so it took for us to cross the room to meet them, Joe reminded me of their history and caught me up on the last twenty years. He had a love, he was crazy about her, she dumped him . . . 19 seconds, 18, 17 . . . Took him years to get over her . . . 10, 9, 8 . . . She was married now. They had two kids . . . 4 seconds, 3. She was an amazing woman—the kind I'd vibe with—2, 1 . . .

"Hey!" A chorus of hellos and hugs ensued. Joe and Yaa were comfortable around each other, even after so much time had passed, and that allowed everyone else to relax—particularly me and John, Yaa's husband. Surprisingly, there was no tension, no nervousness. Only a feeling of family. We all laughed, genuinely, over this crazy coincidence and agreed it must be fate, or something deeper. Huddled off to the side I could see Cassius and their daughter starting to swap Pokémon cards. It was official: The two families had clicked, immediately and seamlessly. And just as immediately, I saw something inside Joe soften.

I don't know exactly what happened to Joe when he saw Yaa, or all the different reasons why he shifted. I never asked Joe how seeing her made him feel. But I suppose that seeing his high school love made him feel at home, as though this strange thing—the thing that landed him at this sort of camp—wasn't just happening to him alone, in some foreign land. If Yaa was experiencing this, and she came from where he came from—then *this,* whatever this was, might just be okay.

After breakfast, we wandered over to a long table where we were encouraged to create name tags for ourselves that included our PGPs—preferred gender pronouns. "Jodie Patterson, She/Her." "Joseph Ghartey, He/Him." "Georgia Becker, She/Her." "Cassius Ghartey, He/Him." "Othello Ghartey, He/Him." "Penelope Ghartey, He/Him." On Penelope's name tag he drew a boy, presumably himself, smiling wide while riding on a green whale. All around him were floating stars.

Most families sign up for trans camp because they want space to be themselves. For trans kids and their families, lives can get derailed by what they can't do: which bathroom they can't use, which bathing suit they can't wear, which team they can't play on, which gender they can't claim. And when they do announce themselves—"I am a trans boy" or "We are a trans family"—they're often treated suspiciously, gingerly. Trans families don't get to be heuristic—making mistakes, learning through trial and error, and eventually finding their way, all without judgment. And trans kids don't get to just be kids—regular, goofy, funny, quiet, amazing kids—without the extra layer of suspicion. But at camp, in this land, among this tribe, kids and their families are free to do as they please. Quiet or loud, extrovert or introvert, grumpy or joyful—in these woods, we can simply be.

Penelope couldn't get away from us fast enough. He'd somehow managed to meet three new friends and get his hands on the activity schedule all before ten o'clock. With his siblings close behind him, I watched Penelope turn around and wave "'Bye, Mom!" before being absorbed into the mass of kids making their way to the gaga ball pit.

I waved back, half-turning to Joe with one eyebrow raised in surprise, and then the two of us made our way over to the center of the room where the adults were gathering. While the kids played and explored, the parents discussed. We split off into small groups and began the work of laying out ideas, sharing hopes, and articulating worries. We sat in circles. We talked in calm voices. We paused for reflection. The process felt very familiar—it reminded me of the meditation group Mama used to take me to in the West Village.

We began, as we often do in spaces like these, with self-introductions:

"Hi. I'm Jodie. I identify as she/her. I'm a mother of five, four of whom are here at camp. Joe's my husband and he's here with me." Joe waved, flashing that smile that got me every time.

"Penelope is our third child and he's a trans boy." My voice cracked. I hadn't even said anything emotional yet, but already my eyes were brimming with tears. "Sorry, I'm nervous. This is our first time around so many trans families. It's kind of amazing."

Throughout our first session, Joe stayed pretty quiet as people talked, outlining their anxieties and fears. Most of the people there were parents, but there were grandparents, aunts, and uncles in the circle, too. Some were quiet, some were outspoken. Some were bankers, others were artists. Some were brown, like us—but most were not. There were even a few trans parents among us.

What was surprising was the variety of men in the circle—there were so many types of men there, so many examples of what it was like to be a father. The men were noticeably a bit quieter, a bit more reserved than most of the women in the room. They may have raised their hands fewer times, or were less assertive in these conversations, but in their own way, the men were engaged. In their own way, they were making their way on the journey, just like Joe.

We put everything out on the table during the sessions, moving words and ideas around. We were having tough conversations that would rattle the infrastructure of any relationship—talk of the body, of gender, of the "labels" that so troubled us. We talked about doctors and procedures, about the future. About things Joe and I had been battling over for years. But there in that space, those things were expected to be discussed—discussed as if they were a right, a must, a necessity.

I glanced over at Joe to see how he was doing, to reassure him we were in this together, but he was leaning forward in his chair, already all the way dialed in.

Then, when it was his turn to speak, he talked to the group about fathers. How they are often the last ones to understand and the slowest to transition. How they aren't the ones to make emotional revelations early on, or to process what was happening around them at the same pace as others in the family. As he was talking, I rifled back through our history—how frustrated I was with him when he insisted on calling Penelope his "plumpkin" and his "princess," long after Penelope expressed dislike for the nicknames. How much I quietly seethed when Joe kept pushing back on me, insisting that we take things slow and not look too deep into what was going on with our kid. How afterward, when Penelope announced himself as boy, Joe told me, over and over, that maybe we should let this whole thing play out without rushing into *doing*. So often, Joe met my urgency with stillness—with "Let's just let Penelope be." So often, I took that sense of calm, that practicality, as a betrayal of Penelope—and of me.

"Dads just experience things in a different way," he continued, looking out at the faces in the room, relaxed in his chair as he said the words. "And what's unfair is that we're made to feel wrong for that. But our way, the Dad way, has value. We need to be able to articulate what we bring. And own it—and be respected for it."

We'd debated and discussed—and outright warred—over

our parenting styles millions of times before. But when he said it this way—in an open forum filled with other dads who nodded in approval, clearly recognizing themselves in Joe—I felt humbled; opened and softer in some way. Maybe he hadn't been working against me all this time. Maybe what I'd been watching over the years was not a man in protest of change but a man processing all the inevitable shifts happening around him. Joe was trying, just as I was. Trying to make sense of something that was hard and complicated, and to proceed with a plan that reflected all his love.

"I'm here to learn how to support Penelope in my own way," Joe announced to the group—and to me. "In the Dad way."

In those small groups, Joe communicated in a way he never could with me. He could talk freely about not wanting to label his kid, not wanting to put Penelope in yet another box. Not wanting any limits set on his family. There, he found understanding, eyes that connected with his while he spoke honestly and emotionally. He could let his guard down and express himself openly, not defensively as we had done too many times in the past.

When Joe finished speaking, the room was silent. After a while, a woman whose name tag read "Candace, She/Her" broke the silence: "I'd sure like to borrow your husband for a day—if that's okay with you, Jodie!" We all laughed, and I looked at Joe with more pride in my heart than I'd felt in a long while, my eyes welling with tears again.

The feeling that there were others out there going through what Joe and I were going through relieved some of the tension between us. That tension, I now understood, had been eating away at our intimacy. It had been one more thing sitting between us each night—a disruptive element in our already fragile love. A love that was tested with every additional experience we continued to throw into our bubbling, heady mix of kids and careers, ambition and growth.

Any moment when two people are on the same page, enjoying the same thing, is a special moment. It can happen anywhere—while you're at home together making a slow-cooked stew, or watching the sun go down over the ocean—these rare, spontaneous times mean everything. They are the reason you stay, the impetus to admit "I was wrong." They are the pull of love. I was always searching for those moments with Joe. And that day, there in the circle at trans camp, the moment found us.

When I suggest something new for my family or friends to try, I often wonder if I'm pushing too hard—if it's more about me than them. I am the pusher of the family—foisting travel, or beliefs, or attitudes, or mantras onto my loved ones that they often meet, even on good days, with annoyance—or, on bad days, with disdain.

At camp, I was just hoping for the best. I wanted the kids, at the end of the day, to have a chance to recalibrate their sense of normal. I wanted Joe and me to unite—to take the walls down so we could approach this new world together, with optimism. And for Penelope, of course, I dreamed for him—always—to feel whole, body and soul. I saw a glimpse into that kind of future for him that summer.

On the last day of camp, Joe and I attended a panel called Growing Up Trans, featuring a boy named Wes. We sat in the back row listening intently as he commanded the stage. At nineteen years old, Wes seemed not only to have survived puberty but to be glowing in the aftermath. At one point during the discussion, someone in the audience asked if he'd ever considered gender reassignment surgery. After a pause, he said, "No. I'm not changing my body. I'm a boy. *This* is my body. So, *this* is a boy's body."

I was mesmerized. Up to that point, a small part of me feared that even with all the self-love and confidence I was pouring into Penelope, it might all be undone when his body began to go through puberty, its next biological chapter. For trans people, that transition can be a dark one, marked by anger and betrayal. As the body becomes more gendered, looking either more "male" or "female," it begins to announce to the world who it's "supposed" to be. At that exact time, many trans people can feel trapped in the wrong body.

In order to allow the child to have more time before making permanent, life-altering decisions about their body, puberty can be put on hold with the help of medicines called blockers. And then down the line, after much deliberation, if the child so decides, hormones can be injected, physical changes begin, and a dramatic reshaping of the body takes place. I thought that that was the only path for us. But here was a boy like Penelope who had opted out of the widely used solutions—hormones, then surgery—and declared himself complete as he was. Maybe Penelope could see it that way, too.

Driving back home the next day, we all had time to think. We now had a new reality to build on. Maybe we were still not all comfortable using the word "transgender." Perhaps that didn't fit precisely. But one word that did resonate with Joe and me over the weekend was "nonconformity." We were a nonconforming family. We would not conform. We would not be broken or bent or forced into any form other than our own natural shape—an ever-evolving shape. Every single one of us would remain free to define our own experience and our own existence as we saw fit. As man, woman, child—and anything in between.

We had seen the future in visuals, and the future looked good.

NINETEEN

The Lab

———

I'M PART DREAMER, YES—but I'm also part realist. I know how important it is for people to explore and imagine beyond what's directly in front of their eyes, but I also try to prepare my kids for the real world—the one in which people aren't gentle, kind, and accepting. I know all five of my children need to learn about the hard truths, those ugly realities that are almost too painful to utter. We tell those realities knowing they're hard, because they're crucial for people who look like us to hear. The fact that many people hate us is a reality we must swallow.

But it's tough to coach a kid to be defensive, especially when it's about who they are. I've always wanted my kids to be open and accepting, not closed off and ready for a fight. And I knew that for Penelope, that fight would be doubly hard. For him—and trans people like him—self-confidence is just half the battle. Every day he engaged with the outside world, he'd likely face people intent on poking holes in his truth. Or violently rejecting him altogether. I wasn't prepared to be the one to tell Penelope—or any of my kids for that matter—that some people on this earth hate other people based on the simple fact of their existence. People hated Penelope for being transgender; hated us for being Black; hated little Black boys who turn into Black men, for nothing less than the history they evoke. I couldn't deliver that blow to my children. What I wanted—needed—was to inform them without breaking them.

In the same way that resistance builds muscle, I wanted to make them stronger from the pressures of life. So, as we opened up the dialogue on big topics more and more within our immediate family, I decided to allow the kids—in the house only—to discuss their opinions completely uncensored. Doing so would allow us to thicken our skins, stockpile our defenses, and get us ready for the real world.

Our home became the laboratory for tough discussions—trans being at the top of the list.

"So, what does transgender mean to you?" I asked the boys one night before bed. It was not long after we returned from camp, and it seemed like a good time to work in a conversation around transgender to see how they were feeling, and where each of them stood. Sometimes I liked to throw out blunt, to-the-point questions in hopes that the kids would respond just as viscerally.

"Well . . . I don't believe in transgender," Cassius started. The strict, meticulous rule abider of the group, he reasoned that while he would always use male pronouns for Penelope, transgender was not scientifically proven. Penelope was still technically, biologically speaking, a girl. Female.

"I respect you, Penelope," he said from his top bunk, staring at the ceiling. "But you can't just change your gender." Hearing this, Penelope sat up, leaning on his elbow to get a better view of his brother. "It's not scientific, Cassius," he said with authority. "It's not an opinion, either. This is just how God made me."

"Well, I don't believe in God *or* transgender, Penelope. So, I'm sorry, but you've lost me on both points." Just like his dad, Cassius was always demanding proof.

Penelope, visibly annoyed, rolled his eyes. "You always have to be so sciencey, Cassius. It's not always about science."

Cassius retorted, in his usual unbothered tone, "*Life* is science. Everything, even you, Penelope, must make biological sense."

"Well, you know what I think, Mama?" Othello chimed in

from the bottom bunk, yawning, eyes nearly closed. "*I* believe in God. God is everywhere—even in my toe!"

Othello was a believer—in Penelope, in God, in the Tooth Fairy, in transgender. Belief, to him, meant hope, and endless possibilities.

That night, they continued for a few more minutes, respectfully bantering back and forth about those big topics—Gender, Religion, Belief—from underneath their cozy blankets adorned with stars, until sleep finally took over.

After our first night in what I liked to call the Lab, nothing became off-limits. We "labbed" about gender, race, God, science— even who got the window seats in our truck. Pinching, teasing, touching, sharing—every conflict, every fight on the basketball court—got handled in Lab format. Sometimes we sat so close together that our knees touched, sometimes we each took a corner of the room to get as much space from each other as we needed. But the core has always remained the same: We talk from our truth, we listen without interruption, and we speak from our heart, not our ego. These were my only rules.

My success rate at complying with these rules, particularly in the beginning, usually hovered around 75 percent. I remain guilty of talking over each and every person in our household on any given day to make my point. But I tried, with the Lab, to set a new standard. "Let him finish," I'd say if one kid tried to interrupt another, too excited to wait his turn. Then, before I could stop myself, I was often blurting out my own two cents, too excited to wait *my* turn. But the Lab wasn't about perfectly following the rules, it was about getting better with each try, practicing what we wanted to be. We were in a state of becoming, and in order to become, you have to do. If you don't do, you will never become. So I used the Lab as a way for all of us to become better thinkers, listeners, and lovers.

We would all do our best not to give in to knee-jerk reactions, or resort to yelling or drowning each other out—which was hard, because things do get heated with such polarizing topics. But I quickly found that sometimes the very things that we think divide us—those drastic and radical ideas—are exactly the points that end up pulling us together.

"Mom, if you don't get that Penelope is normal, you'll just be old and weird," Georgia said to me one day when she saw me stumbling over some point I was trying to make about transgender. She's always had a particular way with me, a bluntness that forces me to be accountable for everything I say I stand for. I have to prove my conviction, each step of the way, and course-correct whenever I'm being hypocritical. She holds up the most scrutinizing mirror, and I see things I've never thought to look at.

For Georgia, trans has never been a big deal. She was processing Penelope as trans at a time when she was coming into her adolescence, trying to investigate her own body—and her own identity. During the rare occasions when Georgia wasn't shutting me down, or retreating into teenagerdom, I got glimpses of who she was becoming—the ideas she was starting to grapple with as she was navigating her way through her changing self. As I did when I was her age, Georgia was trying to suss out her place in the family, in society, among her peers, in relationship to boys. She was figuring out how she felt about belonging to multiple races (Black, white, and Asian), and how she might set about navigating the social nuances of growing up in New York City—the center of the center of the world.

Sometimes we embark on those introspective journeys out of necessity, because, like Penelope, we experience a clear friction between who we are and who we're "supposed" to be. But sometimes we do it simply because we're curious to see what's on the other side. Georgia has always been curious. She wants to know how, why, and what if—and she wants to understand those things in a tactile way. It's always been Georgia's mission to leave no stone unturned, she wants to question it all. For her, nothing is assumed.

It was Penelope who sparked a conversation in Georgia's mind, an internal dialogue about identity: Who are we allowed to be? Who are we not allowed to be? Watching Penelope unfold gave Georgia time to marinate all these questions that were forming within her, without the spotlight being on her. She could privately test the waters and see where she might arrive.

I think people look first to see if obvious, visible diversity is present, and then, depending on how it's received, they decide if they want to reveal their own form of variety. If we don't see those visible differences, we aren't as comfortable announcing our own less obvious nuances. With Penelope, Georgia got a little comfort knowing that her parents—even when they weren't totally on the same page—were at least willing to explore identity without judgment. When she'd see me changing my language to match Penelope's reality, using "he" instead of "she," Georgia would smile at me from across a room. *Good job, Mama,* she was telling me with her eyes. Georgia wanted us all to be better.

Her words about my latest Penelope fumble nagged at me that day. *Old and weird?* Perhaps I'd been missing the point altogether, overemphasizing Penelope's nuances as a trans person simply because of my age. My blinders, my generational presumptions around differences being important stood out to Georgia as awkward and unnecessary. And perhaps they did need to be relegated to "no big deal." But, I told her, "Until lives are no longer at stake, Georgia, and liberties are no longer

being denied, those nuances matter." She nodded, getting it—
then flashed me a smile and raised a clenched fist in solidarity as
she walked out of the room. Politically, Georgia understood
where I was coming from, but she was clearly less agitated by it
all.

There was a whole generation coming up under me whose
definition of "normal" cast a far wider net than that of the generations before. In fact, they eliminated the net completely;
Georgia was proof of that. The things my generation were still
stuck on—gender, identity, sexuality, race—Georgia's generation was chopping up, flipping around, slicing and dicing in an
infinite number of ways.

Penelope spoke to Georgia in a very personal way. He was, I
think, a beacon for what was possible for her: a self far beyond
boundaries.

"Pleppy! You have to come see this photo!" Georgia yelled
from the living room couch one day, photo albums spread all
around her. We've all thought it ironic that Georgia and Penelope favor each other so intensely. Neither of their dads has any
golden-hued features, yet Penelope and Georgia share the same
golden skin, light brown curls that go almost blond in the summertime, eyebrows that fade into their skin tone, and lovely,
kind faces.

Penelope ran over to Georgia, plopping himself down on the
couch next to his big sister. "Guess who this cutie-pie is?"
Georgia held up a photo of a chubby, smiling toddler wearing a
pink swimsuit.

"That's me!" Penelope grinned with delight.

"Nope, it's me when I was young. We're twins! You're the
boy version of me."

Georgia always found a special connection between herself
and her siblings. With Cassius it was intellect—she'd sit with
him for hours in his bedroom reasoning with him, talking him

out of being angry with me for something I'd done, always using logic to get her point across, never frustration. With Othello, Georgia found rhythm—they'd stand in front of our living room mirror while she taught him whatever dance was trending with her friends. Always, he'd master the move in five minutes flat. "Ooooo, get it, Othello! Get it!" she'd cheer him on, taking videos of him on her phone.

"I thought that was meeee!" Penelope flipped through picture after picture, blissfully unable to distinguish between himself and his big sister. Penelope looked up to Georgia, and resembling her was a huge compliment. I loved how it didn't matter to either of them that one is a girl and the other is a boy. All they see is their love, and their aura.

They continued looking at old pictures of Penelope in pink dresses and Georgia in plastic dress-up high heels, exclaiming, "Look how Mama used to dress us! We're so cute!" Georgia never once made the images of Penelope in a dress seem shameful or awkward, she praised each one just the same. I could see what Georgia was doing—she was helping to establish Penelope's total and complete self-acceptance, despite the silly clothing that Mama might have draped over him once upon a time. She placed the mistake on me—"Silly Mama!" she'd say—and then keep all the glory for themselves: "We're so good-looking, Penelope."

Cassius's main line of argument whenever it came to the transgender conversation was that *believing* in something does not make it true: "If you can't calculate it or measure it, it can't be real."

I often got lost in metaphysical discussions with Cash. He's two grades ahead of his age and eats three-hundred-page books for breakfast. Cassius wants to know the chemistry and the makeup of this life. He craves to understand the mystery of existence by examining its elements—the molecules and particles, life's true essence. He takes pride in knowing the size of the earth, the heat of a shooting star, the density of lava, and the combustion point of liquid nitrogen. Things that don't even register to me. He teaches me to examine, to probe and consider the details.

"Do you know that the air around a lightning bolt is hotter than the surface of the sun? Do you know that if antimatter and normal matter collide there will be a gargantuan explosion?" Cassius will follow me around the house all day—and anyone else who happens to be around—asking us questions he knows we don't know the answers to, just so he can bring us up to speed.

That intellectual appetite keeps him really inquisitive, which is a good thing, but it also makes him deeply analytical—to the point where he leaves little room for gray area. Cassius takes after his mama: He likes to be in control. The idea of having someone else's ideas dictating or informing what he believes is a no-go for him. He'd rather come to his own conclusions, through his own experiments. I wouldn't be a bit surprised if he actually does believe in God and transgender, but he'll never admit it—not if he feels cornered, or pressured to conform.

But my heart hurts for Cassius when he tells me he doesn't believe in immeasurable things. "Some things *can't* be proven, not scientifically at least," I remind him. Because more powerful than quantifiable proof is the notion that even without concrete confirmation, things *do* exist—some of the best, most awesome things. Powerful, soul-defining unexplainable things, like love. I'm past the point of wanting more things, to fill up more closets and drawers. If I want for anything, it would be more love.

Unfortunately, we can't *tell* people about love, they have to feel it—even if briefly. Only then does it become real. And only then will they seek it out for the rest of their lives. I've witnessed the reality of love and how it pulls us toward each other, day after day. Forcing us to believe blindly, making us pour our faith into one another. Without knowing exactly where we'll end up, we follow.

Although Cassius thinks practically and logically, making it hard for him to believe in things like God or transgender, I'm seeing something else emerging in him, something surprising. He, more than any of the other kids, loves teddy bears. He sleeps with five in his bed at night, closely snuggled up to them. And in the morning before he leaves for school, he wraps them in blankets so they won't be alone and scared. I quietly watch as he talks to his bears—about his seven-year-old problems, I imagine—and then the expression on his face when they respond. I love that he's having a relationship that doesn't quite make sense.

After watching this for several weeks, one day while sitting in the living room I approached him. "Cassius, do you still not believe in God?"

"No, Mom. I don't."

I paused for a couple of beats, poker-faced. "Well, I've noticed you talking to your bears lately. Do they answer you?" His expression changed to an "I-know-what-you're-about-to-say" look. I smiled. Cassius is smart and could tell what kind of conversation I was steering him toward. One about belief, and the importance of the intangible.

"Yes, Mom, we communicate," he says, leaving it at that. I try not to hit him over the head with the point I'm making. "That's interesting," I say, smiling, "that you and your teddy bears . . . communicate." I shoot him a wink, so he knows I'm on his side.

After that, I started buying Cassius more teddy bears in a variety of sizes so he could travel with them, and he smiled with pure, undisguised happiness every time I brought a new one home. When he thinks no one is looking, even more snuggling takes place with his teddies—and he's cuter than ever before. "Cute" was never a word that I typically used for Cassius. Smart, presidential, exact, but not "cute." But now, I'm starting to see his cuteness overflowing.

Going forward, I remind myself that Cassius, our realist, our scientist, the one who's skipped two grades and sits at the dinner table with a compound microscope next to him, is also a fantasist and a dreamer. He has the ability and the desire to step outside that straightforward reality and go into the other world, the one of teddy bears, and perhaps one day, even God.

It was this kind of boundary pushing that I appreciated seeing and the type of work I was always practicing with my kids—in the Lab and outside it. Erasing the lines of our limitations, redrawing the parameters of what's possible, expanding our definition of normal. Whether it was Georgia telling me I was "old and weird" for not getting it, or Othello finding faith in every inch of his body, growth within these tough conversations always required one fundamental skill: mental flexibility— the ability to see and work through things from alternate perspectives.

With Nain, the sibling connection was and always will be about invisible bonds. The kids' early vocabulary around family has always been rooted in love, not biology—in embracing the multiple ties that bind us. Nain has loved Penelope wholly from the very first day they met. Penelope was calling Nain "brother" before I started calling him "son." And that clarity of love enabled them to move with each other wherever and however they were. Nain never once missed a beat when it came to thinking of Penelope as his brother instead of his sister. For Nain, transgender has always been just vocabulary, semantics. And honestly, the two of them seem to live outside language anyway—cracking up on the couch over some joke I can't even understand, using barely decipherable slang: "Buckets, Penel! I get buckets! All day, errr day"—whatever that means.

All my kids have nicknames—Georgia the Wise Soul; Cassius the President; Othello the Rascal; Nain the Gift. And Penelope is the Rock Star. He's the bandleader, the one who's center stage and believes in himself more than anyone else. He's the kid who can't help but insert himself, announce himself, finessing his way into being seen. I often catch him in the living room perfecting the flick of his wrist in a jump shot, and then practicing the look of satisfaction on his face when the ball swooshes in. Honing flair down to the smallest movements—the eyebrows, the shoulders, the subtle gestures with his hands. And Nain is a bit of a peacock himself—struttin', stuntin', ballin'. Always in search of the next and the new. Together, they make a perfect pair.

Nain likes to practice skateboarding with Penelope, and eventually taught him to "skate goofy." One day, hovering at the top of our brownstone stoop, I overheard the two cohorts in action. "Yo! You gotta skate goofy-style, Penel!"

"What's goofy?" Penel inquired, his eyes huge.

"It's when you do it like this"—and Nain jumped onto his board in the most counterintuitive way—with his left foot at the back of the board instead of at the front, like skating backward. He skated off down the length of the block, gracefully weaving in and out of pedestrians—often just missing them. Penelope exploded down the street toward his brother, abandoning his board. "Yo, Nain! You gotta teach me to skate goofy!"

This idea of doing it differently is like water to a dehydrated body for Penelope, invigorating him. Penelope wants to throw a curve ball, he wants to ride goofy—he wants to stunt, to strut, to ball out. And he responded to all that in his older brother Nain. Because Nain is a rock star, too—the kind of person who

Nain, with his sidekick Othello, and his ever-present skateboard, keeps us "wavy."

lives his life against the grain, and who wants to draw you in so deep that you'll never let him go.

Nain knows things his younger brothers don't—about basketball and music, about life. For the kids, he is, as Cassius recently said, "the coolest adult I know." A kid with extra knowledge, a man-child who found his way into our "we."

In my family, I was constantly learning that you can be right, or you can be with the ones you love. We are a sorted bunch, each of us with a different take on the world. None of us comes to the table with the exact same set of experiences, opinions, or beliefs. But I actually think that's a good thing. I'd rather be a house of many minds—united by our differences and strengthened by our love.

Because the truth is that, at its heart, that's what the Lab is all about: love. It's breaking things apart and moving things around in order to see the people we care about more vividly. Together, as a family, we were learning to unpack big concepts, laying truths on the table and exploring them with honesty, dignity, and respect. The laboratory we were developing was about the art of debating, discussing, and disagreeing without getting rattled. The goal was simply to love each other more.

Even with all of our nuances—Cassius insisting on reason, Othello being all believing, Joe moving slower, me moving faster, Georgia and Nain being the champions—we always, ultimately, relied on our fierce, invisible bonds to move us forward: Toward truth. Toward freedom. And always, toward love.

Stars,

I believe in you. I see you. Try your best each day to find joy in the little things . . . these happinesses will sustain you through life. There is no need to know everything, but you must find the few things you care to know a little something about. Listen. Speak. Do. Love.

xx Mama

TWENTY

Passing

WHEN IT CAME TO PENELOPE'S IDENTITY, Joe and I never considered our family "stealth." The idea of being covert or anonymous never sat easily with us. It reminded me of "passing," a term birthed during slavery and practiced throughout Jim Crow that refers to Black people who chose to live as white without the restrictions, dangers, and threats specific to Black lives.

People who passed were those born racially ambiguous—straight hair, narrow noses, light skin. In short, they could pretend to be white, and thus could claim life, liberty, and justice as white people did. They passed for survival: as a way to gain the jobs, housing, and education Black people were repeatedly denied—and to avoid being killed, beaten, and raped, as Black folks so often were during those times. But in exchange they were forced to turn their backs on their families, friends, and customs. Those who passed took on new identities and new languages, intermingled their DNA with that of new people—white people—and disappeared quietly into the white world, often never to be seen again.

In contrast, my family had always historically chosen to be seen, even those light enough to live quietly, unobtrusively as a white person. My grandmother Gloria marched for our civil rights and was a major leader in the movement. She and my mother and Aunt Lurma marched and sat in jails and then marched again, never stopping until the injustices were dealt with. My father walked into spaces that were forbidden to him, standing next to people bent on showing him that he didn't belong. He was notorious for not giving a damn—often strolling into our posh apartment building straight from a tennis match, sweaty and confident, showing way more Black skin in his Arthur Ashe attire than any of those white folks were comfortable seeing. He made himself known and respected, on his own terms.

Joe and I likened the civil rights work our parents' and grandparents' generations did to what we were doing with gender equality now. More and more, we were talking openly about transgender with our friends and colleagues, even when they were too busy to care but politely listened anyway.

Within the safe environments that we created, it was true, we freely called ourselves a trans family. We wore the title like a badge of honor. But outside those safe zones—of school, of camp, at home—were spaces I knew I could never control, and situations that no amount of labbing it out could prepare us for.

Politically, I'd long resolved to hide nothing about Penelope. I couldn't bear the idea of us passing as a "normal" family, or Penelope getting over as a "real" boy. I spent decades trying to be invisible, hiding behind my dynamic family, strong-willed men, domineering bosses. And now, as a grown woman in my forties, I had no desire to hide or blend in anymore. I'd worked too hard to be seen—we all had.

But fear can be a powerful adversary. No matter how much revolutionary blood runs through your veins or how much pride you have, one very scary interaction, one face-to-face with strangers who hold your freedom in their hands, can dial down even the most rebellious among us. For me, all it took was one weekend, while traveling across borders with my family, to instantly remind me just how intimidating being seen can actually be.

We were taking a trip to Canada with Penelope, Cassius, and Othello. Joe's cousin was getting married, and I saw it as a good excuse to road trip together. I'd been pushing for some family time, and this seemed like the perfect event. Joe and I had been struggling during the months leading up to the trip, sleeping in separate rooms, arguing over our familiar list of disagreements: control, power, intimacy. I saw the trip as a salve. We'd be together for hours on the open road, blasting our favorite radio hits, laughing, and exploring.

Joe drove for most of the hours between Brooklyn and Canada, and after what seemed like days in the car with rambunctious boys emitting the distinct smell of potato chips and sweat, we approached the surprisingly short line of cars at the border checkpoint. While we moved along in the queue, Joe looked over to me and anxiously asked me to "prepare" all the passports.

"Not much to prepare, babe, they're in my bag. Literally all of one second to grab them," I said, opening my purse wide so he could see inside.

But I could tell Joe was tightening up. He got this way whenever he faced authority—police officers in particular. I expect it has something to do with having his head pressed into the cement by an overexcited Boston police officer's knee during an altercation outside a diner when he was in his early twenties. Since then, Joe has preferred to head in the opposite direction whenever police came around.

When we got to the front of the line and pulled up alongside the border patrol booth, I handed the five passports over to Joe, and Joe then handed them over to the officer inside. We watched as the man examined our pictures, one at a time, looking back into the car at our faces to verify what he saw in our passport books. The officer looked into the driver's window, slowly sliding his eyes over Joe and me. Then his eyes moved back to the passenger window, scanning Penelope, Othello, and Cassius in the backseat. The man looked at the passports, moving his eyes across all three boys' documents again, then looked once more at them in the backseat, eyeing the boys more slowly this time. He motioned for us to roll down the back window.

"Who is Penelope?"

Penelope politely raised his hand. The officer looked at Penelope's passport for the third time, silently determining whether this child—the one sporting a Mohawk, basketball shorts, and a T-shirt—was the same "Penelope Ghartey, Sex: F" who was identified in the passport book we'd just given him. (Although we'd talked about officially changing Penelope's gender on the document, it was a long and involved process, and we just hadn't gotten around to it yet.)

I could see the man in the booth observing Penelope, looking him up and down, questioning him with his eyes. And while he did this, I had a visceral urge to leap into the backseat and cover Penelope's body with my own so that the officer could not see, touch, or smell my little boy. I didn't want him to have any access to my kid—I wanted him gone. Fighting the urge to scream obscenities at the man, I reached over the seat and held Penelope's hand tight.

"You'll need to pull your car over to the left, park in the lot, and come inside with me."

We spent the next two hours in a very official-looking waiting room, unaware of exactly what was going on—but quite sure that *something* was. The officer disappeared behind a door with our identities, and all we could do was wait for him to come back and tell us what he had sorted out. While we panicked inside, the kids carried on unaware—absorbed in their gadgets and books, assuming that nothing about this disruption was out of the ordinary. Eventually, Joe and I were called to the counter and asked a series of questions: *Where are you going? Are these your children? How old are you?* We rattled off the answers, and then they asked about Penelope. We responded instinctively, protection mode kicking in:

"Yes, that's our daughter. Yes, she is six."

Our answers felt like a betrayal of what we knew to be true, of how we'd been living over the last several years. Using "she" felt shameful, because Joe and I knew better. But in the tension that filled that moment, we felt safer behind those two words—"she" and "her." As proud of our son as we were, in the seconds when being seen directly conflicted with our being safe—when the fear took over—I no longer wanted to fight for Penelope's right to be a boy. I just wanted anonymity.

Travel has been something I've taken for granted since I was a child. I've traveled all over America and throughout Europe, the Caribbean, and Africa, hopping on planes and crossing borders without a second thought. Without complication, suspicion, or delay, I've moved around the world freely, wherever and whenever I've desired.

And then this moment happened to us—our family marked as suspicious, our freedom to move delayed. I knew we would eventually be released, but I couldn't help thinking about the mental annihilation it would cause Penelope if he, too, were forced to answer questions about himself, his gender—and maybe even his body—by strangers in uniforms. I knew we hadn't broken any laws—that's not what scared me in those moments. It was more the terrifying thought of Joe and me being stripped of our authority in front of our children—no longer free to take our kids on the family trip we'd planned months back, forced to turn around and head back to Brooklyn. On top of all that, the crushing fear that Penelope would think he had been the cause of all this chaos.

This experience was a warning: Freedom can be revoked just like *that* by people imbued with the authority to act based on who they think you are—and who they're convinced you're not. In a few quick, frightening seconds, one's freedom can be taken—just snatched away like a dollar found on the street.

Quietly in our hotel room that night, Joe and I began processing all that had happened at the border.

"I don't know, babe, I was so mad at the officer for staring at Pleppy like that. I mean . . . I literally wanted to bite his head off."

I stood in front of the tiny closet in our hotel, trying to sort out the boys' clothing for tomorrow's activities while the three of them slept in the bed next to ours. Exhausted from the drive, they had conked out early. I smiled at how cozy they all looked, our three little lion cubs, curled around and over one another for comfort.

"Yeah, I hear you. It was the way he was looking at him that worried me, like he was going to *do* something . . ." Joe's voice trailed off. "I don't know what, but something . . ."

I looked over at Joe sitting on the corner of the other bed, next to the boys, and then at our bed, where he and I would be sleeping. It would be the first time in a while that we would lie together. I hung up the shirt I was holding and moved closer to where he sat, wiggling myself in between his legs and placing my hands on his shoulders. From that vantage point, looking down on his face, I could tell just how worried he was. I ran my fingers through his hair, noting the few gray hairs and the thinning patch in the center—both relatively new appearances. He wrapped his arms around my legs.

"Honestly, Joe-Joe, I'm also furious with myself for not changing Penelope's gender marker on that damn passport months ago, like we talked about. We've really got to take care of that—like yesterday." My voice sounded only halfway committed to the daunting idea of walking into the passport office and saying "Gender marker change, please."

"As soon as we get back home we can start that process. But for now let's use a different name for him in public. Something that sounds more boyish." He looked over at Penelope, then up at me. "Maybe something like Li'l Joe, or Joe Junior, or Joe-Joe!" I burst out laughing at the suggestion.

"What's so funny?" Joe could barely keep a straight face himself. "It's obvious he looks up to me. He'd be proud to take my name!"

"Maybe pull back on the vanity—just a tad bit," I teased. "I mean, I love your name—for *you*. But Joe-Joe for Penelope?"

Face-to-face, body to body, and with an intentional lightness we'd forced upon the situation, trying our best to strip it of its ugliness, we decided together that in public Penelope would be called Penel or P—nicknames we'd always lovingly called him over the last years—to attract less attention. It would give us the layers of protection we needed, some armor to buffer us from the interrogating eyes and the unwanted scrutiny.

The next morning, we didn't share with Penelope anything about our conversation; it would be our covert action to move seamlessly toward a little more discretion when the situation called for it.

"Good morning, Othello. Good morning, Cassius. Good morning, P! Who's up for a little boat ride through Niagara Falls?" It was as simple as that.

But even as Joe and I were devising our plan, deep down I knew that we were only buying time. The hatred and confusion, the judgment, the questioning, they would never go away. We knew that a buffer would never be enough.

We had not been entirely successful, had not found the right balance between safety and progress, between off-radar and unequivocal freedom. And perhaps we never would. The border situation was behind us, but it wasn't at all, not in the least, resolved.

TWENTY-ONE

A Boy Named Penelope

WE NAVIGATE OUR WAY through the casino maze: past the smokers and slot machine players, the blackjack and roulette tables. It's eight o'clock on a Saturday morning and we're at Atlantic City's Tropicana Casino & Resort: Joe, Penelope, Cassius, Othello, and me. The Tropicana is a vision of seedy opulence, all winding staircases, beveled mirrors, and heavy gold chandeliers. Waxy palm trees line the hotel lobby and are plunked down sporadically throughout the casino interior, their leaves rustling gently in the air conditioner breeze. With the hotel's salmon-colored tiling and soft white walls, it's as if New Jersey's own Old Havana has been resurrected right here on the boardwalk, minus any of the original's charm.

Clearly, we're not in Brooklyn anymore. Looking around, we appear to be the only Black trans family on earth.

We're here for Penelope's first big karate tournament, the War on the Shore, an annual event that draws crowds in the hundreds, from as far away as Japan. For months, Penelope and his teammates have been preparing for this day. They've spent hours practicing in front of the dojo's one long mirror, while their teacher, Master Bill, weaves between them, making corrections. This is Penelope's big opportunity to showcase his skills beyond our New York safe zone—beyond our carefully cultivated community in Brooklyn. Here, Penelope will be given his first taste of competition on the Outside, with the threat of an unfamiliar opponent—body to body, skill to skill.

• • •

Penelope was barely five years old when we first enrolled him in Master Bill's class. He'd been struggling to see himself in the body he had been given, his frustrations coming out in wild spits and spurts. At home, he tore through each room—slicing at the air and kicking his legs in front of our living room mirror, wrestling his brothers to the ground, unloading his wrath on our couch cushions, and karate-chopping everything and everyone around him, in imitation of the superheroes he admired in the movies. It quickly became apparent that all that energy needed to be redirected somewhere, and I thought formal martial arts training might be the outlet.

My sister and I grew up around karate. Back in the 1970s, our dad frequented a dojo on the second floor of a rickety walk-up building on Broadway, and we often spent afternoons there. Daddy was always taking us places that felt different from our mostly white Upper West Side neighborhood, and the dojo was one of those places. Populated with older Black guys in their forties and fifties like my dad, the men of the dojo embodied the distinctly seventies swagger of Shaft. My sister and I were the only kids—and the only girls—in the place. In my memory, the guys kicking and flying through the air, doing flips and rolls, looked like superheroes.

Dad would teach us the moves he'd learned at the dojo at home, too. The stances, the positioning of our feet. He said he was trying to show us how to find the importance and purpose of our bodies, making them into our greatest weapons of confidence. He'd always strongly believed that you have to train your mental energy in the same way you train your physical energy— the two went hand in hand. Daddy was someone filled with fire and anger at all times, but in all of his fury, he was also aware of the need to force the anger out, knowing if he didn't, it would likely implode. So he channeled that energy into sports, trying to shake loose his daily frustrations. Recognizing similar unrest in Penelope, I thought karate could be a release for him, too.

During his first few months at Master Bill's dojo, Penelope didn't say much. This wasn't like him—at home, he was rarely quiet, never able to help himself from jumping into everyone else's conversations. But as soon as he stepped into the dojo, he became very still, his eyes wide open in observation. He was deferential to the entire environment, to Master Bill's demands, to other kids' seniority. Most of the other students—a mix of about fifteen boys and girls, primarily from the neighborhood—had known one another for at least a few years already. They were a well-formed pack. Penelope was the new kid, the disrupter. He had a rough beginning, often struggling to find his place in the group and to grasp the instructions given to him.

Fortunately, Master Bill—a tall, bald Black man, shockingly in shape at the age of seventy something—was nurturing. He knew that the best route to improvement involved feeling good about yourself, even as you were working through your challenges, and he made sure that that philosophy was felt by his students. In a lot of ways, Master Bill reminded me of the guys at my dad's dojo all those years back. He was an old-school New York cat—worldly but firmly rooted in his culture. And having been immersed in the practice of martial arts and Buddhism since the 1960s, he knew how to impart vital lessons to his students.

"There are no advanced moves on the mat, or in life, kids," he would tell the class, slowly pacing in front of them. "There are just different formations of the basics. The basics are all you need."

Each class began with five minutes of silent meditation. It was Master Bill who first told Penelope that the body is controlled by the mind. And that the only limitations on his capabilities were the ones he placed on himself. For Penelope—for all the kids—Master Bill was a living, breathing wise man. At the same time, he was a teacher who took no pity on you if you were, say, five years old and still trying to distinguish between your right and left. "I said *left* foot, P! *Left* foot! Your *other* left!"

With tears often streaming down his face, Penelope pushed and stumbled through the moves, frustrated but undeterred. After particularly hard days, during the car rides home I'd tell him an aphorism I often repeated to all the kids: "Winners are losers who got back up." We all go down at some point—him, me, even Oprah—but only winners have the resolve to keep trying. I made Penelope repeat the mantra back to me so loudly during these drives that by the time we got home we'd both be laughing.

Penelope began to approach his time at the dojo less like an after-school activity and more like an apprenticeship. When he was there, he was focused. On the mat, he was fierce. In time, Penelope got control of his limbs. He learned the contours of his movements, the far reaches of his strength. He was finally figuring out how to see his body as his ally.

The dojo was good for Penelope. Boys and girls were challenged equally. Everyone was expected to fall, fail, and then get back up again. Like everyone else, Penelope was rewarded when he'd earned it, reprimanded when he fell short of expectation. At home we were practicing embracing transgender—calling it by name, owning it, loving it—but in Master Bill's class, trans was beside the point. Everyone there knew Penelope only as a boy—not a trans boy, or a "boy who used to be a girl," but simply a boy. Unlike the other areas of his life—at home, at school—there, he was no longer "different." At the dojo, he could take his first steps as himself.

Penelope felt powerful and secure in the community he found in his teammates, and with Master Bill. This sense of security went relatively uninterrupted until about a year into Penelope's practice. That day, he was on the mat during an in-class practice spar, about to beat arguably the best boy in class. But before Penelope could win, the boy's mother, who was standing on the sidelines, angrily pointed her finger in his direction.

"That's a girl!" she shouted, loud enough for everyone in the dojo to hear.

Twenty pairs of eyes looked toward Penelope for further explanation. And I watched my son well up with tears. He was embarrassed—called out, by an adult no less, in a place he thought was safe. The class ended at its normal time but with a feeling of confusion. The children were frustrated that their favorite part of the class had been disrupted, and the adults were puzzled by the unexpected outburst. As everyone started packing up their things to leave, I walked over to the mother.

"I need you to remember that Penelope is a boy. That's it—it's not complicated. Just call him what he is."

Without indulging any of her protests, I walked away. Inside I was mad at myself for leaving loose ends. This woman helped out with admin work at the dojo, and she had seen the application I filled out years ago when we first signed up for class, on which I'd listed Penelope as a girl.

No one else made a big deal out of what happened, but I knew I needed to explain Penelope's situation to Master Bill in our own words. Joe and I agreed to send him the same letter I'd written to our family and to MACADEMY, announcing Penelope as a boy.

At the next class after I'd delivered the note, I was nervous. It filled me with anxiety to think about what rejection in that setting could mean for Penelope—who loved Master Bill and had come so far under his instruction. Before class began, I asked Master Bill if he'd read the letter. He took a moment to pull away from what he was doing, look at me, and simply say, "No problem." Then he carried on with the class as usual, treating Penelope as he had always done.

From that point forward, Master Bill never once stumbled over names or pronouns, as most people did (even me, still, sometimes). To him, "transgender" was irrelevant. Like Bishop, I believe he saw Penelope with his heart.

As the kids prepared for the Atlantic City tournament, they worked two hours a day, five days a week, perfecting their sparring techniques and improving their katas (a series of movements that, when done well, can be as elegant and graceful as ballet). Observing Penelope in class in the lead-up to the tournament, I could tell he wanted more than just a fun experience at the competition. This kid wanted to win. After each class, Penelope would come home and continue practicing in our living room while the rest of the family cheered him on. Some nights, Penelope even slept in his uniform.

During the last class before the tournament, the atmosphere at the dojo was subdued. This was the students' final opportunity to collect themselves together as a team and mentally gear up for what was to come. Once they arrived at the competition, everyone would be dispersed. There would be no time for handholding or coaching; the kids would be on their own. And so this was also Master Bill's moment to drill into his students the philosophy of the dojo one last time:

"When you fight on Saturday, I want you to remember that winning means nothing if you're not mindful. You are not trying to win—anyone can score points. You're there to showcase your art. And you will be in excellent form."

As we exited the dojo after practice, Master Bill pulled Penelope aside. "P—you ready for this?" Penelope nodded back, ready to win.

Driving up to the casino the next morning for the day's events, I'm antsy. I keep thinking: What if Penelope's crushed by a bigger, stronger boy? Someone who forces him to confront the fundamental difference between his own body and a body that perhaps has naturally stronger capabilities? I know all mothers want their kids' best to be good enough, that we feel a certain amount of anxiety when our child is placed in an arena of objective judgment. I also know that everyone wants to feel the satisfaction of a win. But when the success of winning is so intricately and deeply tied to your child's validity, as it is with Penelope, the weight of defeat hangs so much heavier. I hated to think about him experiencing the blow of such a personal denial.

On top of that, I'm having flashbacks to the outing incident in class the year before. I wanted to be sure a similar display wouldn't erupt while Penelope was competing. So, as we pulled up to the Tropicana, I turned to Penelope in the backseat and reminded him that, for today, we should probably stick to calling him P or Penel so we didn't confuse anyone.

"Because for most people, Penelope's a girl's name," Joe points out. "And since you're a boy . . ."

Penelope turned away from the window as if he was computing exactly what we were proposing.

"Okay, Mama," he said, turning back toward us. "If it makes *people* more comfortable, they can call me Jack." I knew the name well. Jack was a kid in one of Penelope's favorite television shows, *Kickin' It*. Jack is cool, good-looking, and the leader of the pack. He's also the best among his friends at karate. Penelope looked at me, sealing his statement with a wink. A wink! I couldn't help but laugh.

After five minutes of weaving our way through Tropicana's lobby, we finally arrived at the tournament check-in counter. The woman behind the table held a clipboard and a pencil, poised to mark off our names. The sight of her caused sheer panic inside me. I hadn't thought this out properly. I never anticipated the sign-in scenario. How had I registered Penelope? Had I listed his full name or just Penel? I couldn't recall. My mind racing, I tried to think of the best way to handle this so that Penel wasn't embarrassed. *Okay,* I thought. *Just try to peek at the names on the clipboard . . . upside down . . .*

"Hi! I'm Penelope Ghartey. G-H-A-R-T-E-Y." While I was stuck on strategy, Penelope had taken control. "I'm competing in sparring and katas." I shot a nervous glance at Joe.

"Umm, let's see . . . Yes, welcome, Penelope! You're all registered. Best of luck!" That was it. No dramatics, no confusion. I had never felt so much anxiety from a simple encounter in all my life, but apparently Penel was handling it just fine.

That seemed to be the theme of our interactions whenever we were out in public. I still walked the line between wanting Penel to be himself anywhere—everywhere—and at the same time being afraid of what might happen if he did. I didn't want any of my children to hedge their way through life. But with Penel, I found myself often padding his identity with a little extra protection.

We left the woman and followed the crowd of people, eventually pushing through two huge golden doors to enter the space where the War on the Shore was well under way. On one side of the room, aging martial arts superstars sign autographs in front of cardboard cutouts of themselves, promoting magic protein powders and breakthrough workout videos. On the other end, compact child warriors flip, kick, and *"kiya!"* while their overexcited mothers hover close by.

When we first arrived, without his teammates and Master Bill around, Penel looked a little lost. He spent his first half hour sitting crossed-legged on the floor in silence—eyes downcast and shoulders slumped. He refused to warm up and flatly rejected my attempts at a pep talk. But eventually, the Brooklyn dojo crew emerged into view, bringing with them a bit of New

York swag. Seeing them approaching, Penel immediately perked up. With his teammates by his side, he was ready. "Born ready!" as he and his brothers had been chanting for months.

Contestants participating in the competition range from six to sixteen—boys and girls, all grouped by age, not gender (thankfully). The areas of competition are katas, sparring, and weapons. Penel, in the seven-to-nine age group, will be competing in katas and sparring. Joe and I and the rest of our kids find a spot on the sidelines near Penelope's sight line, and as he takes to the floor for his first activity, I move a little closer to the edge of the mat.

Katas are up first. After asking the judges' permission to begin, Penel takes several steps back and drops into the horse stance: feet planted, legs spread wide and slightly bent, arms straight down by his sides. His fists are clenched, ready for what looks like combat. But then Penel loosens. His moves are fluid but intentional. And his focus is directed inward. He looks like a grown man who has been practicing tai chi on his lawn every morning for the last fifty years. He's strong and clean—and in my mind, transcendent. He's become the Buddhist expression of the "water in the wave," and like water inside a wave, there's no beginning or end to Penel's movements. It's beautiful to watch, and his scores at the end of the round are high.

Next comes sparring. Penel is up against a boy who is much bigger than he is. His size makes him look powerful—as though he could deliver heavy blows. I hold my breath as they move toward each other. The kid has at least a good two inches on Penel, and next to him Penelope looks like David meeting Goliath. They bow and circle each other, and within seconds Penel is hit. Goliath scores easy points by bopping him on the top of the head—a cheap shot. Penel manages to land a chin tap on the boy, but it's obvious that his current strategy isn't enough. He's several points down, sweaty, exhausted—and close to elimination. It's then that Master Bill yells "P!" from the sidelines. They make eye contact, and with only body language uttered between them, Penel nods, understanding. Goliath and Penel regroup and begin again. Penel is moving quickly now, hands high to protect himself, shifting from side to side. Then he starts shuffling his feet—one in front of the other so that his shoulders, hips—his entire body—are in constant motion. Switching directions, bobbing, weaving, swaying. Goliath doesn't know which way to look. Then Penel sees his opening, lunges back, and sends a front-snap kick to the kid's chest. He scores—and then scores and scores again. He wins.

Penel advances to the final round and is now face-to-face with a girl I've dubbed the Ninja, having observed her at the beginning of the day. She's clearly a force: While all the other kids goofed off with their teammates during downtime, the Ninja practiced her katas over and over again—without ever taking a break. Her moves were sharp, fast, and diabolical. I'd never seen a seven-year-old look so serious. For her, this tournament was not a game, either. I knew the Ninja stood between Penel and the gold medal.

Penel is in a zone. After his victory against Goliath, he is *amped*. With the headgear he's wearing, I can see only his eyes—and they are lit. They're speaking a language I learned from my dad. They're saying *I'm about to get mine*.

The round begins. Penel and the Ninja meet on the mat. They bow. Then Penel blasts out of the gate with a spray of chest blows, backing the Ninja halfway across the mat and out of bounds. They start again and Penel jumps from side to side, twisting his body left and right. Then—*whomp*—he lands a roundhouse sidekick to the Ninja's head, followed by another long series of chest blows. Dazed, the Ninja retreats, reconsidering her next move through angry tears. At this point, internally, I am in a state. *Penel could actually win this!* But on the outside, all I can manage to do is squeeze Joe's hand tighter. Penel dominates the next two rounds with fast punches and kicks. After that, there's nothing more the Ninja can do. As she walks off the mat in defeat, we all hear her frustrated yells.

After the match is over, Penel walks over to the Ninja and, showing good sportsmanship, gives her a shoulder pound. He knows what it feels like when it's just not your time. But this is Penel's time. He's won against all the boys and girls in his age group, and he takes the gold in both categories he competed in. He's beaten the biggest Goliath and the toughest Ninja. As our family gathers around the periphery of Penel's winner's circle, Joe and I radiate with pride. We are standing tall and smiling wide, clapping for Penel—and for ourselves. We know, deeply, how much it took to get us here.

When it's time for the medals to be awarded, all the contestants line up at the front of the mat. The officials announce our son's name over the loudspeakers. And when they do, they don't call him Jack. Or P. Or Penel. There, in front of a room full of strangers, he hears "Penelope Ghartey" amplified throughout the room. And then, beaming that broad smile he's had since birth, he steps forward to claim what is rightfully his.

Penelope has won not only the contest, but his own authority—and the right to his full name: Penelope Gloria Adjoa Patterson Ghartey. He's perfect in all ways. And in his moment of victory, I realize that no adjustments should ever be needed to make him more palatable to others. He's a boy named Penelope, and regardless of how confusing people might find that, or how contradictory it might sound, the world will have to take him as he is.

Penelope takes the gold!

TWENTY-TWO

The Loss and the Gain

I'VE INHERITED A LEGACY OF ACTIVISM. "If not me, then who?" was one of my grandmother's favorite responses whenever she was asked why such a nice, pretty lady chose to protest and advocate and be jailed time and time again. She was relentlessly visible in her activism, never thinking to hold her tongue even when she knew her life and the stability of her family might depend on it.

When Gloria's daughters, my aunt Lurma and my mom, came of age, they linked arm in arm and marched with their mother. Gloria was arrested more than twenty-five times; Lurma, an honor student, was jailed more than a dozen times before she turned thirteen, and my own mother, right before leaving to study at Bennett College, did her part, participating in sit-ins and marches, too. Marching was their rite of passage. Gloria recognized very deeply that a new world order—for her, and for her children—was one worth fighting for.

This was the responsibility left to me.

To make this world better, there is still so much left to do. And I want to do it in the most thoughtful way, in a way that makes my children proud of me and of their lineage, and that shows them, in real time, what the Patterson-Becker-Ghartey clan stands for. I want more than gold medals and pedestal visibility. What I want, really, is to change the paradigm.

To do that work, to blow wide open the current narrow definition of gender, I knew I had to do more than just recite numbers and repeat statistics. People don't feel in numbers; we're not moved by politics. We respond to stories. I know I do. It is watching Penelope, day in and day out, and being drawn to him, compelled by his narrative, that shifts my mind to a new way of thinking. The mind is malleable. We're hardwired to look for connections and similarities, and even oddities in our lives, and to shape and reshape stories around them, stories that make the world more united. Narratives over data points. Empathy over fear.

I recall an email conversation between Aunt Lurma and me, in which she offered perspective on what our family was up against if and when we were to speak out publicly on trans issues. She saw it similar to what her generation went through during the civil rights era. She knew that struggle firsthand—what was asked of them, what they endured, how they strategized, and the advancements they eventually won. Lurma helped me weigh out the complicated balance of progress versus hatred versus safety.

Me: A national magazine reached out to me. They're doing a feature on transgender and want to anchor the article with our family. What do you think?

Aunt Lurma: I don't know . . . If you believe Penelope won't shift to feminine—and that this is not a tomboy phase—and if you don't think the attention would be harmful for Penelope at this young age, then I guess allowing such an article would simply solidify your commitment to the cause. But there is so much hate and ignorance in the world, it might be better to wait for such media attention until she is a little older. It's like the question of how soon a child could go out on the picket line in the civil rights movement. Until age twelve, we had to stay in the church basement helping to make signs or serving up sandwiches and juice to the picketers when they came back to rest.

ME: That's the first explanation I can actually understand and support. It means so much to Penel and to me to have his story out in the open. But I do understand waiting a bit to shine the light directly on Penel.

AUNT LURMA: And then there's the delicate issue of how old one might have to be to understand all the nuances and irreversible aspects of such weighty decisions. Right now all your younger ones are too young to understand sexual dynamics in their full array.

ME: I've spoken with several therapists and doctors. Actually, this isn't about sexuality. It's about self-identity. Self-identity begins around two years old. So Penel is actually right on target in terms of the timing of his feelings. He is more expressive and aware than most, but this is the time when we internally begin to define ourselves.

AUNT LURMA: Okay. That's good to know. But is the child old enough to know at that age exactly what it means to be a boy or a girl? That definition is not even the same in every culture, is it? When it comes down to it, the sexual part is the only real hard and fast defining factor regarding saying whether someone is a boy or girl, technically, right?

ME: Self-identity exists even when our organs have been taken away or have never developed properly. Or even if our breasts have been removed. So no, identity isn't about sex or the body. I'm a woman with or without my breasts and even when I'm not having sex (which is often). I just know I am a woman. I have to believe that Penel knows who he is on a basic and internal level, too. But Penel is a transgender boy. That has its own unique nuances. And it's very real.

AUNT LURMA: After a while, "gender" won't have to fit in a little box. It will be like race—defined far differently for these next generations than it was for their forebears.

ME: Exactly.

I sat on that email exchange for a long time—mulling over the questions of timing, of responsibility, of the appropriate level of visibility—for all included. And finally, when Joe began to feel more comfortable with my forwardness, I asked for both Penelope's and his blessing. It was then that I began speaking in public about us.

We can never be sure about what we decide. We never know as parents if we're making the best choices for our family. But we try our best to be aware of all the moving parts—the gains and losses—and then we decide, hundreds of times over, the direction in which we will lead.

There were articles and interviews on national radio and television featuring us, and then more articles that I wrote in the first person. Each time I opened my mouth, I spoke about our family, about gender and identity, as though there was nothing on earth more worthy of discussion, dissection, and contemplation. The zeitgeist seemed to be changing—people were debating and discussing transgender more than ever before. A few days after *Cosmopolitan* magazine released a documentary online about our family, to my astonishment, it climbed to over ten million views on social media, reaching people as far away as Africa. And not long after that doc went viral, the Human Rights Campaign reached out, asking if Joe and I would work with them on their anti-trans hatred initiative. And to our surprise, those videos went viral as well. Clearly, what we had to say was resonating.

I knew that if people could see how our family lived—that we were not crazy, not brainwashing our children, or succumbing to the devil, that we believed in God and spoke prayers of gratitude each night from our pillows; that we laughed during board games, cried on the living room couch over our shortcomings, fought over shotgun in the car, got A's in math, obsessed over books, got lost in Minecraft, and constantly showed up late after the school bell rang each morning; if they could visualize us sitting for dinner at seven thirty each night, Joe and I the leaders of a united team—maybe then people would believe me when I said that every single member of our family was a healthy part of the human experience. Penelope not excluded.

What stands before us, the Goliaths and the Ninjas, are real—and they are not always contained in the safety of a padded ring. The monsters that walk the streets with us are out for blood. I know this because sometimes, when I'm up for it, I open my computer and read what they say about us.

> *This is sad and disgusting. What type of parent forces an unnatural view of sexuality on an IGNORANT child? When we are children we are naïve. There are so many things that I desired as a child that I no longer desire.*

It's the caps that bother me most. The hatred they carry stops my heart; it freezes every time I read words like "ignorant," "unnatural," and "disgusting." At first I picture an older white man with white hair and deep lines around his pursed lips as the author of such venom. But when I read the comments more thoroughly, I realize that that image conveys only part of the truth. All types of people hate us: Black people, white people, men and women, the young and the old, the educated and the ignorant, religious folks as well as nonbelievers have something negative to say. The world as I've seen it can be ugly and divisive, and brutal.

I want to lead our family out of all that ugliness and divisiveness, toward a place where gender as we know it is obsolete. Where any definition we come up with today is understood to be outdated tomorrow. Toward a place where gender, like race, will be defined far differently for these next generations than it was for their forebears.

It was the middle of the week and I sat down for lunch at a favorite café in the Time Warner Center on West Fifty-Ninth Street. I was meeting Tracey, one of my closest friends, for lunch. I was thankful that I arrived early, because it gave me time to unwind before seeing her. As girlfriends do, we'd fallen out of sync over the last year, not because of any particular problem or event, but more, I'd hoped, just because of life—which had taken us in different directions. So much had happened for each of us—sickness, recovery, new baby on her end; advocacy, depression, tumultuous relationship on mine. We needed each other's ear on this day.

Tracey arrived and took the seat opposite me. As always, we clasped hands and locked eyes, as old lovers might do when seeing each other for the first time in years. "Your hair looks cute," I remember saying about her wig, not taking my eyes off her face. The last time I'd seen her, the chemo had taken most of her long, thick, wavy hair.

"I don't know." She paused, moving a few strands of the wig away from her face. "I'm getting used to it. But what I've learned, Jo, during this time, is that I'm sexier than my hair . . . and my tits, for that matter. They were never what I was known for anyway!" I loved how she could turn cancer, something so heavy, into her moment of comic relief—and power.

"You're right, Trace. As I get older, I realize there's much more to focus on than this body."

She nodded in agreement. Then there was a break in our energy while she carefully collected her next words. "But forget the cancer, how about you, Jo? I'm worried about you." I'd always hated that line: *I'm worried about you*. It usually fed directly into a backhanded, unexpected slap.

"Oh, really?" I asked, pulling back in my seat, placing my hands in my lap, prepared this time for the hit. "Why's that?"

"No . . . it's just that Kelly told me you're going through a lot with Joe. You *know* I know how that goes. You're my girl, Jo. What can I do?" If only we could have continued talking about her cancer. Or about *our* difficult husbands, even. We could easily have had another great laugh over the misused privilege our cisgender men wield. At least then we would have stayed on the same side of the fight. But she'd pulled this one on me—placing me over there, on the losing side, the other side.

"Well, unless you want to take him off my hands, there's not much anyone can do. We're juggling a lot." I left it at that.

But she didn't stop.

"All those happy pictures you post of you and Joe, that's got to end." *Why? What did it matter to her?* I thought. Those were happy moments. I remembered each one of them. Sure, those pictures didn't tell an entire story, and maybe an hour later we were fighting and he did storm out of the house, but those kisses and smiles and my hands wrapped around his were real. They showed where my heart was and the place where this family found stability. They were not everything, but they were genuine. And on those days when we were fighting, those images then became goals—everything that I wanted for us. Accomplishments on some days, goals on others.

But what Tracey saw in those photos were masks over an

image she felt she knew better, more accurately, from behind the scenes.

"Maybe, just for some time, to let yourself breathe, you could pull back on all this stuff around Penelope." *Stuff*, as if Penelope and advocacy were just side notes. "Stop posting, stop talking, just stop the constant show—of the family." I wondered if by "show" she really meant *"show-off."* "Honey, be quiet for a bit," she said, reaching out to touch my hand again. And then she asked the question that still gets under my skin: "I'm just curious, Jo, why *do* you always need to talk about it?"

I stumbled a bit, trying to explain to her why it felt like being strangled when I didn't speak up for my child, and how it felt like freedom when I did. I tried to explain the need for a family like ours to be visible until it was no longer a big deal, until 50 percent of trans teens were no longer attempting suicide, until churches and schools and entire communities weren't turning their backs on children like Penelope. "Each one of us deserves to be authentic," I said, "and fully actualized. If the world is questioning Penelope's gender, then it can and will question anything else it may deem suspect: race, class, body, brain, soul. We have to speak up, Tracey. We have to dictate the terms of our freedom. Even when there is a loss."

"But honey, your family is breaking apart. Is it worth it?"

I had laid critical points on the table, but from the look on Tracey's face, they just sat there between us, untouched.

A Black family at the center of a transgender narrative holds its own unique, complicated weight. Yes, our family was fragile, and perhaps we wouldn't make it, Joe and I—but what did that have to do with my advocacy, or transphobia, or all the hatred I was trying to dismantle?

If we were talking about racism, Tracey would never have asked me why I always needed to talk about it, because racism is a torch Black folks have been carrying for years. We know that when we dismantle racism, we will simultaneously fix so many of the cracks causing our families to crumble. It's that much of a negative weight on us. We also know that silence and ignorance are the muscle behind all "isms"—so when it comes to race, we refuse to be silent. For centuries, we've pushed back against it with our voices and with our unflinching presence.

That's when I saw it, etched into the awkward silence between my friend and me. The same "it" that had been simmering on the edges of my conversations with friends and some family for years. A little something Black folks like to call "white people's problems."

"White people's problems" can essentially be explained by breaking down "hard" and "soft" issues, as defined by the Black community. Hard issues are anything that can be most directly tied into the Struggle—racism, poverty, murder, education, and the everyday injustices that make steel out of our skin. Black people have always had to prioritize our circumstances. We are taught to stay focused. To keep our eyes trained on the prize: rising up, moving forward, and ushering in another generation in better standing than the last. These are the responsibilities defined for us by our ancestors. We sing of them in church hymns, shout them at rallies, and demand that they be addressed by our representatives.

Everything else, then, is "white people's problems." These are the soft issues—issues that often deal with the emotional life, and as such should be relegated to side conversations and spoken of only behind closed doors, if at all. To talk publicly in large groups about feelings and identities and souls—to investigate our deeper, personal selves—is a privilege afforded only to the privileged. It's a conversation that, historically, *we* just haven't had time for. Why? Because we still exist in a time when Black lives don't matter.

I knew if I asked, Tracey would protect Penelope at all costs, no questions asked. We had twenty years of history; Tracey and I had solidified our friendship at weddings, on vacations, and through years of late-night confessions and shared secrets. If anyone should understand what I was doing, it would be her, my sister. But I was not naïve, I also knew there was an even stronger collective understanding that whenever we, Black people, picked up the microphone or the pen, there was a list of clearly defined hard issues that we were supposed to endorse— issues that must do one thing only: fortify the Black narrative. Period. Transgender issues are not, nor have they ever been, on that list.

This way of thinking is more insidious than logical, it's intuitive rather than cognitive. But it exists, and I understand it, nonetheless. The tone my friend had taken with me conveyed it all: Everything that I'd been writing, and sharing about our family, and standing up for was actually doing the opposite of what I intended. Apparently, it was chipping away at us— maybe all of us: Tracey, me, our girlfriends, Black families I had never even met. "So many people, Jo, thousands, don't want you to write about this stuff anyway. Just think about it."

If she'd only said: "I know this is hard, but you're doing good work—you're moving us all forward."

The lunch continued, and Tracey didn't offer any more thoughts about my advocacy, only about the things she knew firsthand: the weight that Joe and I were under, the pressures between husband and wife, and the possibility that my time with Joe might be coming to an end. She coached me on how to proceed with care, and again advised me to be a little less in the public eye while it all went down—the demise of my marriage, that is. In between the chewing and the talking and the sipping, I kept telling myself *Choose reserve. Don't explode. Don't write her off, devise a plan instead. Connect the dots for her, for them—for anyone who questions what you're about—so they can see how trans issues don't undermine "Black" issues. And how family fragility shouldn't silence human rights. And mostly how Black transgender families shouldn't have to be perfect before being visible. Visibility on all levels is the goal.*

But until then, we were stuck in a "super wicked problem." I first heard the term in *Time* magazine. It's used by scientists to describe an issue with so many different causes and stakeholders that it's all but impossible to resolve. Environmental issues—big, multidimensional headaches like global warming—are considered super wicked. I immediately connected the article to my family.

Being Black and transgender is a super wicked problem. For my family and others who are similar, fighting trans phobia feels like fighting all the "isms" in the entire world. Not only are we fighting against racism, sexism, classism, and genderism, we're simultaneously expected to defend any presumed attack against the Black family, at all costs. We are expected to reject anything that makes us more vulnerable. I don't even think Tracey knew all that she was asking of me, not fully. If I can't speak up, loudly, repeatedly, in any setting—then nothing will change. The status quo will remain of what Black boys and girls, Black men and women, Black husbands and Black wives are *expected* to be.

The Black family, in whatever state it's in or form it may take, however deeply flawed and vulnerable it may be, needs to address gender. So many Black lives—lives that matter—depend on it.

Sometimes I think there is just too much to peel back. America—Black America especially—may not be ready.

But America wasn't ready for my grandmother, either, or Aunt Lurma, or my father. They weren't ready for Martin or

Malcolm. Some folks weren't ready for Bayard Rustin, or Sylvia Rivera, or Marsha P. Johnson. Or Audre Lorde, Zora Neale Hurston, or James Baldwin. The list of agitators is long. Change agents, those who aren't asking permission, are often not welcomed. But they come for the world anyway. *They* are ready. Penelope, who shares my father's perseverance and my grandmother's grit, is ready. Ready, even when the world is not.

All Black lives matter. My family in our Brooklyn living room.

TWENTY-THREE

This Spot

I NEVER LOOK AT THE OCEAN WITHOUT FEELING AFRAID. I rarely go out far into the water; I just walk in up to my waist and stay put, never venturing farther. The ocean is the unknown—its depth, its darkness. I guess if I could talk to the sharks and breathe in liquid, maybe I wouldn't be so scared. But I am human and can easily drown, or be eaten alive.

Today, at the beach on Martha's Vineyard, I face the water once more. I excuse myself from our beach chairs and blankets, from my friends, and from our kids running like wild things, tackling each other, making starfish in the sand, and I walk into the ocean. Pushing past the cold, past the seaweed tangling around my ankles, past the rough pebbles and shells that dig into my feet, I walk—farther than I normally would. And again, I am scared. But today I'm testing myself. Pushing to know what I have learned.

From all that I've gone through—the fear of losing a child, the poison of tunnel vision, the tug of love, the commotion of life—I know this turbulence around me will always be there, in some form or another. But today I'm facing another truth: The smack of the wave, the snatch of the undertow—they don't answer to me. They have an agenda all their own. I don't control them.

I'd like life to be easier. But it isn't. Sometimes I want to revert—for a split second—to feeling like the Spelmanite who lands the Harvard superstar, and to lie still in that fairy tale. But then I quickly remember the weight of that pathology. Those ideals have nothing to do with life. They don't make the marriage, they don't keep you together. They are irrelevant to the real life that demands your presence.

I've been pulled in so many different directions by so many different forces over the years. Pulled by children, by husbands, by love, by loss and gain, by places and ideas. That constant tug has made me the woman I am. Yet sometimes the pull has been so strong that it's detached me from my spirit. Daddy could do that to me with just a few simple words. His words, his actions, so many times left me undone—unable to think and feel and do all at the same time. For so many years, all I wanted to do, all I could do in fact, was sleep to get away from that feeling. Or run—far away from my nightmares and their relentless monster. Running fast, a body without a brain, running on adrenaline alone.

Joe sometimes did that, too—he could separate me from my spirit in his own way. A big fight, a long silence, a wall rising up between us, and suddenly I'd be floating, light and unbearably disconnected. He saw it, my want to be king. And I'm not sure he ever knew what to do with it. I want to be king. Not king of anyone or anything. Not king over this or that—but king of myself. To be that kind of woman—who protects, gets shit done, fixes problems, and takes care of the business at hand. One who drinks defiance like mother's milk and resists being controlled. That kind of king. And at the same time, I want to be vulnerable, to admit that I've fallen apart, and for that to be okay, too. And then I want to make my way back, back to being whole. I want to be that kind of king.

I've always wanted to be king, even as a little girl. But no one uses that word next to my name. I wanted to be my dad, but that wasn't encouraged. I wanted to be all that "male" implied.

I was eager to be a woman, too. My mom was so graceful at it. My older sisters were so beautiful; Ramona was such a badass. Those feminine qualities were golden and I wanted to have them. At Spelman, I learned how to embody them. But I wanted masculinity, too. Both. Except I wasn't sure if the masculine I craved could be mine. And that made me want it even more.

For as long as I can remember, I'd been sussing out the men—observing how they did things, how they moved through life—and in return what the world did for them. How men sat back and spoke when they wanted to. How they did things without asking permission. How they walked with their shoulders back and one dropped slightly lower. How their gaze was direct and their smiles appeared like a surprise, whenever *they* chose to reveal them—not when someone (strangers, annoying uncles, persistent aunts) commanded them to.

But no one ever said, and perhaps may never say "Okay, Jodie—be a man. Be like your father, or Serge, or Joe." But I observed and tried them on anyway, on my own.

I'd always wanted what they had—attitudes and freedoms dangled in front of me but forever out of my reach. Freedoms denied to me because of my place, because of my parts. Because of the rules. Freedoms transformed into "bitch" or "butch" or "ball-buster," "cold" or "manipulative" when worn on a woman's skin.

I want to be unclosed. I want to spread out like a starfish in the sand and touch every bit of life around me. I see Joe doing that—he's unfolding. Opening up to new worlds far beyond the one of finance he's spent fifteen years in. Beyond Brooklyn. Beyond America. He's traveled to Ghana, South Africa, and Nigeria to test new waters in his career. He's boldly reinserted himself into our kids' daily lives, making himself irreplaceable to each and every one of them. He's spent a year reading and rereading books on spirituality, coding, music, marathon running, cooking, parenting—all the things that make him happy. And, most impressive, he's torn open the narrow idea of what a man is. "When I stop and think, Jodie, about what makes me a man, I just don't know anymore. All the things I used to think defined me—making money, providing, being strong—they don't say enough." Joe, who loves to cook but once expected me to make all our meals, who loves his kids but felt it wasn't his place as the man of the house to gracefully, tenderly show that love—that man no longer wants only to be commander in chief of our home. That title no longer holds enough power. What Joe wants is more, endlessly more. Infinitely more.

And so do I.

All of us can be more than what gender says. More than what society tells us we should be. If we write ourselves off as purely one thing—boys do *this,* and girls do *that*—we will gravely underestimate ourselves, miscalculating our infinite potential.

Joe and I both get it, this new, wider vision of life. We've tried to adjust the terms of our relationship to match our new consciousness. We've tried growing together, and we did; we're better now, smarter than before. But ultimately, irrevocably, we grew apart.

I'm independent, and couple that with the fact that much of this human experience is solo work, I've been in my own head a lot. For better or for worse. Looking back over all my stories, from little girl to wife to mother of five—I see myself solo. Where I stand today, shoulders-deep, alone in the water, doesn't surprise me. Because this love I seek, this life I want, is not something to be merely moved by, or stuck in, or caught up under. This love, this life, must be traversed. Experienced. And in the end, it must make us whole.

There are multiple stories being told simultaneously here. Penelope's story. Our story. My story. Rate the success of the story starring Penelope, and it's pretty damn good. Joe and I have been flexible, we've expanded our vision, and we've put love first. We're beyond 100 percent with our kids. But do we put the same level of energy into the adult relationship? Are we as flexible, as bold, as love-centered with each other? No. What Penelope is demanding is very pure: "Let me be in control of my deepest self." The family gravitates toward that pureness. The world continues to.

Sometimes adults aren't as pure—we're tainted by age, experience, pessimism, expectations, and fairy tales. And sometimes we need to journey in different directions instead of pulling one another to follow.

Today at the beach, I walk even deeper into the ocean, wade in until the water reaches my chin. And then I stop. And I think. And I watch. The water moves around me, the waves come at me, bouncing off my shoulders, splashing in my face.

The ocean is uncontrollable.

But what's mine is mine. This person, this body, this mind. This soul belongs to me. And what I choose to do with it, I determine. I can choose to swim, maybe to wade in or dive under. But I can't stop the water from coming—I, woman, control nothing in this sea. Except myself. I, woman, control this flesh, and more times than not, this heart. I can choose to go into the wave, or even under it. I can float on my back. Or I can drown. But that's not my story or this tale. This tale is of characters that battle, needs that don't match, and ideas that collide. And most centrally, it is about this directive, this mission to control oneself, to claim the only little spot worth claiming. To find the light in the dark and the anchor in the sea. That anchor being me.

Now, here, as I stand deep in the ocean, scared as always, and as I look over myself—touching limbs that have grown back, and a face that is etched with lines—I know that this time around, *I, woman, control this spot.*

Portrit of mom (warriar Queen)
By Penel

Penelope sees me from the inside.

ACKNOWLEDGMENTS

———

This book might never have been written if it weren't for life smacking me in the face, knocking me down hard, and then challenging me to get back up again. Thank you, life.

For years, I'd been tossing around several book ideas (in my head as well as over long breakfasts with my friend Keisha Sutton). The topics ranged from beauty to lifestyle to parenting. But it was because Nadeen Gayle, another good friend, encouraged me to write about myself that this particular book began. Helena Andrews-Dyer, one of the coolest women I know, helped me organize my first thoughts. Bishop Sylveta Hamilton-Gonzales, the founder of my young boys' school and our family's mentor, offered extra TLC whenever we needed it. My village of Bed-Stuy, Brooklyn—full of beautiful people and delicious hangouts like Saraghina, Risbo, Butch & Coco, Zabka, and Casablanca—nourished both body and soul in between writing sessions. I have to especially thank all the "aunties," from Bethann Hardison all the way down, who've had my children's backs over the years—carrying them over their heads as if they were rock stars in a mosh pit. I'm especially grateful to Keturah Drake for asking me the million-dollar question "What if?" She made room in my head for imagining beyond the obvious. *Essence,* Refinery29, *Mother Mag,* BET, *Family Circle,* and *Cosmopolitan* were some of the first to help me tell my family's story, and they prepared me for the deep dive this book would require. Aundreus Patterson deserves to be recognized as my spiritual compass and a man of outstanding faith who kept me on track. To my Spelman sisters—especially Tammy McCall and Loran Hamilton-Warner, our ringleaders—I give thanks for sitting with me in spirit while I wrote *The Bold World.*

However strange it may seem to acknowledge two men I've loved in one paragraph, I will do so because they are so much of why I am, and how this book came to be. Serge Becker showed me early on that there is always another world worth exploring, just beyond. Joe Ghartey taught me to be a badass. It's that exact combination of fearless explorer that helped me investigate and write about the tough topics of family, gender, race, and identity. Together we've raised a blended family with five ethnicities, three languages, and eight children. Because Serge and Joe are men who share in the responsibilities of cooking, taking kids to and from school, cleaning, and overseeing homework, I was able to write my first book.

I couldn't have written *The Bold World* without my sisters, Linda Braxton, Sherri Hunt, and Yeefah Ramona Patterson, who've always exemplified organization, grace, and guts (respectively).

I'm deeply appreciative of my aunt, Lurma Rackley, also a writer, who took the time to comb through each version of the book with loving eyes, looking mostly for accuracy in family details. Throughout the process of writing this memoir, which spans five generations, I relied mostly on my own memory, old journals, letters, and photographs. But at times I needed additional help to place my memories into historical context—particularly during the Jim Crow era. Lurma (and Mama, of course) served as my historians.

An invisible weight presses down on nonconforming families like ours, sometimes splitting us apart at the seams. But when I found my community of advocates—Sonya Shields, formerly at Brooklyn Community Services; Jean Malpas at the Ackerman Institute's Gender and Family Project; Ellen Kahn at the Human Rights Campaign; and Eric Komoroff at Community of Unity—I felt less afraid and more powerful than before. I thank them all for what they continue to do for the world and what they've done for our family.

To Emma Parry at Janklow & Nesbit, my brilliant agent, I'm forever beholden. She told me to think bigger—beyond transgender, beyond Penelope, even beyond myself. She was the first to ask "Who taught *you* to be bold, Jodie?" Because of Emma, my book is more than I dreamed. To the team at Ballantine Books/Random House—they had me on day one, when they showed up fifteen deep in a conference room, ready to press go! Particular gratitude is given to Pamela Cannon for offering space and time for me to write my best book.

Maya Millett has been for me an editor, a sounding board, and a guide. The gratitude and respect I have for her are enormous. She was flexible, bending around my particular ways as a new writer: holding my hand when I needed it, leaving me be when I needed that. Her ability to remember the details of my life even when I'd forgotten them is otherworldly. This book exists because of her hard work. In this regard, I also want to thank Eve Claxton for her fierce creative energy and jolts of optimism, especially when we were down to the wire, way past our deadline, and still without a book title.

To my Gentle Love, for being water over stone.

And to my children, my Everythings, I see you. Ladybug Georgia, President Cassius, Rock Star Penelope, Rascal Othello, the Gift Nain, and also beautiful Ashley Newman, whom I consider one of us—I live through you, because of you, for you. You make me see life differently and bring me back each morning to the woman I want to be. The writing of this book and most of what I do in life is done to make you proud.

ABOUT THE AUTHOR

Jodie Patterson is a social activist, entrepreneur, and writer. She has been lauded for her activist work by Hillary Clinton, *The Advocate, Family Circle, Essence, Cosmopolitan,* and Yahoo!, among others. She works closely with a number of gender/family/human rights organizations including serving as Chair of the Board of the Human Rights Campaign Foundation and is a sought-out public speaker addressing a wide range of audiences about identity, gender, beauty, and entrepreneurship. Patterson was appointed by the United Nations as a Champion of Change and, perhaps most impressively, she is a former circus acrobat who performed in the Big Apple Circus. She lives in Brooklyn, New York, where she co-parents her five children with love, education, and family solidarity.

Instagram: @jodiepatterson
Twitter: @Jodie_GeorgiaNY

To inquire about booking Jodie Patterson for a speaking engagement, please contact the Penguin Random House Speakers Bureau at speakers@penguinrandomhouse.com.